Car Stereo Cookbook

How to Design, Choose, and Install Car Stereo Systems

SECOND EDITION

Mark Rumreich

McGraw-Hill
New York • Chicago • San Francisco • Lisbon • London
Madrid • Mexico City • Milan • New Delhi
San Juan • Seoul • Singapore • Sydney • Toronto

The McGraw-Hill Companies

Library of Congress Cataloging-in-Publication Data
Rumreich, Mark.
    Car stereo cookbook : how to design, choose, and install car stereo
    systems / Mark Rumreich.
        p.   cm.
    Includes bibliographical references.
    ISBN 0-07-144847-0
    1. Automobiles—Audio equipment.   I. Title.

TK7881.85.R85   2005
629.2'77—dc22   2005041672

Cover design by Donna Gray. Cover images courtesy of Rockford Corporation, Matsushita Electric Corporation of America, Blaupunkt USA, Sirius Satellite Radio, Kenwood USA Corporation, Polk Audio, Inc., Alpine Electronics, Inc., JL Audio, Inc., and Clarion Corporation of America.

2 3 4 5 6 7 8 9 0 DOC/DOC 0 1 0 9 8 7 6

ISBN 0-07-144847-0

The sponsoring editor for this book was Judy Bass and the production supervisor was Pamela Pelton. It was set in Vendome by North Market Street Graphics.

Printed and bound by RR Donnelley

 This book was printed on recycled, acid-free paper containing a minimum of 50% recycled, de-inked fiber.

McGraw-Hill books are available at special quantity discounts to use as premiums and sales promotions, or for use in corporate training programs. For more information, please write to the Director of Special Sales, Professional Publishing, McGraw-Hill, Two Penn Plaza, New York, NY 10121-2298. Or contact your local bookstore.

AUG - 2007

THE CAR STEREO
COOKBOOK

To my father, who loved music and always had the time to explain how things work.

CONTENTS

PREFACE

A lot has changed in the world of mobile entertainment in the seven short years since the first edition of this book was published. Innovations in mobile video, digital music players, satellite radio, HD Radio, and 5.1 channel audio have reshaped the mobile entertainment landscape. And the performance and features of all mobile electronics have continued to increase while prices drop.

But with all the exciting innovations, you've got more and harder decisions to make. Whether you realize it or not, there's a war being waged over the radio-sized hole in your dashboard. Automobile manufacturers want you to buy a factory sound system and will do everything in their power to sell you one. Face it, vehicle manufacturers have strategic advantages. They can style the radio to match the dash and tailor speaker placement and equalization to match the acoustics of each vehicle (few go to the trouble, however). They're not above some dirty tricks either. Integrating climate controls and vehicle control functions into the radio, nonstandard equipment mounting sizes, proprietary CD changer protocols and hard-to-interface-with premium factory sound systems have made aftermarket installation more challenging.

But the aftermarket is up to the challenge with high-performance solutions to almost any problem. The aftermarket itself is far from being a uniform front in the car stereo war, however. Numerous aftermarket companies are vying for your hard-earned dollar too.

It's hard to get a straight story on what you really need to get the performance you want. And the rules are constantly changing. That's where this book comes in. It provides the right answers to the growing list of questions—so you can win the war!

ACKNOWLEDGMENT

This book would not have been possible without considerable help from a lot of people, including my wife and family. Thanks to Judy Bass at McGraw-Hill for her support throughout the process and to Donna Gray for an awesome cover design. Extra thanks to Alan Hoover for his thoughtful and painstaking review of the manuscript.

I'd also like to thank all the companies that courteously provided product images and information for the book.

—MARK RUMREICH

INTRODUCTION

The Car Stereo Cookbook provides a comprehensive and well-organized guide to designing, choosing, and installing car audio and video systems. It's geared toward the technically oriented do-it-yourselfer who is interested in mobile entertainment. It assumes some familiarity with car stereos, but you don't need to have a degree in electronics or have installed equipment before.

The Cookbook Approach

Unlike other car stereo books and magazines, which describe complete installations for specific vehicles, *The Car Stereo Cookbook* offers a more a la carte approach. Chapters are organized by the type of project, such as speaker projects or amplifier projects. Projects may be used individually or combined to create a more advanced installation.

 The Car Stereo Cookbook covers an entire spectrum of projects from subwoofers to mobile video and from basic to advanced. It also presents a range of cost options. Step-by-step instructions are provided for difficult procedures and just the right amount of explanation is given to help you make smart choices.

Why Do It Yourself?

There are many reasons to do it yourself—saving money, making sure it gets done right, the freedom to select exactly the products you want, and the satisfaction of knowing that you did the job. This book will help you meet all these goals.

How This Book Is Organized

The first two chapters provide useful preparatory information. Chapter 1, "Before You Begin," describes how to plan your system, from considering upgradability, transferability, and maintaining a factory appearance to drawing a wiring diagram. Chapter 2, "Connectors, Supplies, Tools, and

Techniques," covers popular methods of connecting wires, describes the basic specialty tools useful for car stereo work, and explains how to use a multimeter.

The heart of the book is composed of the project chapters. These cover the following types of projects:

- Speakers and speaker projects
- Subwoofers and subwoofer projects
- Head unit projects
- Mobile video and 5.1 channel audio
- Amplifiers and amplifier projects
- Equalizers and equalizer projects
- Biamping and crossovers
- CD changer projects
- Accessories

Chapter 3, "Speakers and Speaker Projects," starts by explaining what good imaging is all about and how to achieve it. Projects range from adding surface-mount tweeter modules to installing a component speaker system.

Chapter 4, "Subwoofers and Subwoofer Projects," is by far the largest chapter. This is for good reason, since subwoofers play such an important role yet are frequently misunderstood. There are clear explanations of how to choose the right crossover, amplifier, driver, and box. For the more adventurous, box design and construction for sealed, ported, and band-pass boxes are covered.

Chapter 5, "Head Unit Projects," explains what to look for in head units, including satellite radio, HD radio, and MP3 features. It covers installation in any type of vehicle including cars with premium factory sound systems, steering wheel controls, OnStar, and GM vehicles with the Class 2 data bus.

Chapter 6, "Mobile Video and 5.1 Channel Audio," covers ways to add mobile video to your car, what to look for in video equipment, and how to choose the best monitor locations. It also includes how to put together a 5.1 channel sound system.

Chapter 7, "Amplifiers and Amplifier Projects," explores how much amp power you need and how to get more power for your money. Power, ground, and speaker wiring are covered in detail. Projects cover boosting head units of all types and include procedures for properly setting amplifier gains.

Chapter 8, "Equalizers and Equalizer Projects," explains the differences between graphic and parametric equalizers and how to choose the right number of bands for your application. Installing and setting up an equalizer, both with and without a real-time analyzer, are explained in detail.

Chapter 9, "Biamping and Crossovers," details the advantages of biamping, covers the basics of crossovers, and tells you what to look for in equipment. Projects cover biamping with head units of all types and include procedures for adjusting the system.

Chapter 10, "Changer and Player Projects," explains the different methods of interfacing a CD changer, DVD changer, or digital music player to your system as well as what to look for in a changer. Projects cover installation of changers and players with head units of all types.

Chapter 11, "Accessories," separates science from snake oil when it comes to power line caps, premium speaker wire, premium patch cables, and sound-deadening mats. Battery savers, portable music player adapters, and antennas are also discussed.

The last chapter is Chapter 12, "Battling Noise." This chapter explains the common causes of automotive noise problems and how to fix them (or better yet, avoid them).

THE CAR STEREO
COOKBOOK

CHAPTER 1

Before You Begin

This chapter is intended to get you thinking about some of the less obvious, but still important, factors in planning your system.

Ask Yourself Some Preliminary Questions

Here are a few questions you need to ask yourself *before* you start to design your system:

- How long am I going to keep this car? Will I sell the audio and video system with it?
- Is this a one-shot deal, or might I want to upgrade later?
- Do I want a factory look?

Transferability

It's hard to think ahead to the time when you'll be selling (or possibly junking) your car. One day it will happen, and on that day you'll either have to remove your upgraded audio and video system (and possibly restore the original one) or sell it with the car.

Putting in a really awesome mobile entertainment system is almost like installing a built-in swimming pool in your backyard. It's worth every cent to you, but it's hard to get your money back when it comes time to sell. At least with an audio and video system, you can take it with you. Unfortunately, you may leave behind gaping holes in the dash, doors, and deck.

Elaborate systems should be easily uninstallable to an acceptable condition.

This implies a few things. First, don't drill or cut any holes that you can't easily repair, conceal, or accept, unless you're willing to leave what's in them. Cutting the dashboard should be avoided if at all possible. Second, NEVER cut off factory wiring harness connectors. Either splice into the wires or spend a few extra bucks and buy wiring harness adapters. Third, try to choose equipment that is easily transferable to another vehicle. This means things such as buying a subwoofer box that will fit in your next car or truck as well as your current one.

It makes more sense to sell less dramatic upgrades with the car. Things like upgraded speakers or a well-chosen head unit can add value to a vehicle at selling time.

Upgradability

You should also consider what type of improvements you may make to your system in the future. A few extra dollars now may save you hundreds later, as well as considerable time. Some examples:

- Buying a head unit with two or three sets of preamp outputs will expand your options if you later decide to add amplifiers, a subwoofer, or electronic crossover. If you think you might add a CD changer or digital music player down the road, CD changer controls are a must. Choose a head unit that's both XM and SIRIUS ready if you're thinking about satellite radio.

- An amp that has speaker-level and preamp-level inputs, plenty of power, and a flexible and high-quality built-in crossover stands a much better chance of being useful in the next incarnation of your system.

- If you're planning to add a DVD head unit with built-in monitor and are thinking about a navigation system in the future, choose a head unit with navigation input. This will let you connect a compatible navigation unit and share the touch screen of your head unit.

Factory Look

Maintaining a factory appearance is important to many people for aesthetic as well as theft deterrent reasons. Others prefer to showcase their installations and protect their investment with an alarm system.

Having good sound while maintaining a factory appearance is easier than ever before. Today's factory head units can provide excellent performance and can be connected to external amplifiers if you need more power. Factory speakers can be replaced with better aftermarket drivers, and factory-look powered subs can be added to provide a rock-solid bottom end. Add-on CD changers and digital music players that will work with any factory head unit are readily available.

Even if you decide to replace the factory head unit, aftermarket models designed to match the factory styling are available for many vehicle makes. These offer CD changer controls and even plug into the factory wiring harness.

For mobile video, there are monitors and DVD players with built-in monitors designed for factory overhead console replacement. Headrest monitors that are exact matches of factory headrests are available for some vehicles.

Understand All Your Options

It's easy to spend more money than you need to on a car audio or video system. You can avoid making this mistake by understanding all your options before you design your system. This means understanding what's in your car now, what products are out there, and what approaches will meet your needs.

Understand What's in Your Car

The first step to understand all your options is investigating the system you have in your car now.

In some vehicles, it's difficult or impossible to replace the factory head unit. The vehicle manufacturer may have integrated climate controls into the radio face, used the head unit for warning chimes and important dashboard controls and messages, or used a proprietary system to run the amplifiers. In most (but not all) cases, the aftermarket has developed a solution, but the installation will be more time-consuming, complex, and expensive. So it pays to understand your factory system before you start thinking about gear. Crutchfield can help—their sales advisors can tell you if your vehicle requires special adapters or if an upgrade just can't be done.

If you bought your vehicle used, you'll need to understand any changes made by previous owners—you may be in for a surprise (pleasant or otherwise). A previous owner may have upgraded the speakers or added an amp under the dash. On the other hand, maybe the wiring harness was butchered or the CD player has an intermittent problem.

Spotting an aftermarket head unit or sub is easy, but looking for speaker or amplifier upgrades may require a little digging. Take a look at the back of a speaker in the trunk for evidence implying an upgrade of some sort. Look at the fuse block for fuse taps—a sure sign some electronics have been added.

You may have a premium factory sound system, in which case amplified speakers are probably involved. This can be a blessing or a curse, depending on what you want to do. See the appropriate project chapters for more on this subject.

Familiarize Yourself with Available Products and Approaches

The more familiar you are with what products are out there and how to use them, the better you'll be able to design a system that sounds great and is affordable. Study catalogs, surf the Net, and visit your local car stereo shop. Check out the latest products—some could be just the answer you need. And use this book to familiarize yourself with both common and not-so-common car stereo solutions and how to squeeze the most out of each component you buy.

Some of the best car stereo solutions are often the ones that aren't obvious. A few good examples:

- Using amplifier-saving configurations for boosting head units. These can save you the cost of an amplifier with no appreciable loss in performance.

- Adding surface-mount (or flush-mount) tweeters rather than upgrading front factory speakers. This can save money and provide better high-frequency reproduction and stereo imaging.

- Adding a subwoofer to fix a system that isn't loud enough. You'll be able to turn down the bass control to your main speakers and use the subwoofer to provide a rock-solid bottom end. By transferring the burden of bass to the subwoofer, you enable the rest of your speakers to play louder with less distortion. This frequently eliminates the need to boost the head unit with an amplifier.

Design Your System

Whether you're starting from scratch or upgrading, the other chapters in this book should give you the basic information you need to design your system. If you're thinking of upgrading, Table 1-1 can help point you in the right direction.

TABLE 1-1
Upgrade Solutions
to Common
Complaints

Factor	Possible Solutions	Chapter
Not loud enough	Replace head unit with higher-power model	5
	Boost head unit with external amp	7
	Add a subwoofer	4
Poor treble response	Upgrade speakers	3
	Add surface-mount tweeters	3
Want to play MP3s	Install a new head unit	5
	Add a CD changer or digital music player	10
	Use a portable music player head unit adapter	11
Weak bass	Add a subwoofer	4
Boomy/muddy bass	Add a subwoofer	4
	Install an equalizer	8
Poor imaging/staging	Imaging upgrade	3
Want satellite radio	Install a new head unit	5
	Use a plug-and-play tuner	5
Want backseat video	Install an overhead or headrest DVD player/monitor	6
	Use a portable DVD player/monitor	6

Sketch a Block Diagram

As a part of your system design process, you should sketch a simple block diagram of the system you intend to create. The purpose of this diagram is to make sure you haven't forgotten some key piece of equipment (like an amplifier, or maybe a line output converter to convert speaker-level signals to preamp level). The diagram doesn't need to be anything fancy. It should show each piece of equipment in the system as well as the basic connections. Your diagram might look something like the one in Fig. 1-1.

If you're putting in multiple high-power amplifiers, you should include power distribution hardware (such as fuse blocks) in your diagram.

Make Your Shopping List, Then Buy

Once you've finished a simple block diagram of your system, make your shopping list. This will reduce the chances of buying the wrong stuff and having to return it and/or needing to make multiple trips to the store during the middle of your installation.

Your shopping list should include everything on your block diagram, plus tools and supplies you'll need for the job. See Chap. 2 for advice on specialty tools you may want to buy. Don't forget:

- Speaker wire (not needed for most simple head unit installations)
- Power, ground, and remote turn-on wire, fuse and fuse holder (for an outboard amp)
- Patch cords (for an outboard amp)
- Wiring harness adapter, antenna adapter (for a head unit)
- Connectors, heat-shrink tubing, and wire ties
- Solder

As you're deciding which models of equipment to buy, visit your local car stereo shop. They can demonstrate what specific head units, speakers, and subwoofers actually sound like and can calibrate you on how much

FIGURE 1-1

A simple block diagram.

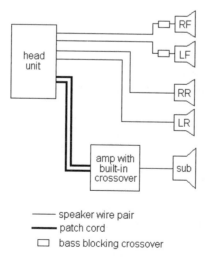

power you need. Be sure to choose a shop that has a reputation for a knowledgeable and friendly staff and that carries quality equipment.

You'll also want to check out Crutchfield's latest catalog and website for the newest products and a wealth of information. Product performance and feature charts show you what to look for and simplify the comparison process. Their website lets you specify your vehicle, then shows you the equipment that will fit it. Or if you prefer, it will show you everything and then tell you whether it will fit. Crutchfield maintains an extensive database, and their well-trained staff can alert you to special adapters and tools you'll need for your project. They also provide detailed, vehicle-specific MasterSheet installation instructions with any car audio or video equipment purchase.

See the list of recommended companies at the end of the book for other mail-order companies.

Read the Manuals and Draw a Complete Wiring Diagram

Once you have all your equipment in hand, it's time to read the pile of literature that came with it. As exciting as it is to dive right in and start installing, it's smarter to read the owner's manuals first. You may discover

FIGURE 1-2

A more complete wiring diagram.

a fundamental problem in your plans due to a bad assumption about a particular piece of equipment.

After you've read the owner's manuals, it's a good idea to draw a more complete wiring diagram for your system. If all you're doing is upgrading factory speakers or a simple head unit replacement with a wiring harness adapter, then you can skip this step. If you're doing a complex system, then a detailed wiring diagram can go a long way toward avoiding hooking things up wrong. You should show every wire with its color and function indicated. Your diagram might look like the one in Fig. 1-2.

Drawing a complete wiring diagram can be the least fun part of preparing for your installation. But the payoff comes when you wire up the system quickly and without errors. Another payoff comes down the road when you need to repair the system or if you decide to upgrade.

Now you're ready for installation!

CHAPTER 2

Connectors, Supplies, Tools, and Techniques

Discovering you don't have the right tool in the middle of a job can be frustrating. In many cases people are not aware that some of the most useful tools even exist, and continue to "drive screws with a hammer."

This section is intended to make you aware of the most useful of the car stereo specialty tools and supplies. Most of the tools only cost a few dollars, and can be used for other projects around the house. The time to buy tools and supplies is *before* you start your car stereo project.

Connectors

Talking about connectors before tools may seem backward, but you should think about connectors first since they may affect what tools you need.

Most car stereo projects involve making lots of connections. Table 2-1 shows the four commonly used methods of making connections—soldering, crimp connectors, Scotchlok™ connectors, and wire nuts.

Soldering

Soldering produces the best electrical connection by far. It provides a low-impedance, corrosion-resistant, mechanically strong connection. Unfortunately, soldered connections are also the most time-consuming, both in soldering and in insulating. And a hot soldering iron always seems to find its way to the upholstery.

TABLE 2-1
Common Connection Methods

Method	Advantages	Disadvantages
Soldering	Best electrical connection	Time consuming, must insulate
Crimp connectors	Good electrical connection, self-insulating, a type for any connection	Can corrode or pull apart if improperly crimped
Quick splice/ Scotchlok	Good electrical connection, self-insulating, easiest way to make a splice	Can corrode, bulky, for splices only
Wire nuts	No special tools needed	Easily become untwisted— not recommended for car stereo

Soldering Tips

Soldering requires skill and patience. To get good results, follow these tips:

- Use only 60/40 (60 percent tin, 40 percent lead) rosin-core solder.
- Make sure the connection to be soldered is free of dirt and corrosion.
- Periodically "tin" the tip of the soldering iron by coating it with solder and brushing off the excess with a cloth until it is smooth and silvery.
- Always heat the connection, not the solder.
- Use the side of the soldering iron tip near the point, not the point itself, to heat the connection. This allows more heat to flow from the tip into the connection.
- A proper solder joint is smooth and silvery, not rough and gray. Rough and gray joints are called *cold* joints because not enough heat was used to melt the solder. Always resolder cold joints.

The traditional way to insulate a soldered connection is with electrical tape, but the adhesive used with most tapes gets gummy after a few years and the tape is likely to slide off. A better solution is heat-shrink tubing. Heat-shrink tubing must be slid onto the wire before soldering; then it is slid over the soldered connection and heated with a butane lighter or heat gun until it shrinks to conform to the connection.

Crimp Connectors

Crimp connectors are the most popular connectors for autosound. There are crimp connectors available to make almost any type of connection imaginable for any type of wire (Fig. 2-1).

Disconnectable terminals are available for ease of disassembly (for repair, for example). To use, simply strip ¼ inch of insulation from the

FIGURE 2-1

A world of crimp connectors: (left to right) spade, ring, male disconnect, female disconnect, bullet plug, bullet receptacle, butt splice, closed end.

end of the wire, insert into the crimp terminal, and crimp with a terminal crimping tool. Try to pull the wire out of the terminal to verify a good connection.

The key to success with crimp terminals is to have the right size connector for the gauge of wire. If you try to use a connector that is too large for the wire gauge, it will not make a good connection and is likely to slide off. Terminals are generally color coded according to the industry standard shown in Table 2-2. If you don't know the wire gauge, use a crimper/stripper to figure it out by stripping some insulation, or just choose the smallest crimp connector that fits the wire. Be sure to use the pull test for each crimp.

A trick you can use when a wire is too small for a connector is to first fortify the wire by twisting additional strands around it (Fig. 2-2). This is useful for super-fine wires or for making a butt connection between two wires of different gauges.

Quick Splice/Scotchlok Connectors

Scotchlok connectors are the best way to splice into an existing wire without having to cut it. There are two types of Scotchlok connectors: original and T-tap (Fig. 2-3). The original type connector opens like a clamshell and has channels for the existing wire and the wire to be spliced into it. The T-tap connector opens like a clamshell, has a single channel for the existing wire, and mates with a ¼-inch male disconnect terminal for the wire to be spliced into it. It's great for applications requiring multiple disconnects or testing.

After the wires are put in their channels, the clamshell is closed with a pair of pliers. Since the connector cuts into the insulation, the insulation should not be stripped.

This connector is often used with power and ground wires. Scotchlok connectors can also be used to connect an aftermarket head unit to a factory wiring harness without cutting off the end of the harness. This is

TABLE 2-2

Color Code for
Crimp Connectors

Wire Gauge	Standard Crimp Connector Color
22–18	Red
16–14	Blue
12–10	Yellow

FIGURE 2-2

(*a*) Fortification trick—before; (*b*) fortification trick—after.

(a)

(b)

useful if a wiring harness adapter isn't readily available and makes it easy if you ever decide to reinstall the factory radio.

There are two keys to success with Scotchlok connectors:

- Be sure to use the right size connector for the wire. Too large a connector will result in a poor (or no) connection. Too small a connector will cut through many of the wire strands, weakening the wire.
- Be very careful when centering all the wires within their channels in the connector to prevent cut wires or bad connections.

Scotchlok connectors are usually color coded as shown in Table 2-3. Most of the original type connectors specify the same wire gauge range

FIGURE 2-3

Scotchlok connectors: (*a*) Original; (*b*) T-tap. (*Courtesy of 3M.*)

(a)

(b)

Wire Gauge	Standard Color
22–18	Red
18–14	Blue
12–10	Yellow

for both wires, but some specify one range for the run wire and another for the tap wire. This lets you splice into a thick wire with a thin wire. T-tap connectors automatically let you splice in any gauge wire by using the proper gauge ¼-inch male disconnect terminal.

If you're unsure about the wire gauge or connector, compare the size of the gap in the metal teeth of the Scotchlok connector against the wire's *conductor* diameter. The gap should be roughly one-third to one-half the conductor diameter.

Wire Nuts

Wire nuts (Fig. 2-4) are the standard connector for home wiring, but are not intended for car stereos. They can easily untwist and cause a short or open circuit. This may result in damaged equipment or equipment that simply fails to operate.

Fuse Taps

When you need a source of power for a new accessory, you can splice into one of the existing power wires. However, a better alternative is to use a

FIGURE 2-4

Wire nuts.

fuse tap. Fuse taps provide an easy way to tap into an automotive fuse block. They come in a number of styles, depending on the type of fuses your car uses.

Taps for AGC Fuse Blocks

For AGC (glass tube) fuse holders, use AGC fuse taps (Fig. 2-5). Temporarily remove an existing fuse, insert the fuse tap, then reinsert the fuse. The fuse tap provides a $\frac{1}{4}$-inch male solderless terminal for the accessory power wire to connect to.

Taps for ATO/ATC Fuse Blocks

For ATO/ATC (blade) fuse holders, you have more styles to choose from.

The *clip-style fuse tap* (Fig. 2-6) is the least expensive option. You temporarily remove an existing fuse, clip the tap onto the fuse, then reinsert the fuse. The fuse tap provides a $\frac{1}{4}$-inch male solderless terminal for the accessory power wire to connect to.

The *lead-wire fuse* (Fig. 2-7) is actually an ATO/ATC fuse with a 7-inch fully insulated lead wire coming out the back. One advantage of this approach is that there is no risk of mechanically overstressing the terminals in the fuse block. Another is that the lead wire can be bent fully back, allowing the fuse box cover to fit back on. A disadvantage of this approach is that since the fuse itself is part of the assembly, you'll need to buy a lead-wire fuse with the proper current rating. If the fuse ever blows, you'll need to replace the entire assembly and redo the accessory connection. If you choose this approach, be sure to order a spare. Lead-wire fuses are available from MCM Electronics.

The *Add-A-Circuit™ fuse holder* by Littelfuse (Fig. 2-8) plugs into the fuse block and has two fuse holder slots built in. The first slot is for the origi-

Tip: Clip-style fuse taps that wrap around the fuse terminal can mechanically overstress the terminals in the fuse block. This can cause nuisance blows due to excessive heat produced by a loose-fitting fuse. A "through the hole" design (shown in Fig. 2-6) avoids this problem.

FIGURE 2-5

AGC fuse tap.

nal circuit and the second is for the new accessory circuit. A fully insulated lead wire is provided for the new accessory circuit. This ingenious design eliminates having to install an in-line fuse holder for the accessory. Its only drawback is its size—you may have difficulty fitting the fuse box cover back on.

Taps for MINI Fuse Blocks

Many newer vehicles use MINI fuses in their fuse blocks. These are miniature blade-type fuses, similar to ATO/ATC fuses, but smaller. For this type of fuse, you can use MINI clip-style fuse taps (Fig. 2-9).

Littelfuse also makes an Add-A-Circuit fuse holder for MINI fuses.

Installation Tips

With any type of fuse tap, you'll need to identify which side of the factory fuse is connected to the battery and which side is connected to the

FIGURE 2-8
ATO/ATC Add-A-
Circuit fuse holder.
(*Courtesy of MCM
Electronics.*)

load. You'll need to use a multimeter for this. Remove the factory fuse, turn the ignition on, and connect the black lead of the multimeter to the vehicle's chassis ground. Touch the red test lead of the multimeter to each of the fuse terminals. The terminal that shows approximately +12 volts is the battery side of the fuse. The terminal that shows approximately 0 volts is the load side.

Now you'll need to decide whether to locate the fuse tap on the battery side or the load side of the existing fuse. For the Add-A-Circuit fuse holder, the lead wire should be located on the load side. For the other types of fuse taps, it's a matter of choice. Using the battery side requires that you add a fuse to the accessory power wire as close to the factory fuse block as possible, for safety reasons. The advantage of this approach is that the accessory cannot cause the factory fuse to blow and the factory circuit cannot cause the accessory fuse to blow. Locating the tap on the load side of the factory fuse is the safest and best approach if the accessory draws only a small amount of current (less than 1 ampere).

When adding a fuse tap, tap a fuse on a circuit labeled IGNITION if you want accessory power only when the ignition switch is on. If you want accessory power all the time, choose a fuse on a circuit labeled BATTERY.

FIGURE 2-9
MINI clip-style fuse
tap. (*Courtesy of MCM
Electronics.*)

Cable Ties

Cable ties (also called wire ties or tie wraps) are so handy, they deserve their own section. They are molded of high-tensile-strength nylon and are used for bundling together wires and cables. The flat, flexible tail is inserted through a ratcheting slot in the head to create a self-locking, permanent loop (Fig. 2-10).

Cable ties come in a variety of sizes—4 and 8 inches are the two most popular lengths for car stereo work (Fig. 2-11). They are most commonly white or black, but virtually every color is available, including neon colors for the fashion-conscious installer.

Uses for cable ties include:

- Bundling wiring together for a neat installation.
- Routing wiring out of sight and out of harm's way by cable-tying wiring to objects along the desired path.
- Securing crossovers or small modules under the dash, inside doors, or in the trunk.
- Marking wires—use different numbers of or different colors of cable ties to identify identical-looking wires. You can also buy special identification cable ties with a built-in writeable tab.

Heat-Shrink Tubing

Heat-shrink tubing is the best way to insulate, moisture-proof, and color-code electrical connections (Fig. 2-12).

Heat-shrink tubing is slid onto a wire before soldering, then it is slid over the soldered connection and heated with a butane lighter or heat gun until it shrinks to conform to the connection.

It's available in almost any diameter and color, in pieces or spools. A 2:1 shrink ratio is standard (the diameter shrinks to half). A 3:1 shrink ratio

FIGURE 2-10

How a cable tie works.

FIGURE 2-11
World of cable ties.

is slightly more expensive but will accommodate large and irregular shapes better. Adhesive-lined heat-shrink tubing uses a special layer of thermoplastic adhesive that flows when heated, to provide a moisture-proof seal.

Specialty Tools

In addition to the usual screwdrivers, wire cutters, pliers, and wrenches, there are a number of tools worth investing in, even if you only install a stereo once. The following tools are especially useful for working on car stereos, although most of them are also useful for other jobs. The list in Table 2-4 includes all my personal favorites.

A **crimper/stripper** (Fig. 2-13) is a necessity if you plan to use crimp connectors. These are often packaged with an assortment of terminals, which is a good way to start. Cheap models often do a poor job of crimping, which can result in bad connections over time. Most crimper/strippers

FIGURE 2-12
Heat-shrink tubing.
(*Courtesy of Parts Express.*)

TABLE 2-4

Useful Tools for Car
Stereo Work

	Tool	Cost	Comments
BUY	Crimper/stripper	$3–10	Must have for crimp connectors
BUY	Soldering iron	$5 and up	Must have if you plan to solder
	Ratcheting offset screwdriver	$12–15	Must have for some jobs
	Hollow-shaft nutdrivers	$10–25	Luxury
	Torx (star drive) driver set	$5–20	Must have for some jobs
	SnakeLight™	$20	Luxury
BUY	24-inch claw pick-up tool	$3	Very handy
BUY	Utility hacksaw	$4	Very handy
BUY	Utility knife or X-Acto knife	$3	Very handy
	Black paint pen	$3	Great for minor chips and scratches
	Window crank clip remover/installer	$4–6	Luxury
	DIN removal tools	$0–3	Needed to remove DIN-E head units
	Test CD	$10–25	Simplifies tweaking your system
BUY	Multimeter	$15 and up	Recommended

cover the range of 22-gauge to 10-gauge wire terminals—more than adequate for most projects. For 8-gauge wire or lower, you'll need to use an expensive impact or lever-style crimper or switch to set-screw-type terminals.

A **soldering iron** can be purchased for as little as $5, and it will do a fine job. More expensive irons offer features such as a built-in stand, interchangeable tips, and temperature control. Most soldering irons are 120-volt models—they plug into a wall outlet (Fig. 2-14). There are two types of sol-

FIGURE 2-13

Crimper/stripper.
(*Courtesy of MCM
Electronics.*)

dering irons of particular interest for car stereo work—the 12-volt iron and the butane iron.

The 12-volt iron (Fig. 2-15) plugs into your cigarette lighter socket. It lets you solder in your car without having to use an extension cord.

Butane soldering irons (Fig. 2-16) start at about $30. They refill using standard butane lighter fuel. Butane models are nice because they can solder where there is no power of any kind and they don't have a cord to get in your way. They also can be used with optional tips such as a hot knife (for cutting plastic) and a hot blower (perfect for shrinking heat-shrink tubing or tape). Optional tips cost about $10 each. A butane iron is really nice if you can afford one.

A **ratcheting offset screwdriver** (Fig. 2-17) is often the only good way to access screws in tight places. Dashboard work (such as installing a new head unit) is the most common situation requiring this tool. Replacing speakers in doors is another job that may require an offset screwdriver.

Skewdriver™ and Skewdriver Jr.™ offset screwdrivers perform the same job, but with a screwdriver handle instead of a ratchet handle.

Hollow-shaft nutdrivers (Fig. 2-18) are useful for removing or installing hex-head screws and hex nuts. The hollow shaft makes them ideal for the shallow nuts on head unit control shafts (such as the volume control). A socket set with a screwdriver handle adapter makes a good substitute for most applications. Metric is standard today on new cars and equipment, but if you're working on older cars, you'll want English sizes too.

Torx (star drive) screws are widely used in cars for dashboards and speaker assemblies. They are also used for many appliances and electronic

FIGURE 2-14

Soldering iron—
120 volts. (*Courtesy of
MCM Electronics.*)

FIGURE 2-15
Soldering iron—
12 volts. (*Courtesy of
MCM Electronics.*)

FIGURE 2-16
Soldering iron—
butane. (*Courtesy of
MCM Electronics.*)

FIGURE 2-17
Ratcheting offset
screwdriver. (*Courtesy
of MCM Electronics.*)

FIGURE 2-18

Hollow-shaft nut-
drivers. (*Courtesy of
MCM Electronics.*)

items, so Torx drivers are good to have around the house. Unlike with flat
or Phillips screws, you must have exactly the right size driver for the screw.
The most common sizes are T10, T15, T20, T25, T27, T30, and T40. T50 is
needed for some seat belt bolts.

To economize, you can buy a Torx key set for as little as $5. For a little
more, you can buy a set of Torx screwdrivers. Yet another option is a set

FIGURE 2-19

Torx bit set.
(*Courtesy of DeWALT.*)

of **Torx bits** (Fig. 2-19) that can be used in a cordless screwdriver. Most ratcheting offset screwdrivers and Skewdrivers come with a set of small Torx bits, so you can kill two birds with one stone by buying one of these.

The **SnakeLight** (Fig. 2-20) is a flexible flashlight particularly well suited to working under dashboards. Its flexible shape lets it fit into tight spots as well as hold itself in place. There are numerous clones available. There are also many other specialty flashlights that have clamps, head-straps, or magnets to give you two hands to work with. A no-hands flash-light is handy to have around the house as well. Be sure to get something bright—a halogen, xenon, or krypton bulb is a real plus.

A **claw pick-up tool** (Fig. 2-21) is indispensable for retrieving small parts dropped inside a car door or behind the dashboard. Another great use for this tool is in starting screws in hard-to-reach spots. It's also very handy for things other than car stereo work, like retrieving a key dropped through a crack in your deck.

A **utility hacksaw** (Fig. 2-22) is the best tool I have found for cutting small holes in dashboards, door panels, or rear decks. It's slow compared to a jigsaw, but doesn't require a flat working surface to rest the saw on. It also reduces the risk of damage from scratching the surrounding area.

A **utility knife** (Fig. 2-23) is useful for cutting and trimming wood, plastic, and upholstery. A **precision knife** (Fig. 2-24) performs the same jobs, but provides better control. A variety of blades are available for preci-sion knives, but the standard triangular pointed blade is best for most jobs.

FIGURE 2-21
24-inch claw pick-up tool. (*Courtesy of MCM Electronics.*)

FIGURE 2-22
Utility hacksaw. (*Courtesy of Stanley.*)

FIGURE 2-23
Utility knife. (*Courtesy of Stanley.*)

FIGURE 2-24
Precision knife. (*Courtesy of Stanley.*)

A **black paint pen** (Fig. 2-25) looks like a magic marker, but it dispenses fast-drying black paint instead of ink. It does a great job of concealing minor chips and scratches and slightly damaged painted screw heads, inevitable during even careful installations. It's perfect for painting the thin metal lip visible along the edge of some DIN mounting sleeves. Black permanent markers work in a pinch, but don't cover evenly and, in some light, take on a reddish cast. Once you use a paint pen, you'll never want to go back. Paint pens are also available in various other colors including white, silver, and gold.

When installing door speakers in vehicles with manually operated windows, you'll need to remove the window crank in order to remove the door panel. Some window cranks are held on with a screw. In GM, Ford, and other vehicles, cranks are held in place by a C type spring clip. A piece of bent coat hanger will do the job of removing the spring clips (just bend a tiny hook in the end and use it to pull off the clip), or you can carefully push it off with a flat-blade screwdriver. A **window crank clip remover/installer** tool (Fig. 2-26) makes the job fast and easy, and helps prevent damage to door panel upholstery. The opposite end of the tool firmly holds the clip for easy installation.

DIN removal tools (Fig. 2-27) are just two U-shaped pieces of solid wire. You'll need them to pull a Euro DIN head unit out of a dash. These are often included with a head unit purchase, but are also sold separately. This is yet another tool that you can make out of bent coat hangers to save a few bucks.

Tweaking your system for the best sound is easier with a good test CD. There are lots of **test CDs** (Fig. 2-28) to choose from—which is best depends on what your project is and whether you have a sound pressure

FIGURE 2-27

DIN removal tools.
(*Courtesy of Scosche.*)

Tip: If your multimeter comes with pointed tip probes, you might want to replace both of them (or just the black one) with an alligator clip or mini-hook-type test clip. This solves the frustrating problem of only having two hands when you're trying to simultaneously make good connections with two probes and read the meter.

level meter to take advantage of some of the test tones. Some test discs are made for a specific purpose such as setting amplifier levels, "system conditioning," or preparing for auto sound competition.

A **multimeter** (Fig. 2-29) is the single most important piece of test equipment you can own. It lets you check connections, inspect speakers, and verify power to equipment. Without it, tracking down problems is like working in the dark.

A multimeter can be bought for as little as $10, a digital model for as little as $20. I highly recommend digital. If you never make mistakes, never have equipment problems, and always have full wiring documentation for the vehicles you work on, then you don't need one. Otherwise, it's a worth-

Recommended Test CDs

"My Disc"

From Sheffield Lab/Autosound 2000. Contains 86 tracks engineered to provide a thorough evaluation of your audio system's performance, the listening environment, and your personal critical listening ability. Contains special tracks that enable you to analyze performance with or without specialized test equipment. There are also six complete music tracks from Sheffield. A detailed 20-page booklet takes you through each procedure track by track.

The Sheffield Lab/Coustic Test Disc

Developed to help installers, competitors, and audio enthusiasts set up and test high-performance auto sound systems as well as home theater systems. Appropriate for the simplest of systems and for the most sophisticated. In addition to narration and musical excerpts, this disc provides test tones for proper channel identification, phasing, and polarity.

FIGURE 2-28

Test CDs. (*Courtesy of Autosound 2000.*)

while investment. Buy a model with an audible continuity checker. Current measurement capabilities are not required.

Using a Multimeter—Wiring Harness Example

The basic functions of a multimeter are shown in Table 2-5.

The best way to explain how to use a multimeter is to dive right in with an example. The following shows how to use a multimeter to figure out a radio wiring harness in a car.

FIGURE 2-29

Digital multimeter. (*Courtesy of MCM Electronics.*)

TABLE 2-5

Multimeter Functions and Their Uses

Function	Common Car Stereo Use
Measure DC voltage	Confirm that power is provided to a component
Measure AC voltage	—
Measure continuity	Verify a connection
Measure resistance	Check a speaker or speaker connection
Measure current	—

Tip: For most vehicles, a wiring harness adapter is available. Wiring harness adapters mate with the existing car harness so you don't need to splice into any wires. Adapters are supplied with a color code cross-reference that identifies all the wires so you don't need to figure them out yourself.

Let's say you plan to replace a factory radio with something better. You've removed the factory radio, and the eight-pin connector (which plugged into the back of the radio) looks like the one in Fig. 2-30.

Step 1: Identify the Power Wires

Turn on your meter and put it in the DC VOLTS mode. Connect the black probe of the meter to a known good electrical ground, such as bare metal on the body of the car or the outer sleeve of the cigarette lighter socket.

Table 2-6 shows the three types of power wires that may be connected to a car radio.

Some or all of these may be provided to the radio. First, we'll look for the BATTERY +12V. With the headlights off and the key out of the ignition, probe each of the terminals inside the connector. In our example, we find that the red wire measures approximately +12 volts.

Next, turn on the headlights and repeat the procedure. In this case, we find that the yellow wire now measures about +12 volts. Finally, put the key in the ignition and turn it to the ACCESSORY or IGNITION position (you don't need to start the car). Now the orange wire measures +12 volts too, so it must be the accessory/ignition wire.

We have identified all the power wires (Fig. 2-31), so the lights can be turned off and the key taken out of the ignition.

FIGURE 2-30

Eight-pin factory radio connector.

black wire	●	●	orange wire
red wire	●	●	yellow wire
green wire	●	●	gray wire
purple wire	●	●	brown wire

TABLE 2-6

Types of Power
Wires in a Radio
Harness

Name	When On
Battery	Always on
Accessory/ignition	On when engine is running (or when ignition switch is in ACC position)
Lights	On when headlights (or dash lights) are on

Step 2: Identify the Ground Wire

Put your meter in the CONTINUITY mode. This mode is often indicated with a musical note symbol. If your meter doesn't have this feature, use the RESISTANCE mode instead. Momentarily connect the two probes of your meter together, and you should hear a beep. If you are using the RESISTANCE mode, you should see a meter reading very close to 0 ohms when the two probe tips are touching. If it doesn't read near zero or jumps around when you move the leads, you have a bad connection.

Tip: Get in the habit of shorting your test probes together before making a resistance measurement to make sure that you get a meter reading near zero.

Once again, connect the black probe of the meter to a known good electrical ground, such as bare metal on the body of the car or the outer sleeve of the cigarette lighter socket. Now probe each of the wires in the connector that have not previously been identified. In our example, we find that the black wire causes the multimeter to beep, so it must be the ground wire (Fig. 2-32).

FIGURE 2-31

Connector with
power wires identi-
fied.

black wire • • orange wire = **ign/acc +12v**
battery +12v = red wire • • yellow wire = **lights +12v**
green wire • • gray wire
purple wire • • brown wire

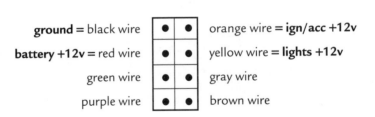

FIGURE 2-32

Connector with
power and ground
wires identified.

ground = black wire • • orange wire = **ign/acc +12v**
battery +12v = red wire • • yellow wire = **lights +12v**
green wire • • gray wire
purple wire • • brown wire

What Is Ground?

Modern cars use a 12-volt DC negative ground electrical system. (When the engine is running, this voltage can actually be as high as 14.4 volts.) This means that the frame, chassis, and body of the car, as well as almost all the electrical circuits in the car, are electrically connected together and to the minus terminal of the car battery. This super-connection is referred to as *electrical ground.*

The advantage of having an electrical system with a common ground is a reduction in wiring. For example, a light bulb only needs one wire rather than two—the second terminal of the bulb is connected to the chassis of the car.

Tip: Most car speakers are 4 ohms, but some are 8 or even 10 ohms. In the case of a 4-ohm nominal speaker, 4 ohms is the impedance for music signals. A multimeter actually measures DC resistance, which is a lower number, such as 3.2 ohms.

Step 3: Identify the Speaker Wires

By the process of elimination, the remaining wires must be speaker wires. Put the multimeter in the RESISTANCE mode.

It doesn't matter which wire we start with. Connect one probe to the green wire terminal. Now, use the other probe to search the other unidentified terminals for one that gives a meter reading between 3 and 10 ohms.

In this example, we find that the purple wire gives a meter reading of 3.5 ohms. (Some meters might show 0.0035 Kohms, which is equivalent, since 1 Kohm equals 1000 ohms.) The other terminals show infinite resistance with respect to the green wire. This reveals that the green and purple wires go to the same speaker.

The only unidentified wires remaining are the gray and the brown ones. Connecting a probe to each gives a meter reading of 3.5 ohms, confirming that these wires go to a second speaker.

We know that the green and purple wires go to one speaker and that the gray and brown wires go to another. We don't know the polarity of the wires or which wires go to which speaker. Sometimes you can tell by

FIGURE 2-33

Speaker polarity tester.

FIGURE 2-34

Connector with all
wires identified.

ground = black wire	●	●	orange wire = **ign/acc +12v**
battery +12v = red wire	●	●	yellow wire = **lights +12v**
left speaker − = green wire	●	●	gray wire = **right speaker −**
left speaker + = purple wire	●	●	brown wire = **right speaker +**

looking at the actual speaker connections inside the trunk or by removing a door speaker. At other times you may need to use the sophisticated speaker polarity tester in Fig. 2-33.

This is nothing more than a flashlight battery with wires connected. Any 1.5-volt battery will work. (Note: do not use a 9-volt battery to check a tweeter's polarity—the higher test voltage could destroy it.) Use tape to hold the wires onto the battery terminals. Connect the minus wire to the green terminal and touch the plus wire to the purple terminal. In this case, we hear a pop coming from the left speaker. Now watch the cone of the left speaker when you connect the battery. Does it move out or in? In this example, it moves out—this means that the plus terminal of the battery is connected to the plus terminal of the speaker. (If it moves in, the plus terminal of the battery is connected to the minus terminal of the speaker.) Repeating this procedure for the gray and brown wires, we complete our chart (Fig. 2-34).

CHAPTER 3

Speakers and Speaker Projects

With today's factory stereos, speakers are often the weak link in system performance. The problem may be a lack of deep bass, a lack of a crisp high end, high distortion, or poor imaging. Adding or upgrading speakers can be the key to improving your system (Table 3-1).

In many cases, it makes sense to keep some or all of the existing speakers and correct their deficiencies by adding surface-mount tweeters or a subwoofer. In other cases, replacing the existing speakers with something better makes the most sense. For exceptional performance (and a price to match), separates can be used.

The following sections present various speaker projects independently. But, in many cases, information of general use may not be repeated in each section. For example, the section on upgrading existing speakers gives advice on choosing drivers. This advice applies just as well to other sections.

The imaging overhaul is presented first because it introduces imaging principles used in all later sections.

Imaging and You

What Is Imaging?

The term *imaging* refers to how well you can "close your eyes and tell where the sax player is standing." In your living room, proper imaging is easily achieved by arranging your speakers and listening chair as shown in Fig. 3-1.

In the recording studio, music is mixed to provide proper imaging for speakers arranged this way—in front of the listener, and forming a 60° angle. It makes sense to optimize music for this speaker arrangement because that's how most people listen to it. This arrangement also makes sense because it duplicates the listening zone of a normal live performance (assuming you have good seats).

FIGURE 3-1
Ideal listening room arrangement.

60 degrees

TABLE 3-1

Popular Speaker
Projects

Project	Comments
Imaging overhaul	Optimizes imaging—may require adding a sub-woofer.
Adding surface-mount tweeters	Low-cost way to improve high-frequency response of moderate-quality speakers.
Upgrading existing speakers	Simple and unobtrusive way to extend high-frequency and bass response plus increase power handling.
Installing speakers in new location	Useful when existing speaker locations are inadequate.
Installing separates	Provides highest sound quality, but expensive and labor intensive.
Adding a subwoofer	Best way to achieve thunderous bass—removes burden of bass from the other speakers, allowing them to play louder and with less distortion. (See Chap. 4.)

A typical listening arrangement for a car is shown in Fig. 3-2.

This setup has the potential to wreak havoc with imaging. For example, the sax player who was supposed to be standing directly in front of you might now seem to surround you. Or, if the back speakers are louder than the front, the sax player may seem to be directly behind you.

This leads to the key question: How much do you care about imaging? For most people, imaging in the car is not a big concern. But for some, it is. Achieving good imaging is not without its sacrifices, either. It puts a big performance burden on the front speakers as primary drivers, since the rear speakers are used only for fill.

FIGURE 3-2

Typical car arrangement.

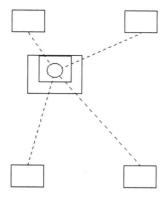

Achieving Good Imaging

For most vehicles, good imaging means sacrificing the easy bass available from trunk-mounted main drivers. For pickup trucks and mid-engine sports cars (where trunk-mounted speakers are not an option), this isn't as much of an issue. In either case, the difficulty of getting good bass out of the front usually makes a subwoofer necessary when good imaging is the goal.

For the ultimate imaging performance in car audio, 5.1 channel audio is now an option. Surround sound is already popular for home-theater systems, and is starting to appear in factory and aftermarket car audio. A hurdle with upgrading to 5.1 is the center channel speaker required in the middle of the dashboard. To achieve the proper surround-sound effect, all five primary channels (right and left front, right and left rear, and center channel) need to be voice-matched. This means that they should all sound the same or you'll hear a change in sound quality as a performer moves across the stage (or behind you). It means that the center channel speaker should ideally be at the same height and use the same driver as the other two front speakers. Upgrading to 5.1 requires other changes, too. See Chapter 6 for more info.

For those who want to perform an imaging overhaul in a four-channel system, here is my three-point program:

- Use the front speakers as your primary drivers. The goal here is to provide good power handling and frequency response down to 150 Hz, where a subwoofer can take over. A crossover can be used to block energy below 150 Hz to the primary drivers. This allows them to play louder with less distortion. You may also decide to upgrade your existing front speakers with drop-in replacements or even go with separates.

- Use the rear speakers for fill. Operating rear speakers at a reduced volume level (with respect to the front speakers) actually expands the stereo image. Rear speakers used for fill don't need to have extended bass, high frequency, or power handling capabilities, so don't buy expensive drivers for this application (you can keep the rear speakers you have). Set the front/rear fader control to the point where you can barely tell that the rear speakers exist.

- Add a subwoofer. A subwoofer takes over the job of providing deep bass where the front speakers normally give out. Removing the burden of bass from the front speakers allows them to play louder and with less distortion. (Chapter 4 has details.)

In those rare cases where the front speakers provide adequate deep bass and power handling, you can consider yourself lucky and forget about adding a subwoofer.

Adding Surface-Mount Tweeters

Inexpensive speakers usually do a good job of reproducing mid-range, but they generally lack good high- and low-frequency capabilities. Adding surface-mount tweeters (Fig. 3-3) is a low-cost way to add a crisp high end to cheap factory speakers not incorporating a tweeter. If the sound of cymbals doesn't shimmer, then your high end needs improvement.

Choosing Tweeters

A pair of surface-mount tweeter modules can cost anywhere from $12 to over $200. I have found that units costing as little as $20 a pair can provide excellent performance. Follow these rules to avoid buying something you'll regret later:

- Buy domes, not cones.
- Do not buy piezo tweeters.
- For high-power applications, ferrofluid is recommended.

FIGURE 3-3

Surface-mount tweeters. (*Courtesy of JL Audio.*)

Dome tweeters offer superior dispersion (which means they radiate well in all directions) and high-frequency response characteristics compared to cones. Cones are an obsolete technology for tweeters. Watch out—if it doesn't say it's a dome, it's probably a cone.

Piezo tweeters are highly efficient and do not require a crossover capacitor, but their advantages end there. Because of their inherently resonant behavior, they almost always exhibit a poor frequency response. Don't buy them.

Ferrofluid allows better cooling of the voice coil and thus provides greater power handling. It also smooths the frequency response somewhat. A ferrofluid-cooled model is recommended for high-power applications.

Another factor to consider is the mounting base. Some models allow the mounting angle to be adjusted by rotating the base. This can be quite helpful when trying to mount the tweeters so they aim toward the ears of the listener.

Placing Tweeters

If you use rear speakers only for fill, you can add surface-mount tweeters in the front only. If you listen to front and rear speakers at nearly equal volume levels, you should add tweeters in the rear too. This will improve the frequency response for backseat listeners and will avoid the problem of "floating" stereo images in which instruments appear to move around depending on the frequency range they are producing. For optimum performance, tweeter modules should be mounted using the following guidelines:

- Mount tweeters near their corresponding full-range speakers.
- Do not mount where a passenger forms an obstacle between you and a tweeter.
- Do not mount too close to your ear (you'll hear only that speaker).
- Mount tweeters as close to ear level as possible.
- Aim tweeters toward listeners' ears.
- Beware of windshield reflections.

Some of these rules conflict in a normal installation, and the practical and aesthetic aspects of mounting must be considered as well, so you must weigh the relative importance of many factors.

Under no circumstances should a tweeter be mounted more than 6 inches from its corresponding full-range speaker. Violating this rule will degrade imaging. Restrict tweeter placement to a 6-inch range in all directions, then consider how to best satisfy the other guidelines. Possible locations include door (Fig. 3-4), dashboard, windshield pillar, and kick panel. Remember, you'll need to run wires to the tweeter from the full-range speaker, so consider ease of wiring.

Windshields can be thought of as sound mirrors for tweeters. If you imagine your tweeter as a lightbulb, then consider what you would see in the reflection of the windshield when sitting in the driver's seat. The apparent image of the tweeter is just as real and powerful as the tweeter itself. If you can see both the lightbulb and its reflection at the same time, you are in trouble—imaging will be smeared. The further apart the apparent image and the actual source, the worse the smearing. If you must mount a tweeter on the top of the dashboard, either mount it very close to the windshield or aim it so that either the direct path or reflected path will strongly dominate over the other.

FIGURE 3-4

Door-mounted tweeters. (*Courtesy of Crutchfield.*)

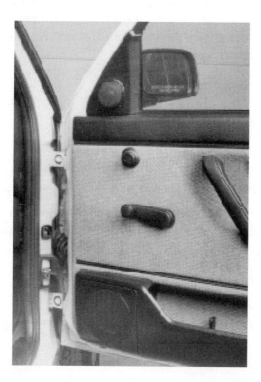

Connecting Tweeters

Surface-mount tweeters should be wired as shown in Fig. 3-5.

The crossover capacitor allows only the high-frequency components of the signal to reach the tweeter. This prevents low frequencies from causing distortion in the tweeter or burning it out. The crossover frequency defines the dividing line between the high frequencies, which are passed to the tweeter, and the low frequencies, which are filtered out. The capacitor should be the non-polarized type (also called bipolar). Table 3-2 shows some common values of crossover frequencies and the corresponding crossover capacitor values for 4-ohm tweeters.

If you want to calculate your own capacitor values, use this equation:

$$C = \frac{1}{2\,\pi\, fR}$$

where f is the crossover frequency in hertz, R is the tweeter impedance in ohms, and C is farads.

Normally tweeter modules are provided with crossover capacitors, but you may wish to use a different value depending on the high-frequency performance of your existing speakers. Experiment to find the value that sounds best, opting for the smallest capacitor value (highest crossover frequency) you find acceptable.

Important: Changing the crossover frequency strongly affects how much power the tweeter must handle. For example, *lowering* the crossover frequency from 8 to 6 kHz subjects the tweeter to roughly 40 percent *more* power. Similarly, *increasing* the crossover frequency from 8 to 12 kHz subjects the tweeter to roughly 40 percent *less* power.

After installing tweeter modules, you may find that they seem too loud compared to the existing speakers. (This is because tweeters are normally more efficient than full-range speakers.) There are three ways you can deal with this:

- Turn down the treble control on the head unit.
- Increase the crossover frequency (by reducing the capacitor value).
- Pad the tweeters using resistors.

Pads are special attenuation circuits designed to maintain the impedance looking into them. In this case, the pad maintains a 4-ohm input

FIGURE 3-5

Wiring for surface-mount tweeters.

TABLE 3-2

Capacitor Values for
Common Crossover
Frequencies

Crossover Frequency	Capacitor Value (4-ohm Tweeter)
6 kHz	6.8 μF
8 kHz	4.7 μF
12 kHz	3.3 μF

impedance so that the crossover works as intended. The circuit for padding tweeters is shown in Fig. 3-6. Table 3-3 shows the resistors to use for 3- and 6-dB pads for a 4-ohm tweeter. Be sure to use power resistors, or you will burn them out. The power ratings shown are adequate for a high-power head unit—power ratings will need to be increased when higher-power amplifiers are used. Mount the crossover and pad components on a small board secured to the car. This will prevent short circuits to ground that could blow your head unit.

Upgrading Existing Speakers

Upgrading your existing speakers is a simple and unobtrusive way to extend high-frequency and bass response. It also lets you increase power handling.

Choosing Speakers

The first step in upgrading is to understand what you have space for. Drop-in replacements are made for almost any size opening, but you

FIGURE 3-6

Circuit for padding
tweeters.

TABLE 3-3

Component Values for Padding Tweeters

Attenuation	R_s (4-ohm Tweeter)	R_p (4-ohm Tweeter)
3 dB	1 ohm	10 ohms
	2 watts	2 watts
6 dB	2 ohms	4 ohms
	5 watts	2 watts

must know the maximum depth as well as the size of the mounting hole. For odd-size factory holes, mounting adapter plates that permit standard aftermarket speakers to fit are available.

Crutchfield has done a tremendous job in this department. Their catalog shows what size speakers (including depth) fit in each factory location in your vehicle. They also provide installation guides that tell you how to access and remove your existing speakers. Their product lineup includes a wide selection of speakers.

When choosing speakers, opt for a two-way model using a dome tweeter (Fig. 3-7). Dual-cone models can't reproduce high frequencies, and the extra driver in three-way models (Fig. 3-8) is more for show than performance. If a speaker is to be mounted off-axis from your ears, choose a model with a pivoting tweeter so you can aim it toward you for better sound. Power handling and frequency response are important, but unfortunately you can't trust most published specs. Even supposedly reputable manufacturers often make exorbitant claims about power handling and frequency response. All other factors being equal, voice coil diameter is a

FIGURE 3-7

Kappa 62.5i two-way speaker. (*Courtesy of Infinity.*)

FIGURE 3-8

Kappa 63.5i three-way speaker. (*Courtesy of Infinity.*)

good indicator of power handling. A typical 1-inch voice coil can be expected to handle about 35 watts, and a 2-inch voice coil about 125 watts. For frequency response, there's something to be said for listening to speakers in a showroom.

Sensitivity is a term for how loud a speaker will play with 1 watt of power. This is important if you are using a normal or high-powered head unit, but not so important if you are using separate power amps capable of higher output power. A decibel or two of difference doesn't matter, but more than that should be weighed in your purchase decision.

Cone material and surround material (Table 3-4) are important in the harsh automotive environment, but it's hard to wade through the hype. Polypropylene cones are extremely resistant to environmental deterioration and are unaffected by humidity. But poly cones are a temperature-sensitive plastic, and become soft in the heat, and hard when cold, affecting their sound. Paper-based cones absorb moisture, so humidity affects their sound. Coatings can be used to improve the resistance to humidity and sunlight, and reinforcement additives such as Kevlar, glass, mica, or ceramic can be used to improve the sonic performance of paper-based cones. Yet

TABLE 3-4

Common Speaker Surround Materials

Surround Material	Comments
Foam	Deteriorates with sunlight and time
⟨BEST⟩ Butyl rubber	Good choice

another option is fiber cones made from woven or nonwoven Kevlar or carbon (graphite) fibers. The problem with pure Kevlar is that it's so lightweight and rigid, it tends to ring like a bell. Materials such as Tri-Laminate, resin laminate, carbon-blended poly, kapok, poly-graphite, graphite-quartz, Foam-Infused IMPP, titanium composite, ceramic metal matrix, Duralam, and mica-injected polypropylene offer the promise of superior performance. Most of these are variants of polypropylene and paper-based cones, and may provide a performance advantage. What they mainly provide is a marketing advantage.

The surround is the soft ring around the outside of the cone with the bulge in it. Choose rubber (Table 3-4) if this driver will be exposed to the sun (for example, if you're mounting it on the top of the dashboard or on the rear deck).

Strive for the most bass possible in front. It will prevent the undesirable effect of all the bass coming from behind you. The keys to good bass in the front (or anywhere, for that matter) are a good driver and a good enclosure. Creating good bass means moving lots of air, so cone area is important too. Choose the largest driver that will fit in a hole. You can buy adapters that let you mount a larger driver in a hole (Fig. 3-9): for example, a 6×9 driver in a 4×10 hole. Depth extender rings that let you install deep speakers in shallow compartments such as kick panels or doors are also available (Fig. 3-10).

Making the Best of the Existing Enclosure

The enclosure will strongly affect your sound quality, especially the bass and mid-range. To a large extent, you are stuck with whatever the car has to offer. Ideally, the enclosure is large, sealed, and nonresonant.

In the case of replacing door speakers, doors are usually large and somewhat sealed, but they are typically resonant. You can reduce the resonance problem by using foam baffles (Fig. 3-11). These are soft foam cups

FIGURE 3-9

6×9 adapters.
(*Courtesy of MCM Electronics.*)

FIGURE 3-10

Depth extender rings. (*Courtesy of Parts Express.*)

FIGURE 3-10

Depth extender rings. (*Courtesy of Parts Express.*)

installed behind the drivers. Foam baffles have the added benefit of reducing road noise (which can pass right through the speaker cone) as well as protecting the back of your speaker against water and dirt that may sometimes find their way inside your door. Applying Dynamat or other sound-deadening material is another effective way to improve the sound of door speakers by reducing unwanted door panel vibrations and road noise.

In the case of replacing dash-mounted speakers, the enclosure is an open-backed cabinet. Open-backed cabinets allow the sound from the back of the speaker to be heard—in this case, from under the dashboard. This causes frequency response ripples (peaks and valleys) in the midrange and cancellation of deep bass. The closer the speaker is to the bottom of the dashboard, the worse the problem is.

Some improvement can be made in the case of frequency response ripples by installing a cardboard box stuffed with damping material (such as fiberglass or polyester batting) behind the driver (see Fig. 3-12). You may be able to use the flaps of the box as a mounting flange; otherwise you must devise your own method of securing the box. It's not important that the box make a tight seal against the dashboard, but it should be secure enough not to rattle or vibrate.

FIGURE 3-11

Foam baffles. (*Courtesy of MCM Electronics.*)

Box with damping
material behind the
driver.

In cases where dash speakers are mounted near the bottom of the dash, it may be best to consider an alternate location.

Installing Speakers in a New Location

Installing speakers in a new location is necessary when existing speaker locations are inadequate. Existing locations may be inadequate for reasons of imaging, inability to accommodate drivers of the desired size, or enclosure volume. This is often the case for front factory speaker openings.

One important rule when adding speakers is that more isn't better. This refers to the number of speakers covering a particular frequency range. For example, you don't want to have a full-range driver in the kick panel and also on the top of the dashboard. Even with good-quality drivers, you should not try to create a wall of sound. Not only will it degrade your imaging, it will create a frequency response with lots of peaks and valleys. (This is because the two drivers have a slightly different time delay to reach your ear, and this produces an interference pattern that cancels some frequencies and reinforces others.) If you need increased power handling, choose a speaker that can provide it rather than using multiple drivers.

The one exception to the "more isn't better" rule is subwoofers. The wavelengths at deep bass frequencies are long compared to the distances between drivers, so interference patterns aren't a problem.

Choosing a Location

There are two main factors for deciding where to put speakers for the best sound: imaging and enclosure. Imaging depends on where the speakers are with respect to your ears. For best imaging, you want to minimize the path length difference between your ears and the speakers (Fig. 3-13). Imaging also involves things like reflections off the windshield or obstructions, such as passengers. Enclosure is the space that the back of the speaker radiates into—ideally it's large, sealed, and nonresonant. Table 3-5 shows common mounting locations for front speakers and their imaging and enclosure traits.

The front edge of the front doors is a popular location for front speakers because of the ease of installation. It provides a good enclosure but is a non-ideal imaging location because of the typically large path length difference. Placing the speakers toward the center or rear of the front doors makes imaging even worse. It causes each listener to hear mainly one speaker and shifts the image too far back. In some cases, it may cause a passenger to block a speaker entirely. If you choose door-mounting speakers, use foam baffles behind the speakers to reduce resonance problems and road noise as well as protect the back of your speakers against water and dirt.

Kick panels (the side panels, under the dash) are one of the best locations for imaging because the path length difference is usually small. Speakers here should be aimed toward the listener for good results. The small enclosure volume usually strongly limits the bass response. This means you will either need to use back speakers to provide deep bass or add a subwoofer.

The dashboard can provide reasonable imaging from a path length difference standpoint, but the top dashboard location suffers from windshield reflections that degrade imaging and frequency response smoothness. Another problem with the dashboard is that it's a poor enclosure—an open-backed cabinet. This allows the sound from the back of the speaker to be heard through the bottom of the dashboard. The combined sound from the front of the speaker and under the dash results in a frequency response with ripples in the mid-range and deep bass cancellation. The cardboard box with damping material, explained previously, helps with mid-range smoothness. Because of the limited bass response, you will either need to use back speakers to provide deep bass or add a subwoofer.

FIGURE 3-13

Path length differences for front speaker locations.

Path Difference = 22"   20"   44"   **Front Door - Front**

Path Difference = 5"   43"   48"   **Kick Panel**

Path Difference = 15"   27"   42"   **Dashboard - Top**

TABLE 3-5

Common Front
Speaker Locations

Front Speaker Location	Comments
Front door—front	Good enclosure but non-ideal imaging location
Front door—center or rear	Good enclosure but very poor imaging location
⟨BEST⟩ Kick panel	Good imaging location (must aim toward ears) Small enclosure makes bass below 150 Hz difficult
Dashboard—top	Windshield reflections degrade imaging. Open-back enclosure produces mid-range frequency response ripples and makes bass below 100 Hz difficult
Dashboard—front or bottom	Open-back enclosure produces strong mid-range frequency response ripples and makes bass below 200 Hz difficult

The best location for rear speakers should be determined by enclosure rather than imaging concerns. This is because in most installations the rear speakers provide the deep bass for the entire system. You should choose whatever location provides the biggest and best sealed box. If you have a trunk, use it!

Center Channel Speakers

For 5.1 channel audio, you'll need a center channel speaker. This is in addition to the right and left front, right and left rear, and subwoofer speakers. Ideally, the center channel speaker should be at the same height and should have the same frequency response as the front speakers.

Unfortunately, most cars don't provide a factory speaker hole in this location, and dashboard real estate is tight. Trying to install a speaker in a dashboard without a factory hole is a difficult project, especially if you want it to look and sound good. In addition to the challenge of mounting a center channel speaker, most amplifiers lack the fifth channel needed to drive it.

Fortunately, there are some clever products to help you solve this problem. Clarion offers a 1/2 DIN (1-inch tall) center channel speaker with amplifier (Fig. 3-14). This mounts in your dash just like any other 1/2 DIN

FIGURE 3-14

Clarion SRK5
1/2 DIN center
channel speaker.
(*Courtesy of Clarion.*)

accessory. The SRK5 has five ¾-inch full-range speakers in a sealed enclosure and two 1-inch mid-bass reinforcement speakers ported to the front of the enclosure. It comes with a 25 watt amplifier. The amp has an internal 200 Hz crossover to prevent overdriving the speaker with deep bass.

Alpine offers another option (Fig. 3-15). The SBS-0715 is a dash-mount center channel speaker. It uses a 2.75-inch full-range speaker and comes with a 20 watt amplifier.

Installing a Door Speaker

The first step in installing a new speaker in a door is removing the door panel. Start by removing the window crank handle (Fig. 3-16). Some handles are held on with a screw, which is sometimes hidden by a snap-on cap. Most are held in place by a spring clip. To remove the clip, you can use a window crank clip removing tool or a piece of coat hanger with a tiny hook bent into the end. Depress the surrounding panel, look behind the window crank handle, and rotate the handle until you see the spring clip. Then gently push it off with the window crank clip removing tool or pull it off with the hook.

FIGURE 3-15

Alpine SBS-0715
dash-mount center
channel speaker.
(*Courtesy of Alpine
Electronics, Inc.*)

NOTE *To reinstall the handle later, first snap the spring clip onto the handle, then push the handle back onto its shaft until it locks into place.*

After removing the window crank handle, remove the armrest (usually secured with a few Phillips-head screws) and any trim around the door handle. The only thing holding the door panel on now should be a half dozen friction fittings and possibly a few more screws.

With all the screws removed, start at a bottom corner and pull the panel straight out. Use a large flathead screwdriver to help pry it off. If a friction fitting breaks, you can get replacements from an auto parts store. Once the corner is loose, work across the bottom and up both sides, being careful not to use too much force. With the bottom and sides loose, the panel should now be hanging by some trim that sticks down into the window well. Lift straight up and it should come free.

Cutting the Hole

Once you've decided on the general location for the new speakers, get out the template that comes with them. You'll find it along with the instructions or printed on the box. Place the template over the area you've selected and make note of any possible obstructions or problems such as an irregular mounting surface.

Check what's behind the surface you're about to cut. Make sure no internal mechanisms will be affected. Be especially careful to check that the speaker will not interfere with the window and window crank mechanisms. Check the clearance with the window rolled down. If it's close, try rolling the window up and down before doing anything permanent. Also try closing the door—the mechanism that holds the door open can sometimes intrude into the speaker mounting cavity as the door closes. The risk of clearance problems is smaller when enlarging a factory location for a speaker than when creating a new opening.

Keeping in mind the general area you've selected for the speaker, check the door to see how much, if any, metal you'll need to cut. Very few doors are solid sheets of metal—there are usually several holes. Double-check the depth available in the door for mounting your speaker. If you think the measurement is too close, you may be able to use a spacer ring.

Metal Cutting Tips

Here are some techniques that will help you make cleaner cuts and avoid damaging your car:

- Instead of trying to cut through the door's hardboard panel and sheet metal at the same time, remove and cut the hardboard panel with an X-Acto or utility knife. Then cut the corresponding sheet metal with a jigsaw equipped with a metal cutting blade. If you try to cut both layers at once, you may rip the panel covering.
- Make sure the blade of the jigsaw (in its most extended position) doesn't reach through the surface you're cutting to the exterior sheet metal of the car. If it does, it will peck numerous dents very quickly! Similarly, make sure the window is rolled up and there are no other obstructions the saw blade can reach.
- If you're cutting metal that will not be concealed behind a door panel, wrap the base of the saw with electrical tape to prevent marring.
- When using a jigsaw or any other power tool, always wear safety glasses or goggles (Fig. 3-17).

FIGURE 3-17

Cutting a door hole with a jigsaw. (*Courtesy of Crutchfield.*)

Locate this same position on the back of the door panel. Tape the supplied template on the exact spot and trace the inside edge with a pen. Lay the panel flat on a clean surface and cut out the circle with a sharp X-Acto or utility knife. Be patient. A dull blade or too much haste here might rip the fabric. Repeat the procedure for the other door, making sure to cut in the same place. You can hold the cut door panel against the uncut one and trace the hole with a pen to guarantee they will be the same.

Frequently the speaker location will partially overlap an existing hole, which can be easily enlarged. If the amount of cutting involved is small, a utility hacksaw can be used. If there is no hole to start with, use a drill to make a pilot hole for the jigsaw blade.

After the hole is cut, but before the speaker is installed, vacuum out all the metal particles and other debris. Particles can get into a speaker and cause buzzing.

If you're going to apply Dynamat or other sound-deadening material, now is the time. You'll first need to clean the surface with solvent to ensure a permanent bond with the adhesive-backed sheets. Using a utility knife or scissors, cut the sheet to the desired shape and size. You may find a cardboard or paper template helpful. Remove the backing from the sheet and apply the material to the prepared surface. On large surfaces, remove the backing in sections, working your way down and across the panel. Using a roller tool (Fig. 3-18) to work the material into the contours of the

FIGURE 3-18
Installing sound-deadening material.
(*Courtesy of Dynamic Control.*)

metal panel helps improve adhesion and damping performance. Use a utility knife to poke holes into any air pockets that may have formed, then roll them out.

Wiring It Up

Before replacing the door panel, don't forget to run the speaker wire. It will have to exit the body of the car in the doorjamb and enter the door as close to that spot as possible. Often there are precut holes (with plugs in them) that will work out nicely. To run your wires from the door into the car body, try to use the factory rubber tubing between the door and the door jamb. If the tube is not present on your car, it may be available from a junkyard. If a factory boot or plugs are not present, you'll need to drill ⅜-inch holes to run the wiring. Before you drill a hole in the door, make sure it will provide access to the speaker location. Sometimes structural steel isolates the front edge of the door. It may still be possible to route this way, but check first.

Protect the wiring from the sharp edges of the holes by using rubber grommets in the holes or flexible tubing run between the two holes. This will keep the insulation from being cut after countless openings and closings of the door. Make sure the wire can't get pinched by the hinge or some other portion of the door jamb. Remember to leave enough slack in the wire to accommodate the door opening all the way.

Once you've finished pulling the speaker wire through the holes, pull the end through the speaker hole you've cut in the door panel and hang the panel from the top (hooked into the window well). If you accidentally broke a strategically located (like a corner) friction fitting when removing the panel, replace it with either a new one, or in a pinch, one taken from the middle of the panel along the bottom.

If your new speaker is designed to be top mounted, you can replace the door panel now. A foam baffle should be installed between the door and the door panel. When the door panel is properly positioned, push the friction fittings back into their seats and replace enough of the screws, armrest, etc. to hold the panel loosely in place. Do not reattach the window crank yet, since you may have to remove the panel again.

Hold the speaker in its new home, mark the screw holes, and remove the speaker. Drill the holes. Connect the speaker wires to the speaker, observing the proper polarity. The positive terminal is usually marked with a + or a colored dot.

Speaker Polarity Tip

It is important to observe the correct speaker polarity when connecting speaker wires. If you attach a set of wires to the terminals of one speaker backward, that speaker will be out of phase and your bass performance will suffer as a result.

NOTE *If EVERY speaker in the vehicle is wired backward, no problems will result, but it is best to wire them properly to make sure future repairs or speaker additions won't inadvertently cause a phasing problem.*

If the positive terminal of a speaker isn't marked, use the speaker polarity tester in Fig. 3-19.

This is nothing more than a flashlight battery with wires connected. Any 1.5-volt battery will work. (Note: Do not use a 9-volt battery to check a tweeter's polarity—it could destroy the tweeter.) Use tape to hold the wires onto the battery terminals.

Connect the minus wire to one speaker terminal and touch the plus wire to the other speaker terminal. Watch the speaker cone when you connect the battery. Does it move out or in? If it moves out, then the plus terminal of the battery is connected to the plus terminal of the speaker. (Otherwise, the plus terminal of the battery is connected to the minus terminal of the speaker.) Mark the plus terminal accordingly.

FIGURE 3-19

Speaker polarity tester.

When supplied, use speed clips (Fig. 3-20) over the new screw holes. They give the screws something extra to hold on to, providing extra support when the door is slammed. Once the speaker is installed, put the grille on immediately to prevent damage to the speaker while you do other work.

FIGURE 3-20
Speed clip.

Installing Separates

Separates (also called component speakers) are individually installed woofers and tweeters (Fig. 3-21). (This is instead of having the tweeter mounted in front of the woofer, as is the case with coaxial speakers.) Normally, separates are sold as matched sets, including woofer, tweeter, and crossover.

The advantages of separates are the quality of the components—especially the crossover—and the flexibility of mounting. The disadvantages are the high cost and the additional installation work.

The quality of component woofers and tweeters is usually superior to that of coaxial speakers, for marketing rather than technical reasons. In other words, there's no reason why component drivers should inherently be any better than those used in a coaxial speaker, other than that this market niche demands it. So don't rush out and buy some amazingly

FIGURE 3-21
Separates. (*Courtesy of JL Audio.*)

low-priced component system assuming you're getting more than you paid for.

The crossover splits the music signal into low frequencies (bass), which go to the woofer, and high frequencies (treble), which go to the tweeter. In a typical coaxial speaker, a simple capacitor is used to prevent bass from going to the tweeter and nothing is used to prevent high frequencies from going to the woofer. This approach is inexpensive and small enough to fit conveniently on the basket assembly of the speaker. Unfortunately its performance is marginal. The crossover module provided with component systems does not have the same size limitation, and because of the marketing niche, some money can be spent on a real crossover. Component crossovers provide filtering for both the woofer and tweeter and are often 12 dB/octave (as opposed to 6 dB/octave for a simple capacitor). The difference can be quite audible, particularly in mid-range smoothness and lower distortion.

Having a separate tweeter provides flexibility of mounting in the sense that you can now mount the woofer in a spot that would be unacceptable for tweeter orientation in a coaxial speaker. Also, you can mount the tweeter in a spot where a woofer wouldn't fit. For example, you could mount a woofer on the bottom front corner of the kick panel, facing the opposite woofer, and a tweeter on the top rear corner of the kick panel, facing the listeners.

Follow the guidelines in the "Adding Surface-Mount Tweeters" section earlier in this chapter for where to mount tweeters. Remember, a tweeter

FIGURE 3-22

Q-Forms kick panel pods—(*a*) before; (*b*) after. (*Courtesy of Q-Logic.*)

(a)   (b)

should not be mounted more than 6 inches from its woofer. Violating this rule will degrade imaging. Restrict tweeter placement to a 6-inch range in all directions, then consider how to best satisfy the other mounting guidelines.

Separates are most advantageous in front, where mid-range performance is most critical and mounting flexibility is more likely to provide a benefit. You may choose to use separates in front and coaxial speakers in the rear to save money without sacrificing top-notch performance.

If you plan to use separates in the front, consider the kick panel pods by Q-Forms (Fig. 3-22). These custom-molded pods are available for many popular vehicles and accommodate a 5¼-inch woofer plus a separate tweeter. The pods aim the speakers toward the listener for good imaging, increase the size of the enclosure to improve bass response, and maintain a factory appearance. They are available from Crutchfield and are priced at about $150 a pair.

CHAPTER 4

Subwoofers and Subwoofer Projects

This chapter is by far the largest in the book. There are two good reasons for this. First, subwoofers ("subs") are one of the most important components in a high-quality auto sound system. Second, there are a tremendous number of options you must choose from every step of the way.

A subwoofer not only gives you a rock-solid bottom end, it lets you play your other speakers louder with less distortion by diverting the burden of deep bass to the subwoofer. A subwoofer is almost a necessity if you use the front speakers for imaging and the rear speakers for fill, because of the difficulty in getting decent bass from the front.

Because subs are so important, manufacturers offer a staggering array of products to support a vast number of approaches. You must choose between everything from powered subs with built-in crossovers to separates, and every combination in between. You can design and build your own box, choose a pre-made one and install your own driver, or buy a ready-made system. There are sealed, ported, bandpass, and other types of enclosures to choose from.

This chapter will cut through the hype and give you the know-how to choose and use the right components, whether you want to buy or build.

System Configuration Options

There are six basic configurations for adding a subwoofer system (Table 4-1). The first two use *speaker-level* crossovers, the rest use *preamp-level* crossovers.

Speaker-level crossovers are used between the amplifiers and speakers and are passive (requiring no power). Preamp-level crossovers are used before the amplifiers and are generally active (requiring power). It's common to see the terms *passive* and *speaker-level* used synonymously in advertising, but preamp-level crossovers can be passive too.

The preamp-level crossover configurations vary only in how they repackage the three basic building blocks of a subwoofer system: crossover, amp, and subwoofer. Separates provide the greatest flexibility; amplified subs with built-in crossovers provide the most convenience. Other options fall in between.

The secret to good subwoofer performance is in the crossover. Regardless of which approach you choose, make sure you satisfy the requirements for a good crossover. This is explained in detail in the section entitled "What to Look For in a Subwoofer Crossover," later in this chapter.

TABLE 4-1

Configurations
for Adding a
Subwoofer

Configuration	Diagram	Comments
Conventional speaker-level crossover, sub		Lets you use a single amp to drive a dual voice coil subwoofer and boost a pair of speakers. Subwoofer level and crossover frequency are not adjustable. Typical 12-dB/octave sub slope is inadequate for most applications. Not recommended.
Tri-way crossover, sub		Lets you use a single tri-way-capable amp to drive a sub-woofer and boost a pair of speakers. Subwoofer level and crossover frequency are not adjustable. Typical 12-dB/octave sub slope is inadequate for most applications. Not recommended.
Separates: crossover, amp, sub		Offers the most flexibility and best performance. (Amp has no built-in crossover or one considered inadequate.)
Amp with built-in crossover, sub		Can save the cost of a separate subwoofer crossover. Built-in crossover may be inadequate.
Separate crossover, amplified sub		Offers potential cost savings and convenience by combining a subwoofer with a matching amp. (Amplified subwoofer has no built-in crossover or one considered inadequate.)
Amplified sub with built-in crossover		The ultimate in convenience. Built-in crossover may be inadequate.

Conventional Speaker-Level Crossover, Subwoofer

A conventional speaker-level crossover connects between any power amp and your speakers. It's a high-power device that generally provides a 6-dB/octave high-pass filter to a pair of main speakers and a 12-dB/octave low-pass filter to a dual voice coil subwoofer (or a pair of regular subwoofers).

This approach lets you use a single amp (rather than two) to both drive a subwoofer and boost a pair of speakers. This would seem to provide a substantial cost savings, but for the same amount of total power, this is not usually the case. For example, the cost of a single 100W × 2 amp for a speaker-level crossover setup is comparable to the cost of two 50W × 2 amps for a preamp-level crossover approach.

In addition, there are a number of performance limitations involved with using a speaker-level crossover. Because a single amp is shared by all drivers, the tweeters are unprotected against clipping of deep bass to the subwoofer (explained in detail in Chap. 9). Unlike most preamp-level crossovers, speaker-level crossovers have fixed crossover frequencies and cannot be adjusted to optimize your system. Furthermore, the subwoofer level is not adjustable with respect to the main speakers with a speaker-level crossover.

Finally, the 12-dB/octave subwoofer slope usually found in this type of crossover is generally inadequate. This is because a 12-dB/octave slope allows mid-bass to be heard, which lets you hear where the sub is located. This degrades imaging. You can fix this deficiency by using an 18- or 24-dB/octave slope, but this generally requires you to design and build your own crossover using coils and capacitors. A 12-dB/octave slope can be acceptable with bandpass subwoofers because of their inherently reduced high-frequency output.

For these reasons, conventional speaker-level crossovers are not recommended for subwoofers.

Tri-Way Crossover, Subwoofer

A tri-way (or tri-mode) crossover connects between a tri-way-capable amp and your speakers. It's a high-power, passive device that generally provides a 6-dB/octave high-pass filter to a pair of main speakers and a 12-dB/octave low-pass filter to a single subwoofer.

This approach lets you use a single amp (rather than two) to both drive a subwoofer and boost a pair of speakers. This would seem to provide a substantial cost savings, but for the same amount of total power, this is not usually the case. For example, the cost of a single $100W \times 2$ amp for a tri-way setup is comparable to the cost of two $50W \times 2$ amps for a preamp-level crossover approach.

In addition, there are a number of performance limitations involved with using a tri-way crossover. Because a single amp is shared by all drivers, the tweeters are unprotected against clipping of deep bass to the subwoofer (explained in detail in Chap. 9). Unlike most preamp-level crossovers, tri-way crossovers have fixed crossover frequencies and cannot be adjusted to optimize your system. The subwoofer level is not adjustable with respect to the main speakers in a tri-way setup. Finally, the 12-dB/octave subwoofer slope found in this type of crossover is generally inadequate. This is because a 12-dB/octave slope allows mid-bass to be heard, which lets you hear where the sub is located. This degrades imaging.

For these reasons, tri-way crossovers are not recommended.

Separates

Using a separate crossover, amp, and subwoofer offers you the most flexibility and the best performance of any of the configurations. You can choose whatever power level you need in an amplifier and pick a subwoofer that is a perfect fit for your vehicle. Most importantly, you can select a subwoofer crossover that provides a steep slope as well as important features usually found only in separate crossovers.

The amplifier in this configuration either has no built-in crossover or has one that is considered inadequate. You may be able to take advantage of an inadequate built-in crossover to reduce the requirements for a separate crossover. See the box to learn how.

Using a Built-In Crossover Together with a Separate Crossover

If you've got an inadequate built-in crossover, you have two choices:

- Bypass the built-in crossover and use a good separate crossover.
- Use the built-in crossover together with a separate crossover.

An inadequate built-in subwoofer crossover can be defeated by choosing the bypass setting. (If there is no bypass setting, setting the built-in crossover to the highest cutoff frequency will usually allow the separate crossover to dominate.) Since the separate crossover will now be doing all the work, you will need to choose a model that meets all your needs. The advantage of this approach is that you then have a single set of controls to deal with, and what you see with them is what you get.

Alternately, you can use the built-in crossover to effectively increase the performance of the separate crossover. This reduces the requirements for the separate crossover and can save money. For example, each crossover by itself might have a 12-dB/octave slope. Using the two together, you can achieve a 24-dB/octave slope (the slopes of two cascaded filters add).

Table 4-2 shows an example of how this works. Suppose both your crossovers are 12 dB/octave and have 80/120-Hz cutoff frequency selection switches. The possible crossover setting combinations and their combined responses are shown in Table 4-2.

TABLE 4-2

Combined Cutoff Frequency of Cascaded Crossovers

Separate Crossover Setting (12 dB/octave)	Built-In Crossover Setting (12 dB/octave)	Combined Filter Response (24 dB/octave)
80 Hz	80 Hz	65 Hz
80 Hz	120 Hz	74 Hz
120 Hz	80 Hz	74 Hz
120 Hz	120 Hz	97 Hz

There are two important things to notice in this table. First, you now have more cutoff frequencies available than either individual crossover provides. This gives you finer control (unless one of the crossovers was already continuously variable).

Second, the crossover frequencies shift to lower values when you combine two crossovers—about 20 percent below the nominally selected frequencies in this case. (This makes sense if you think about it: The two 80-Hz filters were each 3 dB down at 80 Hz, so the combination is 6 dB down at 80 Hz. The 3-dB down frequency of the combined response must be a lower frequency.) This could be good news or bad news depending on the frequency you want and the available frequencies.

Important: For best results with this approach, try to set both cutoff frequencies the same. This will give you the sharpest filter characteristic near the cutoff frequency.

Filter slopes aren't the only things that can benefit from this tactic. Features such as subsonic filters, polarity switches, and 45-Hz bass boost might be included in one crossover, but not the other.

Amp with Built-In Crossover, Subwoofer

Most of today's amps include a built-in low-pass crossover. This can be a great way to save the cost of a separate subwoofer crossover, but you need to make sure the built-in crossover meets your needs. (If it doesn't, consider the previous configuration and see the preceding box.)

Many built-in crossovers use shallow 6- or 12-dB/octave slopes. This may be acceptable if you plan to use a bandpass subwoofer (because of their inherently reduced high-frequency output), but shoot for 18 or 24 dB/octave otherwise. Similarly, many built-in crossovers offer only a single fixed cutoff frequency. This limits your ability to seamlessly integrate a subwoofer into your system. Few models offer subsonic filtering.

Amplifiers with capable built-in crossovers do exist. Alpine's MRP-M350 Class D mono sub amp (Fig. 4-1) provides a 24-dB/octave subwoofer crossover that's continuously variable from 50 to 200 Hz. It has a 15 Hz subsonic filter, adjustable bass boost, and both speaker and preamp-level inputs. Since it's Class D, its higher efficiency produces less heat and can save you money in power wiring, too.

Separate Crossover, Amplified Subwoofer

This approach uses a separate crossover in conjunction with an amplified subwoofer. The amplified subwoofer either has no built-in crossover or

FIGURE 4-1

Alpine MRP-M350 amplifier. (*Courtesy of Alpine Electronics, Inc.*)

has one that is considered inadequate. Either way, this approach offers potential cost savings and convenience by combining a subwoofer with a matching amp. Using a separate crossover guarantees you can obtain the performance and features you need in a crossover without severely limiting your choice of amplified subs.

Amplified subs without built-in subwoofer crossovers are becoming rare as manufacturers realize that they can include a bare-bones crossover for a small incremental cost. Unfortunately, most of these crossovers are inadequate for the job and need the help of an external crossover. You may be able to take advantage of an inadequate built-in crossover to reduce the requirements for a separate crossover. See the box on p. 65 to learn how.

The separate crossover used with this approach may be a subwoofer-only crossover or one with high-pass filtered outputs for the main channels too. If you are using separate amps to drive the main channels, then the latter is the way to go.

Amplified Subwoofer with Built-In Crossover

This approach is the ultimate in convenience. You just connect power and signal leads, adjust your settings, and you're done. Many amplified subs are designed to fit in the trunk or cargo area of almost any vehicle. Other products, such as MTX's Amplified Thunderforms (Fig. 4-2), are custom

FIGURE 4-2

MTX's Amplified Thunderform for GM/Chevrolet extended cab. (*Courtesy of MTX.*)

FIGURE 4-3

Kenwood KSC-SW1
compact powered
subwoofer. (*Courtesy of
Kenwood.*)

designed for specific popular cars, trucks, and SUVs to take advantage of
wasted space and to match the vehicle's interior. If you've only got space
for a shoebox, there's the KSC-SW1 from Kenwood (Fig. 4-3). This is a compact powered sub that puts out surprising bass for its size.

The main concern with all amplified subwoofers is making sure the
built-in crossover meets your needs. (If it doesn't, consider the previous
configuration and see the box on p. 65.) Many of the built-in crossovers
use shallow 6- or 12-dB/octave slopes. This may be acceptable for bandpass
subwoofers, but you need 18 or 24 dB/octave otherwise.

Adding a Subwoofer to Premium Factory Sound Systems

If you have a premium factory sound system (such as Delco/Bose or Ford/JBL)
and want to add a subwoofer, the situation is slightly more complicated than
with standard systems.

You can use any of the four preamp-level crossover configurations outlined
at the beginning of this chapter, but you'll need to use a line output converter
designed specifically for Bose or Ford Premium systems. The line output
converter is needed to convert the signals from the premium factory head unit
to a standard preamp-level signal suitable for crossover inputs.

Line Output Converters for Bose/Ford Premium Head Units

Line output converters are commonly used to convert head unit speaker-level
outputs to levels suitable for the preamp-level inputs of amps.

If you're dealing with a Bose or Ford Premium Sound factory head unit,
you'll want to use a line output converter specifically designed for interfacing
to these units. Using a standard LOC having low input impedance may damage
the output circuit of a Bose or Ford Premium Sound head unit. Using a
standard LOC with a Bose or Ford system can also result in extremely low

output from the LOC because of the relatively low signal levels of many premium factory system head units.

The LOCB.2 by Soundgate will accept any input signal from 350 mV to 6.6 volts and convert it to a 2.5-volt audio output suitable for aftermarket crossovers and amps. It also has a noise-blanking circuit that activates the audio path after turn-on noises have subsided.

Line Output Converters for Systems Using GM's Class 2 Data Bus

In 2002, GM added a new twist to some of its premium factory sound systems—Class 2 data bus control. GM's Premium/Smart Bose system is used in 2002 and later full-size trucks and SUVs. With this system, the head unit provides fixed-level audio signals to the factory amplifiers. The head unit issues commands to each amp via the Class 2 data bus to control volume, fader, and balance. This approach provides improved noise immunity, but makes adding a subwoofer more challenging.

The GMAA line output converter by Peripheral Electronics decodes GM's Class 2 data bus commands and uses them to provide varying output levels to an aftermarket subwoofer crossover and amp. Additionally, the GMAA reads the data bus and generates an amplifier remote turn-on signal so the aftermarket amp turns on and off with the head unit, not with the ignition.

Chrysler/Infinity Systems

Unlike Bose and Ford, Chrysler/Infinity systems use standard head unit technology. No line output converter is needed with crossovers having speaker-level inputs. A standard LOC will do the job of interfacing a Chrysler/Infinity head unit to a crossover lacking speaker-level inputs.

What to Look For in a Subwoofer Crossover

There are a number of considerations for choosing the right crossover for your application. You might choose a dedicated subwoofer crossover with subwoofer outputs only, or one with high-pass outputs too if you use amps to drive your main speakers. If you're thinking of biamping later on, you might choose a three-way model with subwoofer, woofer, and tweeter outputs. (See Chap. 9 for more details.)

The most important subwoofer crossover characteristics are listed in Table 4-3.

The crossover filter slope may be the single most important item to consider. To make it possible to put a subwoofer anywhere in the vehicle, the subwoofer crossover must be 18 dB/octave or higher. Slopes less than 18 dB/octave allow mid-bass and even mid-range to be heard from the

TABLE 4-3

What to Look For in a Subwoofer Crossover

Item	Comments
Crossover filter slope	18-dB/octave minimum.
	12-dB/octave minimum for bandpass boxes.
Cutoff frequency range	75- to 150-Hz minimum range.
	Continuously variable—a big plus.
High-pass outputs	Important if you have amps driving main speakers.
	6-dB/octave slope minimum.
Subsonic filter	Crucial for ported boxes, beneficial for others.
45-Hz bass boost	Useful for improving bass.
Polarity switch	Useful for improving bass.
Speaker-level inputs	Important if your head unit lacks preamp-level outputs.
Preamp-level inputs	Ground loop isolation is a big plus for reducing noise problems.
Output level controls	Of limited value—usually redundant with amp input level controls.
Automatic amp wake-up output	Saves having to run remote turn-on wire from head unit to sub amp.

subwoofer. Since only deep bass frequencies are nondirectional, this gives away the subwoofer location and degrades imaging. Who wants a bass guitar player under the seat? The only exception to this is bandpass boxes, where you can successfully use a 12-dB/octave crossover.

A subwoofer cutoff frequency range of 75 to 150 Hz in three or four steps is adequate for most situations. A continuously variable cutoff frequency control gives you full flexibility to seamlessly blend the subwoofer with the rest of your system. Even with high-pass crossovers on your main speakers, the natural low-frequency rolloff of woofers makes it difficult to predict the best subwoofer crossover frequency. A continuously variable crossover lets you avoid a gap or peak in your mid-bass.

High-pass outputs are an important feature if you have amps driving your main speakers. Using this feature saves you from having to install bass blocking crossovers in line with your main speakers. A 6-dB/octave slope is acceptable, but 12 dB/octave or higher is better. The high-pass slope for the main speakers does not need to be the same as the subwoofer low-pass slope.

A subsonic filter prevents very low frequencies from getting to the subwoofer amp and speaker. These frequencies are too low to be effectively reproduced by a subwoofer anyway, but they use up valuable amplifier and speaker headroom. A subsonic filter protects against unnecessary distortion and speaker damage as well as reducing annoying turn-on thumps. A subsonic filter is important for any subwoofer system, but it is crucial when ported boxes are used because they lack the protective air "shock absorber" of a sealed box.

Five to 10 dB of bass boost at 40 or 45 Hz extends the low-frequency response of most subwoofer systems without overdriving them.

A subwoofer polarity switch lets you select the proper polarity without having to reverse any speaker wires. Choose the setting that gives you the most bass.

If your head unit lacks preamp-level outputs, then speaker-level inputs are an important feature. This saves you from having to buy a line output converter to convert your head unit's speaker-level signals to preamp level. Preamp-level inputs are provided as standard equipment on almost every crossover. If you plan to use them, buy a model with ground loop isolation. This will go a long way toward preventing system noise problems.

Output level controls are usually provided for each set of outputs, but they are of limited value. They are usually redundant with the input level controls found on your amp.

There are many names for automatic amp wake-up output, a useful feature that eliminates having to run a remote turn-on wire from your head unit to your sub amp. It works by monitoring the DC voltage on a speaker wire from the head unit, and provides a signal to activate the subwoofer amp when the head unit is on. This can be a big time-saver when you're adding a subwoofer system in the trunk by tapping into the rear speaker wires and you have no other reason to pull the head unit out.

One final point. The important thing is to obtain the performance you need in your combined system. Many of the features listed above may be included in your power amp. If your amp has a subsonic filter, for example, you don't need to have one in the crossover too. If neither do, you can add one externally if you want to.

Choosing a Subwoofer Amplifier

Most of what you should know about choosing amps is contained in Chap. 7. That chapter also contains information on installing amps, amplifier power and ground wiring, remote turn-on hookup, and speaker wiring. There are two additional points worth covering here: how much power you need in a subwoofer amp and the best amplifier/subwoofer configurations.

How Much Power Do You Need?

The appropriate power for a subwoofer amp mainly depends on how much power is used for the rest of the system and the subwoofer crossover frequency used.

The typical frequency distribution of power in music is shown in Table 4-4.

Notice that less than half the power in music is above 300 Hz. This means that at least half the power in music is below 300 Hz. To make sure you're covered, use the following rule of thumb:

Rule of Thumb: The sub amp power should equal 1.5 times the power to the front speakers.

For example, suppose you are using a 50W × 4 amp to drive your main speakers. The rule of thumb says you should use a sub amp that can provide roughly 1.5 × (50 watts + 50 watts) = 150 watts to your sub. This could mean a 75W × 2 amp driving a dual voice coil sub or an amp that produces 150 watts when bridged to a single sub.

TABLE 4-4

Frequency Distribution of Power in Music

Frequency	Maximum Power Above That Frequency
300 Hz	50%
600 Hz	25%
1200 Hz	10%
2400 Hz	5%

This rule of thumb is quite generous with power to the sub for typical situations, but not all situations are typical. Consider using more power for your subwoofer amp if:

- Your subwoofer crossover frequency is higher than 150 Hz.

- Your subwoofer sensitivity is exceptionally low.

- Your subwoofer is installed in a trunk that is sonically isolated from the passenger compartment.

- You like music with lots of deep bass.

The Best Amplifier/Subwoofer Configurations

You should choose the right amplifier configuration to provide efficient power transfer to your speakers based on the number of subwoofers you plan to use and their impedances. Only by doing this are you getting the amplifier power you paid for.

Subwoofers are commonly available in 4-ohms, dual 4-ohms, and dual 2-ohms. Amplifiers usually support bridging and are 2 ohm stable, but there are exceptions. Because of the many possible combinations, the best configurations are shown for convenience in Table 4-5.

Table 4-5 shows maximum power and rated power configurations for both one- and two-subwoofer systems. Rated power configurations provide acceptably efficient power transfer to your speakers with little risk of overheated amplifiers. Rated power configurations are so named because they give you the rated power nominally specified using a 4-ohm load. Maximum power configurations provide the maximum power transfer to your speakers that is still safe for your amp. Maximum power configurations typically provide 50 percent more power transfer than rated power configurations for a given amp.

Configurations other than those shown may not provide satisfactory power to the speakers or may risk blowing the amp. For example, using rated power configurations with higher-impedance speakers than those shown is throwing away amplifier horsepower. Using maximum power configurations with lower-impedance speakers than those shown will most likely overheat your amp.

If the thought of having to choose an amplifier based on a subwoofer configuration bothers you, JL Audio has a solution with their "Slash"

Tip: An amp used in a maximum power configuration runs hotter, so be sure to mount it where it will have good air circulation.

TABLE 4-5

Amplifier/
Subwoofer
Configurations

Note: Configurations with the same letter (such as b1 and b2) use the same hardware, but are configured differently. For example, b1 and b2 both use a two-channel amp with a 2-ohm dual voice coil sub. Both provide the same performance, but you may prefer one method of wiring to another (or may not have a bridgeable amp).

Bridging

Bridging converts a stereo amp into a mono amp, which gives you more power than the sum of the two stereo channels. Of course, you must use an amp that is bridgeable to do this. As an example, a 50-watt per channel stereo amp might be bridgeable to a 150-watt mono configuration. Similarly, a 50-watt per channel four-channel amp might be bridgeable to a 150-watt per channel stereo configuration.

You must use a 4-ohm or higher speaker load when bridging. This means you can't run two 4-ohm woofers wired in parallel, for example. This is because a bridged amplifier "sees" a speaker load of half the actual value, so a 4-ohm speaker looks like a 2-ohm equivalent load. Very few amps can handle using anything less than 4 ohms in the bridged mode.

Be sure to follow the instructions included with the amp for the correct bridging procedure and connections—not all amps are alike.

Series and Parallel Wiring

If you want to try your hand at creating your own amplifier/speaker configurations, you will need to calculate the combined impedance of series- and parallel-wired speakers.

Series wiring refers to connecting multiple speakers (or the two sets of terminals on dual voice coil woofers) as shown in Fig. 4-4.

FIGURE 4-4
Series-wired speakers.

Notice that the plus terminal of one speaker (or set of terminals) is always connected to the minus terminal of the other. This is so both speakers (or voice coils) are driven in phase with each other. Calculating the combined impedance of series-wired speakers is easy—just add up the individual impedances. This is true for any number of speakers.

Parallel wiring refers to connecting multiple speakers (or the two sets of terminals on dual voice coil woofers) as shown in Fig. 4-5.

FIGURE 4-5
Parallel-wired speakers.

Notice that the plus terminal of one speaker (or set of terminals) is always connected to the plus terminal of the other. This is so both speakers (or voice coils) are driven in phase with each other. Calculating the combined impedance of parallel-wired speakers is more complicated. You need to add up 1 over each of the individual impedances, then take 1 over the total. This formula works for any number of speakers.

Once you understand the two basic calculations, you can calculate the impedance of combined series and parallel configurations. All you need to do is break the problem down by calculating simple series or parallel pieces of the configuration first. By substituting in the calculated values for these pieces, you'll be able to calculate the next level up until you're done.

The key to maximizing power in amplifier/subwoofer configurations is to present each amplifier with the lowest impedance load it can safely handle. This is usually 2 ohms for nonbridged amps and 4 ohms for bridged amps, but you should check the specs of any amp you plan to use.

You should avoid series wiring of speakers, with two exceptions—series wiring of the two voice coils of a dual voice coil subwoofer and series wiring of two opposing drivers mounted in an isobarik system. Wiring drivers in series otherwise can cause the back EMF of one driver to modulate the other driver, increasing distortion.

series of amps (Fig. 4-6). JL Audio's Regulated Intelligent Power Supply (R.I.P.S.) detects the impedance of the subwoofer load and delivers the same maximum power to impedances from 1.5 to 4 ohms and for power supply voltages from 11 to 14.5 volts.

Subwoofer Enclosure Options

When it comes to choosing a subwoofer enclosure, there are two factors involved—the amount of assembly you prefer and the type of enclosure

FIGURE 4-6

JL Audio 500/1 amplifier with R.I.P.S. (*Courtesy of JL Audio.*)

that is best for your installation. These two factors are interrelated, since the type of enclosure you choose might depend on the amount of assembly you prefer, and the amount of assembly you prefer might depend on the type of enclosure.

Subwoofer Amount of Assembly Options

If you plan to use one of the powered subwoofer configurations, then your subwoofer and box are already designed and assembled for you. Otherwise you have the flexibility to choose the amount of assembly you prefer. The three possibilities are shown in Table 4-6.

A ready-made subwoofer is by far the easiest approach, and is sure to look professional. For people who have no interest in delving into box science or construction, this is the way to go. Unfortunately it's no guarantee of good sound quality. If you choose this route, either buy a product with a solid reputation or audition before you buy. Don't trust specs to tell the whole story—a lot of manufacturers bend the truth in the way they specify performance.

If you're willing to spend the extra money, some manufacturers such as JL Audio and MTX offer ready-made subwoofers custom designed for popular makes of trucks and sport utility vehicles (Fig. 4-7). The fiberglass enclosures are contoured to precisely fit behind a seat and are carpeted to match the vehicle's interior. The sound is tailored to match the vehicle's acoustics as well.

Installing component drivers in a prefabricated box gives you the flexibility to choose both enclosure and drivers without having to build the

TABLE 4-6

Subwoofer Amount of Assembly Options

Amount of Assembly	Comments
Ready-made subwoofer	The easiest approach, and sure to look professional. No guarantee of good sound quality.
Component woofers in a prefab box	Gives you the flexibility to choose both enclosure and drivers without having to build the box yourself. Can save money compared to ready-made and provide better performance.
Build your own box	If you have basic woodworking skills, can save a lot of money. Lets you create any size and shape enclosure you wish, making best use of odd space.

FIGURE 4-7

JL Audio Stealthbox.
(*Courtesy of JL Audio.*)

box yourself. If you choose your speakers wisely, you can save money compared to ready-made and get better performance. (Advice on choosing a speaker and box is given later in this chapter.) Prefabricated boxes are available in a variety of sizes, shapes, and types (sealed, ported, bandpass) to accommodate almost any size driver or drivers. They generally come carpeted and have speaker terminals installed.

Some prefabricated boxes are custom made for specific applications. An example is the Q-Customs Camaro/Firebird/Trans Am enclosure (Fig. 4-8). It's designed to fit precisely in the rear storage well and accommodates a pair of 12-inch woofers.

If you have basic woodworking skills, building your own box can save a lot of money. It also lets you create any size and shape enclosure you wish, making best use of whatever odd space is available. Box design and construction are covered later in this chapter.

FIGURE 4-8

Q-Customs
Camaro/Firebird
enclosure—
(a) before; (b) after.
(*Courtesy of Q-Logic.*)

(a)   (b)

Types of Enclosures

There are many types of speaker enclosures you can choose from, including sealed, ported, bandpass, and transmission line. Whether you plan to buy a ready-made subwoofer, use a prefab box, or build your own, it's important that you understand the fundamental differences.

If you've ever seen a pair of 6 × 9 speakers wedged between the rear window and deck of a car, with no enclosure, you may have wondered: Why use a box at all? The basic answer is that the back of a speaker makes as much sound as the front, but of the opposite polarity. If you happen to be sitting where you get an equal amount of sound from front and back, the two will totally cancel each other out and you'll hear nothing! In practice, speakers without any enclosure will provide some high frequencies and mid-range, but no deep bass. This is because the sound from the back of the speaker gets delayed due to a longer reflected path to your ear. This causes sound cancellation at some frequencies (especially low ones) but reinforcement at others.

Using an enclosure is the practical solution to this problem. The most popular enclosure types for subwoofers are shown in Table 4-7.

Free-Air. Free-air (or enclosureless) subwoofers are designed to be mounted on the rear deck or behind the backseat, using the trunk as a large speaker enclosure. The idea here is for the trunk to isolate all of the sound from the back of the speaker, thus avoiding the problem of sound cancellation explained previously.

Assuming you have a trunk and a suitable mounting location, free-air subwoofers eliminate the need to build or buy a box. The problem is that most trunks do not provide good sonic isolation. This means that sound from the back of the speaker can be heard in the passenger compartment, canceling out deep bass. To check this for yourself, have a friend with a deep voice talk into your open trunk from the outside. You should be listening inside the passenger compartment with the windows rolled up. If you can barely hear your friend, then a free-air subwoofer will work in your car. Otherwise, choose one of the other options.

Sealed. Using a sealed box effectively prevents sound from the back of the speaker from being heard, but also affects the sound coming from the front of the speaker. The air inside a sealed box acts like a spring, effectively changing the behavior of the speaker. How this affects the sound depends on the size of the box and the particular driver.

Sealed boxes offer a number of advantages over the other enclosure types. They are the easiest box type to design and build. Sealed systems

TABLE 4-7

The Most Popular Enclosure Types for Subwoofers

Enclosure Type	Diagram	Comments
Free-air (trunk is enclosure)		Requires a trunk as the enclosure. Eliminates the need to build or buy a box. Poor performance in most cases due to poor sonic isolation of trunk causing deep bass cancellation.
Sealed		Easiest box type to design and build. Woofer is protected against turn-on thumps and subsonic bass. Provides the deepest bass if you must use a small enclosure. Cannot provide bass as deep as the other enclosure types for large enclosures.
Ported		More difficult to design and build than sealed systems. Provides no woofer protection against turn-on thumps and subsonic bass. Can provide bass at least an octave deeper than sealed boxes for a given driver. Requires a much bigger box than sealed systems.
Bandpass		More difficult to design and build than either sealed or ported systems. Produces sound over a narrow frequency range, reducing the requirement for a steep low-pass slope in a subwoofer crossover. Runs the risk of sounding like a "one-note" system. Requires a much bigger box than sealed systems.
Transmission line		Elaborate and expensive construction required to create the internal labyrinth structure. Possible to achieve deeper bass than with a sealed box. Not recommended.

are the least sensitive to using a box that is a little too big or small, or to drivers that are different than their published specs. This is a big benefit if you are planning to use component woofers in a prefab box. The spring effect of air in a sealed box provides woofer protection against turn-on thumps, subsonic bass energy, and going over bumps.

Sealed boxes provide the deepest bass if you must use a small enclosure. The big drawback of sealed boxes is that they cannot provide bass as deep as the other enclosure types for larger enclosures. However, the low-frequency rolloff characteristic of sealed systems is relatively shallow compared with that for ported and bandpass systems, resulting in useful deep bass below the "official" –3-dB cutoff frequency. Exactly what defines a small enclosure and how deep a sealed box can go is covered in the "Box Design" section later in this chapter.

Ported.   Ported enclosures make constructive use of the sound from the back of the speaker. Because of this, it becomes possible to achieve deeper bass than with a sealed box. In a ported system, the sound from the back of the speaker produces a resonant output at the port, much like producing a tone by blowing air across the mouth of a soda bottle. The port is tuned to provide constructive reinforcement of bass at the proper frequency.

Ported systems are more difficult to design and build than sealed systems. They are more sensitive than sealed systems to using a box that is a little too big or small and to drivers that are different than their published specs. Ported boxes provide no woofer protection against turn-on thumps, subsonic bass energy, and going over bumps.

The big plus of ported boxes is that they can provide bass at least an octave deeper than sealed boxes. That's the difference between 80-Hz bass and 40-Hz bass. However, a much bigger box—typically five times bigger—is required to get that octave improvement.

A primary factor in whether to use a ported box or a sealed box is how big a box you can tolerate. Small boxes should always be sealed, and large boxes should generally be ported. What is considered a big or small box is explained in the "Box Design" section later in this chapter.

Bandpass.   Bandpass enclosures are based on ported enclosures, except that the direct sound from the speaker is blocked off using a secondary sealed chamber. This means all you hear is the tuned output from the port. Unlike the other enclosure types, bandpass boxes only pass sound over a narrow frequency band. This reduces the requirement for a steep low-pass slope in a subwoofer crossover. Like the tone from a soda bottle, however, bandpass designs run the risk of sounding like "one-note" systems.

Bandpass systems are more difficult to design and build than either sealed or ported systems. They are very sensitive to speaker parameters, box volumes of the sealed and ported sub-enclosures, and port tuning. Because of this, using component woofers in a "one size fits all" prefab bandpass box is insanity.

Bandpass systems produce deep bass that is comparable to that of equally sized ported systems. Like ported systems, bandpass systems require big enclosures. A unique property of bandpass systems is that they allow you to trade efficiency for bandwidth by changing the sealed fraction of the box. Very efficient bandpass designs have inherently narrow bandwidths, resulting in a "one-note thump monster." The efficiency/bandwidth trade-off is shown in detail in the "Box Design" section later in this chapter.

Transmission Lines.   Even though the way they work is different than ported enclosures, transmission line enclosures also make constructive use of the sound from the back of the speaker. Doing so makes it possible to achieve deeper bass than with a sealed box.

Transmission line enclosures delay the sound from the back of the speaker through a labyrinth structure. The delay is chosen to provide constructive reinforcement of bass at the proper frequency.

Transmission line enclosures utilize elaborate and expensive construction to create the internal labyrinth structure. They do not offer any advantages over properly designed ported enclosures and often have coloration problems in the mid-bass region. Their design typically involves more trial and error than science to produce a satisfactory result. For these reasons, transmission line enclosures are not recommended.

Choosing a Driver

Whether you buy a pre-made box or build your own, you will need to choose your own subwoofer driver.

Choosing a driver and buying or building a box are interrelated because your choice of driver affects the size and type of box required. Most people choose a driver, then buy or build a suitable box. The problem is that you can end up needing a box that is bigger than you have space for or not the type you want. This section will help you avoid that problem by showing you how you can quickly and easily estimate what box you would need for a specific driver. It will also cover power handling, sensitivity, and other factors influencing your choice of driver.

Power Handling

How much power a subwoofer driver can handle is limited by two things—the diameter and maximum excursion of the cone and the power rating of the voice coil. Either factor can be the weak link in power handling.

At low frequencies, a subwoofer has to move lots of air to create loud bass. How much air it can move is proportional to the area of the cone multiplied by the maximum excursion of the cone. Since area is proportional to cone diameter squared, large drivers have the potential to move a lot more air than small ones. Cone excursion means how far out the cone can realistically move before distortion or damage to the speaker occurs. This is shown as Xmax on subwoofer spec sheets.

Voice coil power handling depends on the diameter of the voice coil, the gauge of wire used, and other factors affecting how much heat the voice coil assembly can handle and effectively dissipate.

Tip: Be careful when reading manufacturers' literature—some list Xmax as total excursion, others as one-way excursion, still others as one-way + 15%!

When choosing a driver, make sure its power rating exceeds that of the amplifier you'll be driving it with. Unfortunately, many manufacturers make exorbitant claims about power handling for their subwoofers. If it seems too good to be true, compare the Xmax and voice coil diameter specs against a reputable driver with the same size cone. If the driver in question claims higher power handling with similar specs or similar power handling with a smaller Xmax or voice coil diameter, watch out.

Sensitivity

Sensitivity tells you how loud a speaker will play at a specified power level. This number is given in decibels and is normally measured at 1 meter using 1 watt. A typical value is 90 dB, and higher numbers are better.

For example, a subwoofer with 90-dB sensitivity is 3 dB better than one with 87 dB. This means that it is 3 dB louder—equivalently, it would require 3 dB less amplifier power to play at the same volume level. Table 4-8 illustrates how sensitivity affects how much power you would need to produce the same volume level.

Table 4-8 shows that the 87-dB driver would require 200 watts of power to play as loud as the 90-dB driver using 100 watts. This seems dramatic, but you may not achieve the big benefit you expect, since high-sensitivity drivers often produce higher cutoff frequencies. This means that the gains you pick up in sensitivity may be lost in having to boost the deep bass frequencies.

TABLE 4-8

How Sensitivity
Affects Required
Power

Sensitivity	Required Amp Power
87 dB	200 W
88 dB	158 W
89 dB	126 W
90 dB	100 W
91 dB	79 W
92 dB	63 W
93 dB	50 W

The bottom line is not to overemphasize the importance of sensitivity. Consider it along with bass response to paint a more complete picture.

Bass Response

The bass response of a subwoofer system depends on two things—the driver itself and its enclosure. In general, the larger the enclosure you are

Pioneer TS-SW124D shallow-mount sub

If you crave the performance of a full-size sub but don't have space for a big box, the TS-SW124D (Fig. 4-9) may be just the ticket. It's a 12-inch sub that's only 4 inches deep, and has the power handling and excursion of a thick sub. Not only is the driver thin, it's optimized for use in small boxes. This is great news for pickup truck owners looking to put a sub behind their seat without giving up leg room.

FIGURE 4-9
Pioneer TS-SW124D shallow-mount subwoofer.
(*Courtesy of Pioneer.*)

T/S Parameter	Units	Meaning
f_s	Hz	Resonant frequency of driver
Q_{ts}		Total Q at the resonant frequency
V_{as}	ft³*	Volume of air having the same compliance as driver

*Some manufacturers provide V_{as} in liters rather than ft³. Divide the number of liters by 28.3 to convert to ft³.

willing to use, the lower the bass response will be for a properly designed sealed, ported, or bandpass system. For free-air applications, bass response depends only on the driver.

The most accurate way to compare the bass response potential of various drivers is to simulate the frequency response of each in your intended application. This would entail a large amount of work, not to mention the fact that you may not have even decided what size your intended enclosure should be.

However, you don't need to go through all that work. You can calculate a single number for each of the drivers you're considering that lets you compare its bass response potential to that of the others. Better yet, you can do this without knowing anything about your intended application, other than whether it's free-air or not.

Introduction to T/S Parameters.   When you want to compare the bass response potential of various drivers (or, later, design a subwoofer box), there are three magic numbers that tell you everything you need to know about a driver. These are called the Thiele/Small (T/S) parameters.

T/S parameters are normally provided in mail-order catalogs or printed right on the box in stores. If you can't find them, ask the retailer—you can't do anything without them. Table 4-9 lists the T/S parameters:

The problem with T/S parameters is that they don't tell you much in their raw form. You need to use your calculator or computer to do something useful with them.

Comparing Woofers for Sealed, Ported, and Bandpass Applications.   To compare woofers for sealed, ported, and bandpass applications, here's the calculation you need to perform:

$$f_{fb} = f_s \sqrt{V_{as}}$$

f_{fb} indicates how low the bass response would be for that driver in a reference-size evaluation box. (Lower numbers are better.) Suppose you are trying to decide between the two 10-inch subwoofers in Table 4-10.

Calculating f_{fb} for each driver provides the results given in Table 4-11.

This shows that the Polk driver provides bass response about 15 percent lower than that of the Rockford Fosgate driver. (This would come as a big surprise if you used f_s to judge bass potential.) This holds true regardless of what the box volume is, so long as you are comparing both drivers using the same box volume. This simple calculation lets you compare woofers without knowing the size or type of your box.

If you know your box size and type, the actual cutoff frequencies for sealed and ported systems can be estimated using these equations:

sealed box: $$f_3 = 0.8 f_{fb}/\sqrt{V_b}$$

ported box: $$f_3 = 1.0 f_{fb}/\sqrt{V_b}$$

where f_3 is the cutoff frequency and V_b is the box volume in ft^3.

Tip: Avoid drivers with unusually high Q_{ts} values—anything above 0.8 is too high. High values are caused by undersized magnet structures and usually result in frequency responses with a large resonant peak.

These equations show that a larger box provides a lower cutoff frequency. Furthermore, it takes a box that is 4 times larger to lower the cutoff frequency by a factor of 2. Suppose you have space for a 1.1-ft^3 box behind the seat of your truck and you have chosen to use a ported box. The approximate cutoff frequencies for the above subwoofers would be as shown in Table 4-12.

Comparing Woofers for Free-Air Applications. To compare woofers for free-air applications, the calculation is different:

$$f_{ob} = f_s/Q_{ts}$$

f_{ob} indicates how low the relative bass response would be in a gigantic box. (Lower numbers are better.) Calculating f_{ob} for the same two 10-inch subwoofers used previously provides the results shown in Table 4-13.

In this case, the Rockford Fosgate driver is better—it provides a relative cutoff frequency about 10 percent lower than that of the Polk driver. The actual cutoff frequencies can be estimated using:

$$f_3 = 0.9 \, f_{ob}$$

Calculating for the previously mentioned subwoofers gives us the values in Table 4-14.

TABLE 4-10

T/S Parameters of Two Contending Subwoofers

Model	f_s	Q_{ts}	V_{as}
Rockford Fosgate P110S4	30 Hz	0.51	1.77 ft^3
Polk Audio dB104	37 Hz	0.57	0.85 ft^3

TABLE 4-11

Relative Bass Response of Two Contending Sub-woofers

Model	f_{fb}
Rockford Fosgate P110S4	39.9
Polk Audio dB104	34.1

TABLE 4-12

Bass Response Comparison in a 1.1-ft^3 Ported Box

Model	Cutoff Frequency in 1.1-ft^3 Ported Box
Rockford Fosgate P110S4	38.0 Hz
Polk Audio dB104	32.5 Hz

TABLE 4-13

Relative Free-Air Response Comparison

Model	f_{ob}
Rockford Fosgate P110S4	58.5
Polk Audio dB104	64.9

TABLE 4-14

Actual Free-Air Response Comparison

Model	Free-Air Cutoff Frequency
Rockford Fosgate P110S4	52.6 Hz
Polk Audio dB104	58.4 Hz

Notice that these cutoff frequencies are actually worse (higher) than those obtained using the 1.1-ft^3 ported box. This demonstrates that free-air applications usually sacrifice deep bass compared to properly designed sealed and ported systems. This is true even for the best of trunks, where sonic isolation is not an issue.

The Infinity Kappa Perfect10 VQ subwoofer (Fig. 4-10) offers a unique variable Q_{ts} feature, which allows you to optimize the driver for use with a variety of enclosures—sealed, ported, bandpass, and free-air applications. The sub is shipped with two metal polepiece inserts, which can be plugged into the motor assembly to vary the Q_{ts}. Using no insert provides a Q_{ts} of 0.63, making it most suitable for free-air applications. The small insert provides a Q_{ts} of 0.42, most useful for medium-size sealed and ported boxes. The large insert provides a Q_{ts} of 0.32, most useful for small sealed and ported boxes.

Cone and Surround Material

Cone material (Table 4-15) and surround material (Table 4-16) are important in the harsh automotive environment, but it's hard to wade through the hype. All of the cone materials listed in the table are capable of excellent performance, so I'll emphasize the differences. Polypropylene cones are extremely resistant to environmental deterioration and are unaffected by humidity. But poly cones are a temperature-sensitive plastic, and become soft in the heat, and hard when cold, affecting their sound. Paper-based cones absorb moisture, so humidity affects their sound. Coatings can be used to improve the resistance to humidity and sunlight, and rein-

FIGURE 4-10

Infinity Kappa Perfect10 VQ variable Q subwoofer. (*Courtesy of Infinity.*)

TABLE 4-15

Common
Subwoofer Cone
Materials

Cone Material	Comments
Paper-based	Humidity-sensitive performance
Polypropylene	Temperature-sensitive performance
Fiber	Expensive
Metal	Subject to dents

TABLE 4-16

Common Subwoofer
Surround Materials

Surround Material	Comments
Foam	Deteriorates with sunlight and time
⟨BEST⟩ Butyl rubber	Good choice

forcement additives such as Kevlar, glass, mica or ceramic can be used to improve the sonic performance of paper-based cones. Another option is fiber cones made from woven or nonwoven Kevlar, carbon (graphite), or glass fibers. Metal cones (usually aluminum or magnesium alloy) are strong and light, and offer good environmental stability. They also help conduct heat away from the voice coil. You'll need to be careful not to dent them. Materials such as Tri-Laminate, resin laminate, carbon-blended poly, Kapok, poly-graphite, graphite-quartz, Foam-Infused IMPP, titanium composite, ceramic metal matrix, Duralam and mica-injected polypropylene offer the promise of superior performance. Most of these are variants of polypropylene and paper-based cones, and may provide a performance advantage. What they mainly provide is a marketing advantage.

The surround is the soft ring around the outside of the cone with the bulge in it. Foam deteriorates with sunlight and time—choose rubber if your subwoofer will be exposed to the sun.

Dual Voice Coil Subwoofers

A dual voice coil speaker (Fig. 4-11) is simply one in which two separate voice coil windings and sets of terminals are provided. It's more expensive to wind and terminate dual voice coils, but you typically pay only a small premium compared to a similar single voice coil speaker.

FIGURE 4-11

JL Audio 10W3V2-D4 dual voice coil subwoofer. (*Courtesy of JL Audio.*)

The main advantage of dual voice coil speakers is wiring flexibility. A single dual voice coil driver offers the user three hookup choices: parallel, series, and independent. In a parallel hookup the drivers' impedance will be half that of each individual coil (a dual 4-ohm speaker would be a 2-ohm speaker in parallel). A series hookup results in twice the impedance of each single coil (a dual 4-ohm speaker results in 8 ohms if its coils are wired in series). Finally, you can wire each voice coil to a separate channel of your amplifier, which can be useful if your amplifier is not mono-bridgeable or if you are bridging a four-channel amplifier down to two channels to run your sub.

Tip: For independently wired DVC subs, adding a choke coil in series with each winding of the subwoofer (Fig. 4-12) will prevent power amp oscillation problems. The interwinding capacitance or mutual inductance of DVC subwoofers can cause some power amplifiers to oscillate. The oscillation can be at almost any frequency, from very low ("motorboating") to very high—even ultrasonic. Ultrasonic oscillation is not directly audible, but results in reduced headroom and increased distortion. In some cases, oscillation can result in amplifier overheating or destruction.

FIGURE 4-12

A choke in series with each sub-woofer winding.

You can purchase choke coils inexpensively or wind your own. Twenty turns of #22 wire around a ¼-inch bolt (keep the bolt in) will provide about 20 μH of inductance—a good value. Make sure the DC resistance is less than 0.1 ohms to prevent signal loss to the subwoofer and ensure adequate power handling of the choke.

If a dual voice coil subwoofer is wired to two independent channels, the inputs to both channels should ideally be the same (summed mono). If there is any difference between the signals driving each coil, the voice coils effectively fight each other. This results in wasted amplifier power, reduced headroom, and increased distortion.

A common misconception with regard to dual voice coil speakers is the assumption that nothing changes if you use only one of the voice coils. With only one coil hooked up, a dual voice coil speaker will suffer a loss in reference efficiency of about 3 dB as well as a significant shift in its Thiele/Small parameters (Q_{ts} will go way up). This renders any enclosure calculations inaccurate unless you measure the speaker parameters with only one coil hooked up. Failure to account for the different parameters of a dual voice coil speaker with only one coil powered can result in very poor performance.

Box Design

Whether you buy a pre-made box or build your own, this section will show you how to design or choose the right box for your driver.

Computer Programs for Box Design

There are many excellent computer programs for helping you design a speaker box. Many of them are available at little or no cost. *The Loudspeaker Design Cookbook* by Vance Dickason lists and describes the most well known of these programs.

Even if you plan to use a computer program, this section will give you an intuitive understanding of how box size and enclosure type affect the bass response. If you don't have a computer, this section has everything you need to design your enclosure.

Step 1: Calculate f_{ob} and V_{of} from the T/S Parameters

As explained in the "Choosing a Driver" section earlier in this chapter, there are three magic numbers that tell you everything you need to know

Subwoofer Design Toolbox

The Subwoofer Design Toolbox by MFR Engineering (Fig. 4-13) is an easy-to-use but powerful program for designing subwoofers, for Microsoft Windows (95 or higher). Its convenient tab interface lets you choose from box design, port design, enclosure design, and woofer selection tools.

FIGURE 4-13
Subwoofer Design Toolbox. (*Courtesy of MFR Engineering.*)

Box designs can be sealed, ported, or bandpass. Context-sensitive design hints and recommended values assist beginners and pros alike. The enclosure design tool helps you design rectangular and wedge-shaped boxes. The woofer selection tool lets you quickly compare woofers without having to design a box for each of them.

With the Subwoofer Design Toolbox, it's easy to compare frequency responses of different box designs on a single graph. Frequency response printouts can be in color or with symbols enabled to improve readability with black-and-white laser printers.

Features of particular interest to automotive applications include free-air modeling, multiple port design, and isobarik loading. The Car Response feature lets you see the effect of operating your sub in a wide range of vehicle sizes.

about a driver for the purposes of box design. These are called the Thiele/Small (T/S) parameters. As mentioned earlier, T/S parameters are normally provided in mail-order catalogs or printed right on the box in stores. They are listed again in Table 4-17 for convenience.

The first step in designing your box is calculating the following two parameters, plugging in the T/S parameters of your driver:

$$f_{ob} = f_s / Q_{ts}$$

$$V_{of} = V_{as} \cdot Q_{ts}^2$$

These two parameters will be used many times throughout the design process.

TABLE 4-17
Thiele/Small
Parameters

T/S Parameter	Units	Meaning
f_s	Hz	Resonant frequency of driver
Q_{ts}		Total Q at the resonant frequency
V_{as}	ft^{3*}	Volume of air having the same compliance as driver

*Some manufacturers provide V_{as} in liters rather than ft^3. Divide the number of liters by 28.3 to convert to ft^3.

Step 2: Label the Frequency Response Diagram for Your Driver

The next step is to refer to the appropriate frequency response diagram. Choose the diagram with the nearest Q_{ts} value to your driver, as well as the desired enclosure type (Figs. 4-14 and 4-15). For each value of Q_{ts} from 0.2 to 0.8, there is a combined sealed and ported diagram and a separate bandpass diagram.

Once you've identified the proper diagram, it's time to label the frequency axis of the diagram using the value of f_{ob} calculated in Step 1. Relabel 0.1 f_{ob}, 1 f_{ob}, and 10 f_{ob} frequency points with their calculated values. Label intermediate points of 0.2 f_{ob} through 0.9 f_{ob} and 2 f_{ob} through 9 f_{ob} for more detail. You might want to make a photocopy of the diagram, or you can write directly in the book with pencil.

Similarly, you'll need to label the enclosure volume for each curve, using the value of V_{of} calculated in Step 1.

Step 3: Choose Your Box Size and Type

Once you've labeled the curves, you'll have a graphic representation of what is possible for your driver. You can now choose the best trade-off between box size and bass response for your needs.

Sealed and Ported Boxes.   For both sealed and ported boxes, you can see that increasing the box size results in deeper bass. Notice that the smallest boxes are sealed and the largest ones are ported. This is because porting helps large boxes, but hurts small ones.

FIGURE 4-14

Frequency response
diagrams for sealed
and ported drivers.
(a) Q_{ts} = 0.2;
(b) Q_{ts} = 0.3.

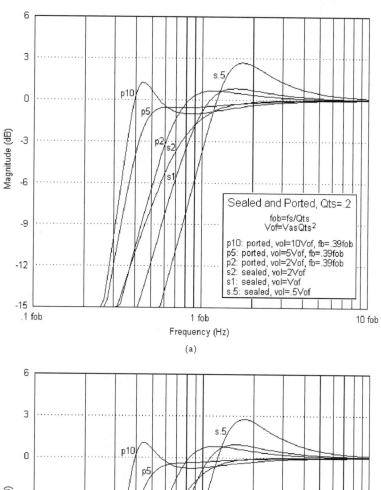

Sealed and Ported, Qts=.2

fob=fs/Qts
Vof=VasQts²

p10: ported, vol=10Vof, fb=.39fob
p5: ported, vol=5Vof, fb=.39fob
p2: ported, vol=2Vof, fb=.39fob
s2: sealed, vol=2Vof
s1: sealed, vol=Vof
s.5: sealed, vol=.5Vof

(a)

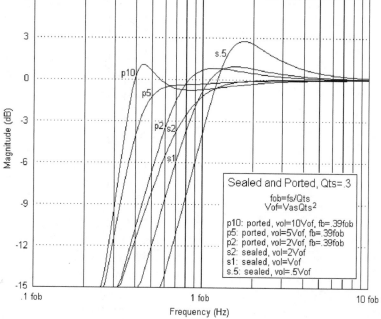

Sealed and Ported, Qts=.3

fob=fs/Qts
Vof=VasQts²

p10: ported, vol=10Vof, fb=.39fob
p5: ported, vol=5Vof, fb=.39fob
p2: ported, vol=2Vof, fb=.39fob
s2: sealed, vol=2Vof
s1: sealed, vol=Vof
s.5: sealed, vol=.5Vof

(b)

**FIGURE 4-14
(continued)**

Frequency response
diagrams for sealed
and ported drivers.
(c) $Q_{ts} = 0.4$;
(d) $Q_{ts} = 0.5$.

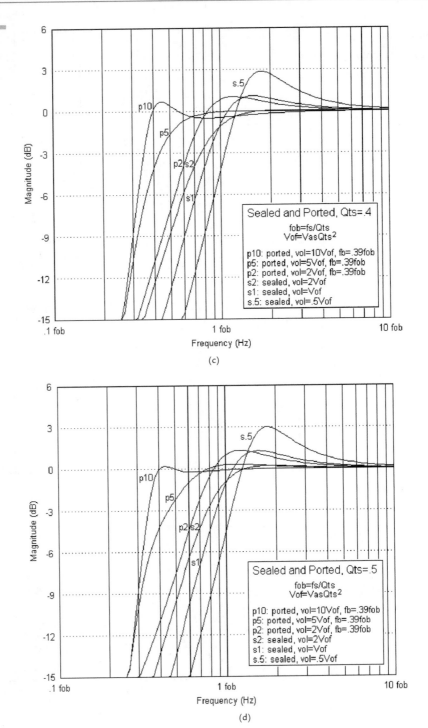

(c)

(d)

FIGURE 4-14
(continued)

Frequency response
diagrams for sealed
and ported drivers.
(e) $Q_{ts} = 0.6$;
(f) $Q_{ts} = 0.7$.

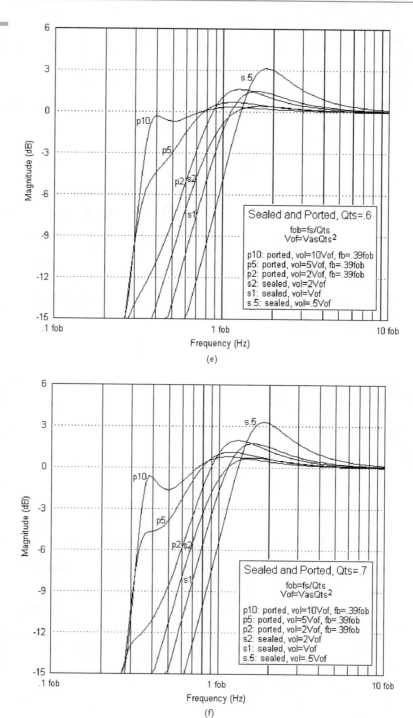

(e)

(f)

FIGURE 4-14
(continued)

Frequency response
diagrams for sealed
and ported drivers.
(g) $Q_{ts} = 0.8$.

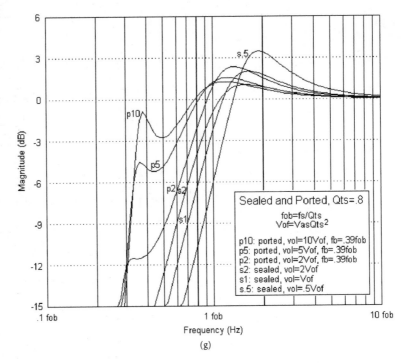

(g)

FIGURE 4-15

Frequency response
diagrams for band-
pass drivers.
(a) $Q_{ts} = 0.2$

(a)

FIGURE 4-15
(continued)
Frequency response
diagrams for band-
pass drivers.
(b) $Q_{ts} = 0.3$;
(c) $Q_{ts} = 0.4$.

**FIGURE 4-15
(continued)**

Frequency response
diagrams for band-
pass drivers.
(d) $Q_{ts} = 0.5$;
(e) $Q_{ts} = 0.6$.

(d)

(e)

FIGURE 4-15
(continued)

Frequency response
diagrams for band-
pass drivers.
(f) $Q_{ts} = 0.7$;
(g) $Q_{ts} = 0.8$.

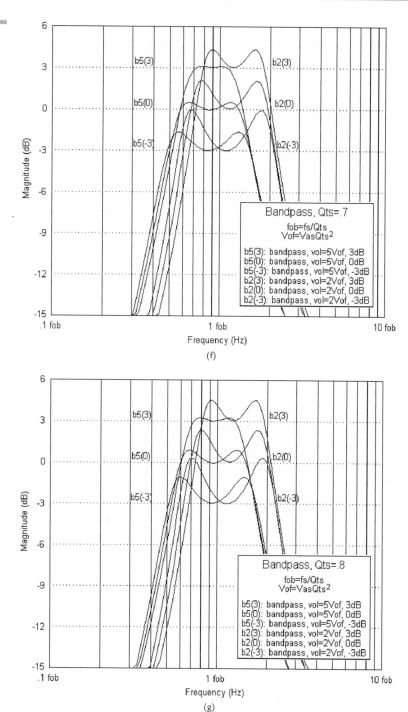

(f)

(g)

Rule: Use a port when the box volume is greater than 2 V_{of}.

2 V_{of} defines the boundary between small and large boxes for a particular driver. For box volumes near this boundary, sealed or ported boxes can be used successfully. Larger boxes should be ported and smaller boxes should be sealed.

For sealed and ported boxes, you are not limited to the six curves on each diagram. You can easily use a box size that is between those shown. In that case, your results will be between the nearest two curves. You can also use a box that is slightly smaller or larger than any of those shown, with predictable results.

Bandpass Boxes.   As with sealed and ported boxes, increasing the size of bandpass boxes results in deeper bass. With bandpass boxes, however, you have an additional degree of flexibility—you can trade sensitivity for

How Low Do You Need to Go?

Deciding how low in frequency you want your subwoofer to go is usually a compromise between performance and practical box size. It's easy to weigh the acceptability of a particular box size, but how do you weigh the importance of bass response?

FM radio broadcasts are limited to between 30 and 50 Hz. With CD players, you can expect response down to 20 Hz or even lower. This doesn't mean your music goes that low, it just means that your CD player can pass it if it does.

In spite of the fact that humans can hear (or feel) bass below 20 Hz, 30 Hz is the realistic lower limit of recorded music. The truth is, very little recorded music (including CDs) contains much below about 40 Hz. Between 40 and 60 Hz, kick drums, tympani, and the low incisive "chunk" of bass guitars kick in. Between 60 and 100 Hz is where you find the power of drums and the deep, tight, strong bass that makes rock solid.

Table 4-18 gives you some idea of what to shoot for.

TABLE 4-18

Subwoofer Response Goal

Subwoofer Response	Comment
30 Hz	Overkill
40 Hz	Realistic goal for auto sound
50 Hz	Respectable performance

bandwidth by changing how much of the total box volume is used for the ported section.

There are six curves shown for each of the bandpass diagrams. The three to the left use a box volume of 5 V_{of}, and the three to the right use a box volume of 2 V_{of}. For each of the two box sizes there are three curves: 3 dB, 0 dB, and –3 dB. (0 dB on these diagrams is identical to 0 dB on the sealed and ported diagrams, so you can directly compare them.)

The 3-dB bandpass designs play 3 dB louder than the 0-dB designs (or require half the amplifier power to play at the same level). The price you pay for using them is their narrow bandwidth. Narrow bandwidths can leave a hole in the system frequency response if the subwoofer's high-end response doesn't extend high enough to cover the low-end response of the main speakers. Narrow bandwidths can also cause a "one-note thump" subwoofer sound.

For bandpass boxes, you must choose one of the six curves shown on each diagram. If you want a different box volume or sensitivity, you'll need to use a computer program to design it.

Step 4: Calculate the Port Tuning Frequency

Once you've decided on a curve for your driver, you'll need to calculate the port tuning frequency. This applies only to ported or bandpass boxes—no additional calculations are needed for sealed boxes.

The port tuning frequency is normally referred to as the box frequency. Its symbol is f_b. The box frequency will be needed for port construction.

Ported Boxes. For ported boxes, calculating the box frequency is easy. Here's the formula:

$$f_b = 0.39\ f_{ob}$$

Bandpass Boxes. For bandpass boxes, refer to Table 4-19 or Table 4-20 for the value of f_b/f_{ob} that applies to your design. (You will also want to make note of the ported fraction of volume entry from the table. This tells you how to partition your box internally.) To calculate the box frequency, plug the value of f_b/f_{ob} from the table and the f_{ob} of your driver into this formula:

$$f_b = \frac{f_b}{f_{ob}}\ f_{ob}$$

TABLE 4-19

Bandpass
Design for Box
Volume = 2 V_{of}

Q_{ts}	+3 dB		0 dB		−3 dB	
	Ported Fraction of Volume	f_b/f_{ob}	Ported Fraction of Volume	f_b/f_{ob}	Ported Fraction of Volume	f_b/f_{ob}
0.2	0.578	1.107	0.490	1.010	0.402	0.936
0.3	0.568	1.117	0.478	1.024	0.390	0.954
0.4	0.552	1.130	0.460	1.042	0.370	0.977
0.5	0.535	1.151	0.440	1.069	0.348	1.008
0.6	0.510	1.175	0.412	1.100	0.322	1.048
0.7	0.485	1.209	0.385	1.142	0.295	1.095
0.8	0.455	1.248	0.355	1.190	0.268	1.150

Sealed/Ported Box Design Example

For this example we'll design a box for the JL Audio 10W3V2-D4 10-inch subwoofer. The T/S parameters for this driver are listed in Table 4-21.

TABLE 4-20

Bandpass
Design for Box
Volume = 5 V_{of}

Q_{ts}	+3 dB		0 dB		−3 dB	
	Ported Fraction of Volume	f_b/f_{ob}	Ported Fraction of Volume	f_b/f_{ob}	Ported Fraction of Volume	f_b/f_{ob}
0.2	0.565	0.707	0.475	0.649	0.388	0.606
0.3	0.540	0.724	0.445	0.671	0.355	0.632
0.4	0.502	0.749	0.405	0.704	0.315	0.672
0.5	0.458	0.787	0.358	0.749	0.270	0.724
0.6	0.405	0.834	0.308	0.806	0.228	0.787
0.7	0.355	0.894	0.262	0.872	0.192	0.859
0.8	0.305	0.963	0.222	0.947	0.162	0.937

TABLE 4-21

T/S Parameters
for JL Audio
10W3V2-D4

Model	f_s	Q_{ts}	V_{as}
JL Audio 10W3V2-D4	28.4 Hz	0.499	1.71 ft³

Calculating f_{ob} and V_{of} from the T/S parameters, we obtain:

$$f_{ob} = f_s / Q_{ts} = 56.9 \text{ Hz}$$

$$V_{of} = V_{as} \cdot Q_{ts}^2 = 0.426 \text{ ft}^3$$

Since Q_{ts} is 0.499, we will use the $Q_{ts} = 0.5$ sealed/ported diagram. The frequency axis of this diagram can now be relabeled based on $f_{ob} = 56.9$ Hz. Similarly, the enclosure volumes can now be relabeled based on $V_{of} = 0.426$ ft³. The result is shown in Fig. 4-16.

A reasonable goal for bass response is –3 dB at or below 40 Hz. Looking at the curves, you can see that the p2 curve just makes this goal and that the p5 curve exceeds it. Even the largest sealed box (s2 curve) doesn't quite make it. The p2 curve is –3 dB at about 37 Hz and the p5 curve is –3 dB at about 26 Hz. The box sizes required for these two designs are 0.85 and 2.13 ft³, respectively. Assume our application has room for something a lit-

FIGURE 4-16

Relabeled
sealed/ported
diagram.

tle bigger than the p2, but not as big as the p5. A 1-ft³ box seems like a good choice.

Since we decided on a ported design, we also need to calculate the box frequency:

$$f_b = 0.39 \, f_{ob} = 22.2 \text{ Hz}$$

The box frequency will be needed for port construction. The "Box Construction" section later in this chapter explains how to build a port.

Bandpass Box Design Example

Now we'll design a bandpass box for the same driver used in the sealed/ported example. The T/S parameters for the JL Audio 10W3V2-D4 10-inch subwoofer are repeated in Table 4-22 for convenience.

Calculating f_{ob} and V_{of} from the T/S parameters, we obtain:

$$f_{ob} = f_s / Q_{ts} = 56.9 \text{ Hz}$$

$$V_{of} = V_{as} \cdot Q_{ts}^2 = 0.426 \text{ ft}^3$$

Since Q_{ts} is 0.499, we will use the $Q_{ts} = 0.5$ bandpass diagram. The frequency axis of this diagram can now be relabeled based on $f_{ob} = 56.9$ Hz. Similarly, the enclosure volumes can now be relabeled based on $V_{of} = 0.426$ ft³. The result is shown in Fig. 4-17.

We must choose from one of two box sizes here—we cannot choose an in-between size as we did in the ported example. In this case, the three b2 curves use a 2 $V_{of} = 0.85$ ft³ box and the three b5 curves use a 5 $V_{of} = 2.13$ ft³ box.

For bandpass systems, a reasonable goal is bass response from 40 to 100 Hz. (This means that the −3-dB frequencies should be below 40 Hz and above 100 Hz, respectively. Note that the −3-dB points are properly referenced to the center frequency level of each curve; thus they are at 0 dB for the +3-dB curves, −3 dB for the 0-dB curves, and −6 dB for the −3-dB curves.)

Looking at the curves closely, the b2(3), b2(0) and b2(−3) designs meet the 40- to 100-Hz goal. The b2(3) and b2(0) designs are the top contenders over

TABLE 4-22

T/S Parameters for JL Audio 10W3V2-D4

Model	f_s	Q_{ts}	V_{as}
JL Audio 10W3V2-D4	28.4 Hz	0.499	1.71 ft³

FIGURE 4-17

Relabeled bandpass
diagram.

the b2(–3) design because of their higher sensitivities and flatter passband responses. The b2(0) provides deeper bass, but less efficiency than the b2(3)—either one would be a good choice.

Although all three of the b5 curves easily meet the 40-Hz goal, they fall short at the 100-Hz end. If your main speakers have no problem providing output down to 70 Hz and you have space for a bigger box, then you could use any of the b5 designs and get deeper bass from the subwoofer.

To determine the box frequency, we need to refer to the proper table. Choosing the b2(0) design, we will use Table 4-19. The 0-dB columns for $Q_{ts} = 0.5$ give us:

$$\text{ported fraction of volume} = 0.440$$

$$f_b/f_{ob} = 1.069$$

This lets us calculate the ported volume and box frequency as follows:

$$\text{ported volume} = 0.440 \ (0.85 \ \text{ft}^3) = 0.37 \ \text{ft}^3$$

$$f_b = (f_b/f_{ob}) \ f_{ob} = 1.069 \ (56.9 \ \text{Hz}) = 60.8 \ \text{Hz}$$

These two numbers will be used for box and port construction. The "Box Construction" section later in the chapter explains how.

How Do Vehicles Affect Bass Response?

The interior volume of cars and trucks can be small enough to affect the bass loading of a subwoofer, particularly when all the windows are rolled up. The good news is that you will usually end up with deeper bass than you expected in your car, especially for sealed boxes. The bad news is that you may have built a larger box than you needed, or tuned your port suboptimally.

The smaller the car, the bigger the bass boost. A midsize car can boost 40 Hz bass by 4 dB, and a compact car by 6 dB or more. Some subwoofer design software lets you specify the size of your vehicle and see how it affects your bass response. The question then becomes how much to include this effect in your box design—the free bass boost disappears when the windows are rolled down.

Multiple Drivers in One Box

Using two or more identical woofers in a single subwoofer cabinet can provide a number of advantages over single subwoofer boxes. Multiple driver formats can be used with sealed, ported, or bandpass designs. The five basic configurations are shown in Table 4-23.

Standard. The standard configuration can be thought of as two identical subwoofer systems joined together with the separating wall removed. This doubles the size of your enclosure and the power handling as well. Because the cone area is doubled, the acoustic sensitivity is 3 dB higher than that of a single driver.

This approach can be used with sealed, ported, or bandpass designs. Follow the same box design procedure as you would for a single driver, but assume that you are using a driver having a V_{as} value twice that of an actual single driver. This method will end up giving you a box that is twice the original size, and any port calculations will come out right.

Push-Pull. The push-pull configuration is a simple variation of the standard configuration, and shares the characteristics explained above. The only difference is that the direction of one of the two woofers is reversed (and the polarity of its speaker connections is reversed as well, to drive both speakers in phase acoustically). This type of setup will cause even-order nonlinearities to cancel, and will result in substantially lower distortion.

A disadvantage of this approach is that you must look at the back of one of your drivers. Some driver manufacturers enhance the appearance of their subwoofer backs just for this purpose. This is only a cosmetic con-

TABLE 4-23

Multiple Driver Con-
figurations

Configuration	Diagram	Comments
Standard		Sensitivity is 3 dB higher than that of a single driver. Doubles the size of your enclosure with respect to that of a single driver. No woofer back is exposed. Even-order distortion products are not canceled.
Push-pull		Sensitivity is 3 dB higher than that of a single driver. Even-order distortion products are canceled. Doubles the size of your enclosure with respect to that of a single driver. Woofer back is exposed.
Front-to-front isobarik		Allows you to cut the size of your enclosure in half with respect to that of a single driver. Even-order distortion products are canceled. Sensitivity is 3 dB lower than that a single driver. Woofer back is exposed. Best isobarik configuration for subwoofer applications.

**TABLE 4-23
(continued)**

Multiple Driver
Configurations

Configuration	Diagram	Comments
Back-to-back isobarik		Allows you to cut the size of your enclosure in half with respect to that of a single driver. Even-order distortion products are canceled. No woofer back is exposed. Sensitivity is 3 dB lower than that a single driver. Construction is more difficult. Heat from both drivers is trapped, reducing power handling. Not recommended.
Piggyback isobarik		Allows you to cut the size of your enclosure in half with respect to that of a single driver. No woofer back is exposed. Sensitivity is 3 dB lower than that a single driver. Even-order distortion products are not canceled. Construction is more difficult. Heat from front driver is trapped, reducing power handling. Not recommended.

cern—the sound coming from the back of a subwoofer is just as good as that from the front at subwoofer frequencies.

Front-to-Front Isobarik. Isobarik (which means constant pressure) designs were first described by Harry Olson in the early 1950s. The primary benefit of any isobarik configuration is that it allows you to cut the size of your enclosure in half with respect to that of a single driver. This can be valuable if you are trying to squeeze a subwoofer box into a tight space. It comes at the price of having to buy a second driver and power it. The acoustic sensitivity of an isobarik pair is also 3 dB lower than that of a single driver (due to the doubling of the effective cone mass). This is 6 dB lower than the standard or push-pull configurations for the same number of drivers and amps.

Of all the isobarik configurations, front-to-front is the most useful for subwoofer applications. (The back of a driver is as good as the front for deep bass.) In addition to cutting the enclosure size in half, the front-to-front setup also provides the even-order distortion canceling characteristic of the push-pull configuration.

Isobarik loading can be used with sealed, ported, or bandpass designs, although in practice bandpass isobarik designs can be particularly difficult to get right. Follow the same box design procedure as you would for a single driver, but assume that you are using a driver having a V_{as} value half that of an actual single driver. This method will end up giving you a box that is half the original size, and any port calculations will come out right.

When mounting the drivers, a spacer must normally be used between the two drivers to prevent the two surrounds from touching each other. You can use a ring of medium-density fiberboard (MDF) with appropriately spaced holes to pass the mounting bolts/screws through. Lay the bottom driver in the box after wiring it up (this driver should have its leads wired normally). Lay the MDF ring on top of this driver. Invert the second driver over the first, line up the mounting holes, and screw the whole assembly to the enclosure. The outer driver should have its leads wired in a reversed fashion. This will assure that both drivers are moving in the same direction when a voltage is applied. If you hook everything up and get no bass from your subwoofer, chances are that you've got a driver's polarity reversed.

Back-to-Back Isobarik. The back-to-back isobarik configuration requires a tunnel subenclosure to tightly couple the two drivers. The chief advantage of this approach over the front-to-front isobaric is cosmetic—you get to look at the front of a woofer rather than the back. As with the push-pull and front-to-front isobarik configurations, even-order distortion products are inherently canceled.

Because of the relatively large mass of air coupling the two drivers, accurate frequency response predictions become more difficult. The tunnel makes construction more challenging as well. A further disadvantage of this approach is that the heat generated by both magnet structures is essentially trapped in the subenclosure. This will greatly reduce the thermal power handling of both drivers. For these reasons, this configuration is not recommended.

Piggyback Isobarik. The piggyback isobarik configuration also requires a tunnel subenclosure to tightly couple the two drivers, although it is smaller than that required for the back-to-back isobarik. As with the back-to-back isobarik approach, you get to look at the front of a woofer rather than the back. Unlike with the other isobarik configurations, even-order distortion products are not canceled.

The piggyback isobarik setup shares a number of disadvantages with the back-to-back isobarik. Because of the relatively large mass of air coupling the two drivers, accurate frequency response predictions become more difficult. The tunnel makes construction more challenging. The heat generated by one of the magnet structures is essentially trapped in the subenclosure. This will greatly reduce its thermal power handling and will cause a performance imbalance between the two drivers as one heats up more than the other. For these reasons, this configuration is not recommended.

Box Construction

Whether you buy a pre-made box or build your own, this section contains useful information on mounting drivers, damping enclosures, and constructing ports.

Box Materials and Shapes

Important: When calculating the volume of an enclosure, be sure to use the internal (not external) dimensions. Subtract the volume of items that reduce the internal volume, such as bracing and the back of the woofer itself. For ported boxes, the volume of the port should be deducted too. These volume adjustments normally amount to about a 5 percent reduction in the internal box volume.

A good speaker box should be both rigid and nonresonant. Choosing the right box material is an important step in ensuring this.

Subwoofer boxes should be constructed of ³/₄-inch-thick particle board or medium-density fiberboard (MDF). Both of these materials are rigid, nonresonant, uniform, easy to work with, and, best of all, cheap. MDF is approximately 35 percent stronger than particle board, but is more expensive and harder to find. Other materials such as hardwood, plywood, or oriented strand board (OSB) may be used, but none are as good as particle board or MDF.

Rectangular boxes are the easiest to build, but to take advantage of an odd-sized space, you may want to use a wedge or other shape. For subwoofers, the shape and relative dimensions of the box do not affect performance. You can build a perfect cube, a tall, thin box, or a pyramid—it doesn't matter, so long as the volume is the same. (This is not true for full-range loudspeakers, where the shape influences mid-bass and higher-frequency response.)

If you want a cylindrical enclosure, use large cardboard tubing called Sonotube® (manufactured by Sunoco for forming concrete pillars). It's available at construction supply outlets. The cylindrical shape provides superior rigidity even though its wall thickness is only $\frac{1}{4}$ to $\frac{1}{2}$ inch. You can also use large-diameter PVC pipe, available in diameters as large as 12 inches from pipe suppliers. Cut circles of particle board or MDF to fit inside the ends and fasten with Liquid Nails or similar construction adhesive.

Assembly and Bracing

The most popular method of box construction today is to build a six-sided box without removable access panels. This provides maximum strength and makes the box more airtight. Access to the inside of the box is provided through the speaker cutout. The speaker must be mounted from the outside with this method.

Bracing refers to fastening strips of wood (usually 2×2 lumber) along internal seams, across panels, or between panels. Bracing strengthens the box and improves its performance by reducing the sound radiated by the box itself. Corner bracing is important where the precision of cuts for the box pieces was limited due to the use of a hand saw, jigsaw, or circular saw. Bracing across panels is beneficial for large enclosures (greater than 1 ft^3).

Because of the speaker cutout, the front panel is usually the weakest. It should either be braced or constructed from a double thickness of particle board. If you use the double thickness approach, you may want to pre-cut the speaker cutout in each thickness before gluing them together, depending on the capabilities of your jigsaw.

All box joints and bracing should be glued generously and then nailed or preferably screwed together. Use a wood glue such as Elmer's® Carpenter's Wood glue. Two-inch drywall screws work well for this application. If you don't have an electric drill and screwdriver bit for driving screws, you can use 6d (2-inch) finishing nails.

Bandpass Box Construction

Bandpass designs present some unique challenges when it comes to box construction.

In other types of designs, the woofer is attached from the outside so the box can be constructed without any removable access panels. This is not the case for bandpass boxes. Furthermore, a bandpass system requires sealed and ported chambers. The normal construction technique for a bandpass box is to build the outer cabinet, then add an inner partition to create the two chambers. The removable access panel can be on the sealed side or the ported side (Fig. 4-18). If you want to see your woofer in action, you can use ⅜- or ½-inch-thick Plexiglas for the access panel. It should be sealed with foam gasket material or nonhardening caulk and then secured with a generous number of screws.

For the most part, woofer direction isn't critical. The front of a woofer provides the best high-frequency response. For full-range systems, good high-frequency response is an asset, but for bandpass systems it's a liability. For this reason, it's better to have the back of the woofer in the ported chamber. (If you use a crossover with a steep slope, this factor shouldn't matter.) A second benefit of this orientation is that it provides better cooling for the motor structure of the driver. This points to putting the access panel on the sealed chamber.

Constructing Ports

Ports can be constructed of PVC pipe (the large-diameter plastic pipe plumbers use). You can also buy prefab speaker ports that you trim to the desired length (Fig. 4-19). There is also an adjustable type that has a sliding outer tube (Fig. 4-20). The advantage of prefab ports is their attractive appearance—they have a contoured mounting flange and are black. The disadvantage is that the length you need in the diameter you want may not be readily available. Another kind of prefab port worth considering is the Aeroport flared port tube (Fig. 4-21). The two flared ends reduce port turbulence and provide increased linearity and greater output with less port noise. The ports come 12-inches long—you trim the center tube for

FIGURE 4-18

Removable access panel construction.

Fixed prefab ports.
(*Courtesy of MCM
Electronics.*)

Adjustable prefab
port. (*Courtesy of MCM
Electronics.*)

the desired length. The cost of Aeroports is higher than standard prefab
tubes, but the benefits are real.

Here's the equation to calculate the port length you need:

$$L = \frac{2117\ D^2}{f_b^2 V_b} - 0.732D$$

Aeroport flared port
tube. (*Courtesy of Light-
ning Audio*)

where port length L and internal diameter D are in inches and box volume (V_b) is in ft^3.

All you need to do is plug in the internal diameter of the port you want to use, the box frequency (calculated in the "Box Design" section), and the box volume. (For a bandpass enclosure, the box volume refers to the volume of the ported section only.)

What port diameter should you use? PVC pipe is available in a number of diameters, including 1.5, 2, 3, 4, and 6 inches (inner diameter). Prefab ports cover a similar range, but often have oddball diameters. Small-diameter ports limit the amount of air passing through them and thus have reduced effectiveness. They are also more prone to audible vent noise. In general, the bigger the better, but as a practical matter, try to use a port diameter that is one-third to one-half the woofer diameter. This is especially important for bandpass boxes because all of the output is from the port.

Large port diameters usually generate extremely long ports, so you may need to limit yourself to a smaller practical diameter. PVC elbows let you create a PVC port that is longer than the box itself by having one or more 90 degree bends. Prefab ports don't offer this flexibility. Use a hacksaw to cut PVC pipe to the desired length and use PVC cement to attach elbows.

If long port length is a problem, there are other options:

For ported boxes:

- Increase f_b. This usually provides a good solution, but you'll need speaker design software to check the resulting frequency response. A 40 percent increase in f_b will give at least a 50 percent reduction in the port length.

- Increase the size of the box. This will reduce the required port length and give you deeper bass too.

- If all else fails, consider using a different driver (with a higher f_{ob}).

For bandpass boxes:

- Choose a design curve with higher sensitivity. For example, use b2(3) instead of b2(0). This will reduce the required port length.

- Choose a design curve with a smaller box. For example, use b2(0) instead of b5(0). This will reduce the required port length. Speaker design software is a big help here because it will let you choose any size smaller box—you're not limited to the two sizes in the charts.

- If all else fails, consider using a different driver.

FIGURE 4-22

Minimum port spac-
ing.

3" min

Tip: Allow adhesives to cure before installing your woofer, since the fumes released by some sealants during curing may have an appetite for foam sur-rounds.

Ports may be located on any side of the enclosure. Ports should be placed a minimum of 4 to 6 inches from the woofer to prevent interaction between the cone and the vent. The back of the port should be a minimum of 3 inches from the opposing wall to prevent a reduction of airflow (Fig. 4-22).

To install the port, hold the small end of the port tube against the box where you want it to go and trace around it with a pencil. Use a jigsaw to cut just inside the pencil mark to provide a snug fit. You will then need to file or sand the hole to make it exact. Use Liquid Nails or a similar construction adhesive to glue the tube to the hole.

Port Design Example

Now we'll finish the port design for the bandpass box used as an example in the "Box Design" section. For the JL Audio 10W3V2-D4 10-inch sub-woofer, we previously calculated the ported volume and box frequency:

$$\text{ported volume} = 0.440 \ (0.85 \ \text{ft}^3) = 0.37 \ \text{ft}^3$$

$$f_b = (f_b/f_{ob}) \ f_{ob} = 1.069 \ (56.9 \ \text{Hz}) = 60.8 \ \text{Hz}$$

Plugging these in to the port length equation, we get:

$$L = \frac{2117 \ D^2}{f_b^2 \ V_b} - 0.732D$$

$$= \frac{2117 \ D^2}{(60.8)^2 \ (0.37)} - 0.732D$$

$$= 1.548D^2 - 0.732D$$

$$= 11.74 \ \text{inches for 3-inch PVC}$$

$$= 21.84 \ \text{inches for 4-inch PVC}$$

Multiple Ports

Multiple ports can be used when the look of several smaller ports is preferred to that of a single large port.

There are two widely used methods for calculating the length of multiple ports for a single chamber. Only one method is correct—but, unfortunately, it is the least commonly used.

The incorrect method says that the effective port diameter is equal to the square root of the sum of the squares of the actual port diameters. This is equivalent to saying that we can simply add the cross-sectional areas of multiple ports together and treat them as a single port with the combined cross-sectional area. This sounds reasonable, but it can lead to errors, as we'll see below.

The correct way to figure out how long each port should be follows this simple two-step procedure:

1. Divide the chamber volume by the number of ports you wish to use for that one chamber.

2. Use that as your V_b (box volume) in the port formula, and calculate how long each port should be.

Let's take the previous example using the JL Audio 10W3V2-D4 10-inch subwoofer. We'll replace the 3-inch diameter port with four 1.5-inch diameter ports and see what the two methods give us.

Incorrect Method

According to this method, the effective port diameter of four 1.5-inch ports is equal to that of a 3-inch port, since both have the same total cross-sectional area. Plugging this into the port formula yields a port length of 11.74 inches—the same result we calculated previously.

Correct Method

We want to use four ports, so we divide 0.37 cubic feet by 4. V_b now becomes 0.0925 ft³. Plugging this into the equation using a port diameter of 1.5 inches gives us a port length of 12.84 inches.

The incorrect method neglects the fact that the end effect (the 0.732D term of the port equation) changes with port diameter.

Since our woofer has a diameter of 10 inches, we would like to have a port diameter of one-third to one-half that, or 3.3 to 5 inches. For this system, a 3-inch diameter PVC port would need to be 11.74 inches long, and a 4-inch diameter PVC port would need to be 21.84 inches long. Considering that the ported section of the box is only 0.37 ft³, even the 3-inch diameter PVC port will be difficult to fit in the box without a PVC elbow. Using the higher sensitivity b2(3) curve is the other option—it reduces the required 3-inch diameter port length to a manageable 7.57 inches.

Speaker Terminals

Speaker terminals should be used rather than running wire through a hole drilled in your speaker box. This reduces air leakage and lets you easily disconnect your speakers.

The most popular terminal types are the spring-loaded pushbutton type (Fig. 4-23) and binding/banana posts (Fig. 4-24).

The spring-loaded pushbutton types are cheaper and easier to use, but provide less reliable connections and break fairly easily (Table 4-24). Both types accept standard speaker wire, but binding/banana posts also accept spade lugs and banana plugs (Fig. 4-25). These can be soldered onto the ends of speaker wires for a superior connection.

It's best to recess mount terminals. This lets you mount the terminals on the bottom of your box or on a side of it that rests against a wall. It also reduces the chance of breaking the terminals or accidentally releasing them. Recessed mounting cups with built-in terminals are commonly available, but their thin plastic construction allows sound to radiate through them from inside the enclosure. The best approach is to cut a 3-inch round or square hole where you want the terminal, then glue and screw a piece of ¾-inch particle board behind it (inside the box). Mount your terminal to the recessed particle board panel.

> **Tip:** Do not tin the ends of your speaker wires with solder unless you actually solder them to spade lugs, banana plugs, or the like. Solder is a relatively soft alloy and will readily cold flow under pressure, causing compression connections (such as binding posts or unsoldered crimp connectors) to eventually loosen.

FIGURE 4-23
Spring-loaded push-button terminal.
(*Courtesy of MCM Electronics.*)

FIGURE 4-24
Binding/banana posts. (*Courtesy of MCM Electronics.*)

TABLE 4-24

Types of Speaker Terminals

Speaker Terminals	Comments
Spring-loaded pushbutton	Cheaper and easier to use
Binding/banana posts	Provide better connection, less prone to breakage

Make It Airtight

It's important to make your speaker enclosure as airtight as possible. This applies to sealed as well as ported and bandpass enclosures. Air leaks degrade the box performance and can cause whistles and other noises.

Caulk all internal box seams, the speaker terminals, and the port where it enters the box. Use a siliconized exterior latex caulk for long life and easy cleanup.

Air leaks frequently occur where the woofer mounts to the box. Ironically, woofers have a gasket on their front face, but most woofers are mounted from the outside of the box so this gasket is on the wrong side. Install a foam gasket or use a nonhardening caulk between the box and the woofer to prevent air leakage. DO NOT use regular caulk or silicon rubber sealant to glue the woofer to the box. You will destroy the woofer when you later try to remove it for access inside the box. (Trust me, you WILL want to get inside the box again—you may need to replace a broken speaker terminal or a foreign object may have mysteriously found its way through the port inside your subwoofer box.)

In addition to using a gasket or nonhardening caulk to prevent air leakage, the woofer should be mounted tightly to the box. Wood screws are acceptable, but their holes easily strip out if you aren't careful. A better alternative is to use tee nuts and machine screws. Tee nuts (Fig. 4-26) are inserted into the back of a drilled screw hole and then tapped in with a hammer so their prongs hold them in place. For a high-tech look, use socket-head-cap (Fig. 4-27) or button-head-cap (Fig. 4-28) machine screws.

For isobarik boxes with front-to-front woofers, both woofers are normally mounted outside the box, as shown in Fig. 4-29. When mounting

Tip: Allow caulk to cure before installing your woofer since the fumes released by some sealants during curing may have an appetite for foam surrounds.

FIGURE 4-25

Banana plugs.
(*Courtesy of MCM Electronics.*)

FIGURE 4-26
Tee nuts.

FIGURE 4-27
Socket-head-cap
machine screws.

FIGURE 4-28
Button-head-cap
machine screws.

FIGURE 4-29
Isobarik gasketing.

spacer ring

foam gasket
or
non-hardening
caulk

the drivers, a spacer must normally be used between them to prevent the two surrounds from touching each other. You can use a ring of medium-density fiberboard (MDF) with appropriately spaced holes to pass the mounting bolts/screws through. Use a foam gasket or nonhardening caulk where one woofer meets the box and where each woofer contacts the spacer ring. Tee nuts and machine screws are highly recommended for mounting.

Enclosure Damping

Enclosure damping refers to using fiberglass, polyester, or dacron batting or similar materials to line or stuff a speaker enclosure.

Enclosure damping is traditionally used for two reasons. First, it reduces the effects of internal reflections within a speaker enclosure, which can cause resonant peaks and dips in the frequency response at mid-bass and higher frequencies. One to two inches of fiberglass are normally used to line the internal walls of an enclosure for this. This is important for full-range systems, but because subwoofers are used only for very low frequencies, lining them with damping material provides no benefit.

The second use of enclosure damping is to increase the effective size of a sealed box. Fully stuffing a sealed box can increase its effective size by 15 to 25 percent. This can be a useful technique where space is extremely tight, but otherwise isn't worth the trouble. Care must be taken to keep damping material out of and away from the rear basket of the speaker itself. If you plan on stuffing, use only materials that do not shed short fibers. These can find their way into the voice coil gap and cause rubbing and distortion in the speaker. Enclosure stuffing should *not* be used for ported or bandpass boxes.

Finishing Touches

Many products are available to give your handcrafted subwoofer box a professional appearance and protect it from damage. These include custom carpet (Fig. 4-30), corner protectors (Fig. 4-31), handles (Fig. 4-32), and grilles (Fig. 4-33).

Speaker carpet is available in colors to match every automotive interior. It provides a more durable finish than paint and conceals minor imper-

FIGURE 4-30

Custom carpet.
(*Courtesy of MCM Electronics.*)

FIGURE 4-31

Corner protector.
(*Courtesy of Parts Express.*)

FIGURE 4-32

Handle. (*Courtesy of MCM Electronics.*)

FIGURE 4-33

Grilles. (*Courtesy of MCM Electronics.*)

fections in the cabinet. Carpet is normally applied to all sides of a speaker box using spray adhesive, hot glue, or a staple gun.

Plastic corner protectors reduce damage to the box and other objects if you bang a corner against something. They also make corners look better—it's difficult to make a corner carpet seam look good otherwise. Plastic or metal speaker grilles protect your expensive woofers from damage from objects in your trunk, dropped screwdrivers, and pets.

Installation

Refer to Chap. 7 for how and where to install the amp for your subwoofer system. In general, the subwoofer crossover should be located close to the subwoofer amp to prevent ignition noise pickup.

Installing a subwoofer system also involves installing the subwoofer box and adjusting the system. This section tells you how.

Bass Blocking Crossovers

Adding speaker-level bass blocking crossovers in line with each of the main (especially the front) speakers is recommended when it's impossible to use a preamp-level high-pass crossover for those channels. This is the case with most head unit speaker outputs. This will reduce the burden of deep bass on the head unit and main speakers, allowing higher volumes with less distortion. The subwoofer will pick up the slack.

For systems where head unit preamp outputs are used for the subwoofer, simply install a bass blocking crossover in series with each speaker (Fig. 4-34).

FIGURE 4-34

Bass blocking crossover locations.

Bass Blockers

Bass blocking capacitors (or bass blockers) are commonly used as a low-cost method of keeping deep bass from getting to front speakers. Ironically, bass blockers may actually *increase* the amount of deep bass getting to the speakers.

How can this be? If the impedance of a speaker looked like a 4-ohm resistor at all frequencies, then bass blocking capacitors would work as advertised—they would produce a 6-dB/octave high-pass filter with the specified cutoff frequency. In reality, the impedance of a speaker looks nothing like a 4-ohm resistor near the resonant frequency of the loaded driver. The capacitance of the bass blocker interacts with the inductance of the speaker below resonance to produce a low-frequency response peak that can easily be 3 dB higher than with no bass blocker at all!

The bottom line on bass blockers is: DON'T USE THEM! If you want to block deep bass to a speaker and must use a speaker-level filter, use a second-order crossover for the job. Second-order crossovers are relatively immune to the problem just described because they put an inductor in parallel with the speaker. This inductor effectively swamps out the high impedance of the speaker near resonance. Second-order crossovers also provide a superior 12-dB/octave slope.

Tip: If you can't find a capacitor with the value you want, you can wire capacitors in parallel (Fig. 4-37). The capacitance of parallel-wired capacitors is equal to the sum of the individual values.

When using head unit speaker outputs for the sub, be sure to connect the subwoofer crossover inputs to the head unit side of the bass blocking crossovers to prevent blocking bass to the subwoofer (Fig. 4-35).

Bass blocking crossovers should be second-order high-pass filters. You can buy them pre-made or build your own (Fig. 4-36). In either case, you'll need to know the nominal speaker impedance (usually 4 ohms) and decide on the cutoff frequency you want. Use something close to 100 Hz for most applications. Choose a higher frequency when the main speakers are weak in bass or unusually small.

If you want to build your own, refer to Fig. 4-36. The formulas allow you to calculate capacitance and inductance values for any speaker impedance (R) and cutoff frequency (F) you want. The table in Fig. 4-36 shows three possibilities, based on standard capacitor values and 4-ohm speakers. Capacitors should be of the nonpolarized (bipolar) type.

Trunk Sonic Isolation Check

If you plan to use your subwoofer box in the trunk, you should perform the following check.

Have a friend with a deep voice talk into your open trunk from the outside. Alternately, you can use a boombox in your trunk. You should be

FIGURE 4-35

Don't block bass to
the subwoofer!

listening inside the passenger compartment with the windows rolled up.
If you can hear your friend loud and clear, then you'll have no problem
using a subwoofer in the trunk. If you can barely hear your friend, then
you may want to provide a better path for the sound to get from the
trunk to the passenger compartment.

One method is to cut a hole in the rear deck and conceal it with a
speaker grille. Another is to cut a hole in the panel behind the back seat.

Secure Your Subwoofer

Whether you've got a tube enclosure that wants to roll around or a box
that wants to slide, it's important to secure your subwoofer. If you've got
a hatchback, station wagon, sports utility vehicle, or van, the enclosure can
become a projectile in a collision, and must be firmly attached.

FIGURE 4-36

Build your own bass blocking crossover.

Bass Blocking Crossover

$$C = \frac{.1125}{R\ F}$$

from head unit

to speaker

$$L = \frac{.2251\ R}{F}$$

Freq (Hz)	C (µF)	L (mH)
188	150	4.8
141	200	6.4
94	300	9.6

Table values shown for a 4-ohm speaker

FIGURE 4-37

Parallel-wired capacitors.

```
┌─100 uF─┐
│        │        ────150 uF────
└─50 uF──┘    =
```

Nylon tie-down straps are available for this purpose and include vehicle mounting hardware. They do a great job of securing any size and shape enclosure without screwing into it. Velcro® hook and loop fasteners (Fig. 4-38) work well for keeping boxes from sliding around in the trunk. By stapling the "hook side" of the strips to the subwoofer box, the vehicle's carpeting can act as a suitable "loop side." Either of these approaches lets you easily remove the subwoofer when you temporarily need some extra room.

A final option is to use flat or 90 degree mounting brackets, available at any hardware store (Fig. 4-39). These are screwed or bolted to the subwoofer and vehicle. Bolt the brackets through the metal of the floorpan or the frame of the vehicle, with large diameter washers for reinforcement.

FIGURE 4-38

Velcro. (*Courtesy of MCM Electronics.*)

FIGURE 4-39

Mounting brackets.

Turning It On the First Time

IMPORTANT: Before turning the system on for the first time, turn the volume controls of the subwoofer amp and the head unit to minimum.

Set the crossover cutoff frequency control to the highest frequency. After turning the system on, slightly increase the head unit volume to check that sound is coming from each of the main speakers. If it is not, check for shorted or open connections.

If sound comes from each of the main speakers, increase the subwoofer power amp level control. Listen for bass from the subwoofer. If little or nothing is heard and you are using speaker-level crossover inputs, try setting the head unit's balance control all the way to one side. If this produces bass, one of the subwoofer crossover's inputs has been connected to the system backward. If bass is still not heard, check for +12 volts at the subwoofer crossover power wire and power amp supply and remote turn-on wires. Inspect for shorted, open, or reversed speaker connections.

System Adjustment, or the Secret to Tight Bass

Proper system adjustment is just as important as choosing the right components and hooking them up correctly. In fact, a properly adjusted inexpensive system easily sounds better than a more expensive one not adjusted right.

The secret to achieving tight bass with a system having a subwoofer is to set and keep the head unit's bass control slightly below the central flat response position. The subwoofer is then adjusted to fill in.

This provides two important benefits. First, it reduces the burden of bass on the main speakers and amps. (The subwoofer will pick up the slack.) This lets you play the stereo louder with less distortion. Second, it provides tighter, less boomy bass. Vehicle interior acoustics are notorious for overemphasizing upper bass frequencies. By turning the bass control down, you reduce this boomy-sounding upper bass. Adjusting the subwoofer crossover cutoff frequency for optimum sound allows the subwoofer to fill in with a deep, solid-sounding bottom end.

Perform the adjustments in this order for best results. Use your favorite, CD, cassette or radio station. Use several sources to get a good average.

Initial Settings. Preset the subwoofer crossover to 100 Hz. If there is a bass boost feature, turn it off for now. Adjust the subwoofer amp level control to the point that sounds best, erring on the side of too little bass.

Crossover Polarity Switch. If there is a subwoofer polarity switch, set it to whichever position gives you the most bass. The effect is usually small.

Crossover Bass Boost. If you plan to use the bass boost feature, turn it on now. In general, it will help extend the system bass response and provide tighter-sounding bass. If you later find that your subwoofer sometimes distorts, you should turn the bass boost off.

Crossover Cutoff Frequency and Power Amp Level. Now fine-tune the cutoff frequency of the subwoofer crossover and the level control of the subwoofer power amplifier to provide the most natural-sounding bass. The bass control of the head unit should be slightly below the flat position as you do this.

You will find that you need more bass when you are driving to overcome the masking effects of road noise. (See the box on road noise masking in Chap. 8.) Try to find a level that is a good compromise for all conditions. After you're satisfied with the settings, you can use the bass control of the head unit to compensate for individual cassettes, CDs, and radio stations.

Bass Transducers

Bass transducers are a relatively new development in car audio. Working on the principle that low bass is mostly felt and not heard, bass transducers directly vibrate the chassis of your vehicle. An example of a bass transducer is the Aura Bass Shaker (Fig. 4-40).

Bass transducers are most effective when bolted to the floor beneath the seats. This provides good coupling to the entire vehicle. (Mounting them directly to the seats may seem like a better idea, but you can feel where the source of the vibration is.)

Bass transducers have a 4-ohm impedance, and are designed to be driven like ordinary subwoofer drivers. Any car stereo amp with the desired power can be used—25 to 50 watts per channel is normally recommended. Although not strictly required, a crossover is advised to prevent any audible vibrations. (An amp with built-in sub crossover is ideal.) As with a subwoofer, the level of the amplifier must be properly set for a realistic effect.

Since bass transducers produce vibration rather than sound, they are best used in conjunction with subwoofers rather than instead of them. What bass transducers can give you is the sensation of extremely powerful bass with zero boominess.

Bass transducers are ideal for open-air vehicles such as convertibles, Jeeps, or Trackers. In these vehicles it is almost impossible to achieve the sensation of solid bass with traditional subwoofers alone because you are radiating into open air. Bass transducers are also well suited for vehicles lacking the space for a large subwoofer, such as two-seater sports cars and small pickup trucks. By using a bass transducer, you can get away with using a smaller subwoofer having a higher cutoff frequency.

CHAPTER 5

Head Unit Projects

Head unit is the industry name for an in-dash radio or receiver. Adding or upgrading a head unit along with a new set of speakers is one of the most popular car stereo projects—not surprising since the head unit is the heart of any car stereo system. In many vehicles, head unit projects are easier than ever with convenient wiring harness adapters and mounting kits.

If you have a premium factory sound system (such as Delco/Bose or Ford/JBL), OnStar, or a 2000 and up GM vehicle with the Class 2 data bus and want to replace your head unit, the situation may be more complicated. See the sections at the end of this chapter for details.

Why Choose an Aftermarket Head Unit?

Even if your factory system is top of the line, chances are good it's missing many of the features you wished you had. MP3 compatibility, satellite radio, HD radio, and mobile video are a few examples. Another advantage of aftermarket head units is easier integration with equipment such as disc changers, digital music players, amplifiers, and video components. If you're interested in mobile video and 5.1 channel audio, Chap. 6 covers all the options.

Pick One That Fits

Before shopping for head units, you'll need to determine what size, mounting method, and depth your vehicle can accommodate. First, it's important to understand the basics of how the aftermarket head unit industry supports the wide diversity of mounting applications with just a few standard sizes.

Size and Mounting Method Basics

Factory head units come in many sizes and use a number of different mounting methods. Automobile manufacturers are constantly inventing new sizes and mounting methods, which makes it more challenging to use aftermarket head units. Most aftermarket head units today will directly fit in Euro DIN, ISO-DIN, and wide-face ISO-DIN vehicle applications. With the proper mounting adapter kit, these units will also fit virtually any other late-model vehicle. For older vehicles, universal shaft-style head units must be used to avoid the need for major dashboard modification.

The most important types of head units (size and mounting method) are shown in Table 5-1.

Aftermarket DIN-compatible head units are of the correct size and provide means to support both Euro DIN and ISO-DIN mounting standards. A front adapter plate is included to support the wide-face ISO-DIN-J applications. (Without the adapter, you would have a gap on each side of the head unit in ISO-DIN-J applications.)

Universal shaft-style radios are required for many pre-1984 vehicles. They can also be used in almost any later vehicle with the proper mounting adapter.

Even though DIN head units can be made to fit almost every late-model vehicle with the proper mounting adapter kit, there are cases where this gives the look of a small head unit in a big panel. This is where GM- and Chrysler-style aftermarket head units come in. These are designed to fill the large factory openings in many GM and Chrysler vehicles without a mounting adapter kit.

TABLE 5-1
Common Head Unit Size/Mounting Methods

Name	Comments
Euro DIN	Most common size and mounting method. Flat front design. Fits through a rectangular hole in dash and snaps into place with locking tabs.
ISO-DIN	Same size as Euro DIN, but mounts to a side-support factory frame using screws. Common in Subaru, Toyota and Nissan.
ISO-DIN-J	Same as ISO-DIN, but with wider face. Common in Toyota, Nissan and Mitsubishi.
Universal	Shaft style, fits three-hole dash opening. Mounts from behind dash. Required for many vehicles prior to 1984.
GM	Front-mount, oversized-face design. Found in many 1982–present GM vehicles.
Chrysler	Front-mount, oversized-face design. Found in many 1981–2002 Chrysler, Plymouth, and Dodge vehicles.
Double DIN	Twice the height of ISO-DIN. Used for combined CD/cassette units. Found in late-model Toyota and Nissan.

What Does DIN Stand For?

DIN stands for *Deutsche Industrie Norm*, which means "German Industry Standard." The DIN head unit standard was created in the seventies and has been widely adopted in Europe. It is used throughout the world for aftermarket head units.

Determining What Your Vehicle Can Accommodate

In addition to head unit size and mounting method, you also need to check mounting depth. Head units have a typical mounting depth requirement that ranges from about 6 to 7 inches. Vehicles can have a mounting depth of as little as 5½ inches to as much as 12 inches. This means that not all head units with the proper face size and mounting method will automatically fit your vehicle. In cases where depth is a problem, a mounting adapter kit with a molded extension may be available.

One way to determine what size, mounting method, and depth your vehicle can accommodate is to inspect and measure the vehicle yourself. This requires familiarity with each of the sizes and mounting methods listed in Table 5-1 and forces you to remove your old head unit before you buy a new one. An easier alternative is to consult with a car stereo shop or use a head unit application guide. Crutchfield takes it a step further. Their website lets you specify your vehicle, then shows you the head units that will fit it. Or if you prefer, it will show you everything and tell you whether it will fit. The Crutchfield catalog (Fig. 5-1) contains a wealth of information on the many head units they carry.

FIGURE 5-1

Crutchfield catalog.
(*Courtesy of Crutchfield.*)

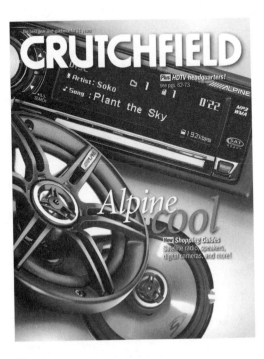

Cassette, CD, Satellite Radio, and HD Radio

Deciding whether to choose cassette, CD, satellite radio, or HD Radio is a matter of personal preference and cost. Many, but not all combinations are possible, and the features for each format vary considerably from head unit to head unit. Read the "Performance and Features" section to know what to look for in each format.

If you want both CD and cassette, you have two options. You can put a cassette receiver in the dash and add a CD changer in the trunk or elsewhere. The other option is to install a combined CD/cassette head unit. Most of these require a double height (double DIN) dash opening, so they only fit in some vehicles. The Sanyo FXCD-1350 (Fig. 5-2) manages to fit it in a standard single-DIN package.

Performance and Features

It's easy to get confused over all the features and performance aspects of head units. This section explains what each feature is all about. For convenience, features are categorized as general features, radio features, cassette features, CD features, satellite radio, and HD Radio.

General Features

The features in Table 5-2 are important to consider in any head unit, regardless of how often you listen to the radio or whether you choose cassette, CD, satellite radio, or HD Radio.

FIGURE 5-2

Sanyo FXCD-1350 combined CD/ cassette single DIN head unit. (*Courtesy of Sanyo*)

TABLE 5-2

Head Unit General Features

Performance/ Feature	Comments
Theft deterrents	Many deterrents are available: fully and partially detachable faces, concealable faces, and security code systems.
CD changer controls	Key feature if you want to add a CD changer, DVD changer, or digital music player now or in the future.
Sound shaping	Tools that go beyond basic bass and treble controls—equalizers, preset eq curves, time alignment, built-in crossovers, and more.
Detailed display	Range from single-color, no-frills display of information to animated displays with full-motion color graphics.
Preamp outputs	One, two, or three sets of RCA jacks on the back of the head unit to connect an external amp.
Preamp output voltage	Higher voltage makes it easier to get noise-free performance. Typical range is 1 to 5 volts.
Balanced line driver outputs	High performance, but expensive alternative to preamp outputs.
Remote control	Hand-held and mounted types.
CEA compliant power	Look at CEA compliant power rather than peak power for a more accurate indication of performance.

Theft Deterrents. There are a number of types of theft deterrents available in today's aftermarket head units:

- Fully detachable face
- Partially detachable face
- Concealable face
- Security code

A fully detachable face lets you take the entire head unit faceplate with you, leaving only a blank panel behind. A partially detachable face lets you take only the essential controls, leaving the bulkier ones behind. The disadvantage of detachable faces is that you need to remove and carry the faceplate with you.

On some Pioneer units, a built-in alarm system is armed each time the faceplate is removed and disarmed when it is reinserted into position. When the alarm is activated, the system emits an ear-piercing tone through the audio system speakers inside the car.

Concealable face head units have a manually operated or motorized fold-down face. Kenwood's 3D MASK Pro head units automatically display a blank panel when the ignition is turned off. This approach eliminates the hassle of removing and carrying faceplates; however, it leaves a complete functional head unit for thieves.

User-programmable security codes are commonly used on high-end factory units and a number of aftermarket head units. If power to the unit is ever removed, the security code must be entered to reactivate it. Instead of entering a number, Eclipse head units have you choose one of your CDs as a key CD. This disc must be loaded to reactivate the unit after loss of power.

CD Changer Controls.   This is a key feature if you think you might want to add a CD changer, DVD changer, or digital music player now or in the future. Head units with CD changer controls have a special connector on the back for a direct audio connection with the changer or player, for the best possible sound. They provide all the buttons and displays needed to support full operation of the changer/player as well.

In general, you'll need to choose a changer/player from the same manufacturer as the head unit for compatibility. Some controller/changer combinations have special programming features. For example, you can specify exactly which track will play on each CD, a great way to eliminate songs you don't like. Some let you assign each disc a name that will appear on the dash display when that disc is loaded.

There are alternate ways to add a changer or player to a system, but none are as good as using a head unit with CD changer controls. See Chap. 10 for details.

Sound Shaping.   These are tools that go beyond basic bass, treble, and loudness controls. Look for built-in graphic or parametric equalizers or selectable preset equalization curves. Some head units even provide digital time alignment so the sound from each speaker reaches your ears at the same time, to improve imaging.

SRS WOW® is a collection of sound-enhancing tools found in some Kenwood head units. It improves the bass performance of small speakers, raises the sound stage to ear-level, and creates a convincing 3D surround effect.

Pioneer's Front Image Enhancer provides an enhanced imaging mode for a more authentic sound stage. This is achieved by using the front speakers as primary drivers and the back speakers for deep bass and rear fill. When you want maximum volume or have passengers in the back, you can turn the feature off.

Built-in crossovers can now be found in many head units. 12 dB/octave high-pass filters are a great way to prevent deep bass from overdriving front speakers, and are better and more convenient than speaker-level bass blocking crossovers. Subwoofer crossovers are also frequently provided, but don't look to them to be sufficient for the job—at best they'll let you get away with using a sub amp with an otherwise too shallow crossover slope.

Detailed Display.   Basic displays give you a single-color, no-frills display of information. Custom color displays let you choose the color you want, to match or complement your dash. If you want to add excitement, choose an animated display with full-motion graphics. Some even let you add your own images, for the ultimate in customization.

Preamp Outputs.   RCA jacks on the back of the head unit that allow you to use a standard patch cable to connect an external amp. (Speaker outputs can be also used to provide signal to some amps, but preamp outputs provide a low-noise, low-distortion interface to any amplifier.)

Many head units have a single set of preamp outputs. Head units with two sets of preamp outputs provide increased flexibility for boosting with amplifiers. Having two sets of preamp outputs means the head unit fader control can remain functional for most configurations. Some head units have three sets of preamp outputs, one of which is intended to be used for a subwoofer amp.

If you plan to boost your head unit with external amps, see Chap. 7 for details on how the number of preamp outputs affects your system configuration options.

Preamp Output Voltage.   A higher preamp output voltage makes it easier to get noise-free performance from external amps. The typical range is 1 to 5 volts.

Balanced Line Driver Outputs.   Balanced line driver outputs go one step beyond high-voltage preamp outputs for providing noise-free performance with external components. They provide differential 16-volt drive, which essentially allows externally induced noise to be subtracted out. Balanced line driver outputs must be used with crossovers and amps having balanced line driver inputs. Balanced signals are normally routed using special XLR connectors and cables. Not for the budget conscious.

Remote Control.   There are two categories of remote controls for head units: hand-held and mounted. Hand-held remotes are useful if you want to control the head unit from outside the vehicle or from anywhere in a van or RV. Mounted remotes may be of the type mounted on the steering wheel within reach of your thumb (Fig. 5-3), or they may be mounted on the console or steering column. The idea is to make it easier to control your stereo without taking your hands off the wheel or your eyes off the road.

CEA Compliant Power.   The amount of continuous power, measured in watts, that an amplifier produces. The higher the number, the louder your music can play without distorting. Manufacturers often show peak power ratings on the faces of their products. Peak power measures the instantaneous power at the peak output voltage of the amplifier. Look at CEA compliant power for a more accurate indication of performance. See Chap. 7 for more details.

Radio Features

If you spend a lot of time listening to the radio, you'll want to choose a head unit with good FM performance and features. Look for a tuner with low FM sensitivity and high FM selectivity. If you like to channel surf, go for lots of presets and features like preset scan and automatic preset pro-

FIGURE 5-3

Blaupunkt Thummer™ remote control. (*Courtesy of Blaupunkt.*)

Low-Power, High-Power, and Very High Power Head Units

For head units, there are actually three distinct power categories (Table 5-3). These correspond to three types of internal circuitry commonly used for head units. The power categories arise because of the 12-volt electrical system of the car.

Low-power amps are the least expensive type, and are found in many older factory and low-cost aftermarket head units. Their power is limited by the fact that one amplifier output terminal is ground (0 volts) and the other terminal has a dynamic range of roughly 12 volts (its maximum swing is limited by the 12-volt power supply). This restricts the CEA compliant power to approximately 5 watts per channel.

High-power factory and aftermarket head units achieve roughly 4 times the power of the low-power amps by driving both plus and minus output terminals via separate internal amps. By driving the minus output terminal with an inverted version of the signal at the plus terminal, the effective output voltage to the speaker is doubled. Doubling the speaker voltage results in 4 times the power, and is good for a CEA compliant 18 watts per channel. This also explains why you can't ground one side of the speakers when using high-power head units—the minus side of the speakers is actually being driven by an internal amplifier.

To achieve power levels greater than high-power head units requires a power supply voltage greater than 12 volts. DC-to-DC converters are used for this purpose and can provide any desired voltage. The practical limitation to power levels is packaging—it's hard to fit all the required circuitry in a head unit–sized package and safely dissipate the heat generated. Very high power head units require amplifier-type power wiring to the battery, due to the high current draw.

TABLE 5-3

The Differences Between Low-, High- and Very High Power Head Units

Head Unit Type	Internal Circuitry	Power Category
Low-power	12-volt supply, single-ended	5 watts per channel typical
High-power	12-volt supply, internally bridged	18 watts per channel typical
Very high power	DC-to-DC converter supply	>18 watts per channel

The Panasonic CQ-C9901U (Fig. 5-4) is an example of a very high power head unit. It produces 60 watts per channel using a DC-to-DC converter and Tripath Class-T® amplifiers. The Tripath switching amplifiers provide the high efficiency needed to keep the heat down in the head unit package.

FIGURE 5-4

Panasonic CQ-C9901U very high power head unit.(*Courtesy of Matsushita Electric Corporation of America.*)

gramming. Check out what RDS has to offer too. Table 5-4 gives a summary of the various radio features.

AM/FM Presets.   These user-programmable push buttons let you go directly to the station you want. Some head units have as many as 36 presets available.

Diversity Tuning.   Uses two antennas and a special tuner to improve reception. It works by automatically selecting the antenna with the best reception. The speed of the selection process is so rapid that you cannot perceive it.

Systems with diversity tuning have excellent multipath rejection. Multipath is that swishing sound you hear when driving around large buildings or the suddenly bad reception you sometimes get when you're stopped at a traffic light. It's caused by a reflected version of the radio signal interfering with the direct signal. Diversity takes advantage of the fact

TABLE 5-4

Head Unit Radio
Features

Performance/ Feature	Comments
AM/FM presets	User-programmable push buttons let you go directly to the station you want.
Diversity tuning	Uses two antennas and a special tuner to improve reception.
FM mono/ stereo switch	Allows you to improve the signal-to-noise ratio during weak signal conditions.
RDS	Enables your head unit to display the station name and other text. Allows station tuning by format. Works only for FM stations transmitting RDS.
Preset scan	Plays a brief sample of what's on each of your preset radio stations.
Station scan	Plays a brief sample of what's on each strong station.
FM mono sensitivity	Tells you how weak an FM station a tuner can pick up.
FM selectivity	Tells you how well a tuner can reject the signal of a nearby interfering radio station.
FM stereo separation	The ability of an FM tuner to recreate the proper stereo image.
Automatic preset programming	Automatically loads your presets with the strongest available signals.

More About Multipath

The nature of a multipath signal is such that the received radio signal can drastically change strength over a distance of only 5 to 10 feet. This is because the typical half-wavelength of an FM signal is about 5 feet, and cancellation often occurs as two signals travel different path distances to reach the same point (hence "multipath"). If there is cancellation at one point, then about 5 to 10 feet away there is usually a useful-strength point.

that it is extremely likely that there is good reception at one of the antennas at all times.

FM Mono/Stereo Switch. Allows you to revert to mono mode during weak signal conditions to improve the signal-to-noise ratio. On some head units, operation is automatic.

RDS. Enables your head unit to display the station name, song title, and artist and other text messages that many FM radio stations now include with their broadcast signal. Also allows you to tune radio stations by music format, such as rock or jazz.

More About RDS

RDS stands for *Radio Data System*. This term is commonly used to refer to the European system as well as the newer, slightly different U.S. system. (The official name of the U.S. system is RBDS, short for *Radio Broadcast Data System*.) Over 1,500 U.S. FM stations use RDS, most of them in the top 50 markets.

RDS is a system for sending digital information along with the regular FM program. You can receive it using one of the newer tuners that have RDS decoding and an alphanumeric display built in. The RDS data stream can carry lots of useful data, such as:

- Station name (WFBQ or Q95)
- Format (country, rock, jazz, etc.)
- Song title and artist or other text
- Time of day
- Traffic alerts
- Weather alerts

Some stations use RDS just for its basic features, displaying their station name and format on RDS radios. With an RDS radio (Fig. 5-5), a scan looks first for RDS stations. If you further scan by format, then the radio will only stop at RDS stations that identify themselves as broadcasting that format. All of the rest are ignored.

RDS can also update some head units' clocks. With a unit capable of receiving the traffic and weather alert features of RDS, you can be alerted with reports even while listening to a CD.

FIGURE 5-5

Blaupunkt Casablanca MP54 CD/MP3 head unit with RDS. (*Courtesy of Blaupunkt.*)

Preset Scan. Touch a button and your receiver automatically plays a brief sample of what's on each of your preset radio stations. Touch the button again when you hear something you want to stay with.

Station Scan. Touch a button and your receiver automatically plays a brief sample of what's on each strong station. Touch the button again when you hear something you want to stay with.

FM Mono Sensitivity. This figure tells you how well a tuner can pick up weak FM radio signals. Lower values are better. Expressed in decibel femtowatts (dBf).

FM Selectivity. Alternate channel selectivity tells you how well a tuner can receive a desired radio station's signal while rejecting the signal of a nearby radio station. It is rated in decibels. Unlike the spec for sensitivity, the higher the number for selectivity the better. A good figure is 75 to 80 dB.

FM Stereo Separation. A measure of the ability of an FM tuner to recreate the proper stereo image. Normally specified at 1 kHz and measured in decibels. Anything 30 dB and above should be considered acceptable.

Automatic Preset Programming. Different manufacturers have different names for this feature. Activate it and the tuner automatically loads your presets with the strongest available signals. This makes finding stations easier when you're traveling.

Cassette Features

If you listen to a lot of tapes, look for a wide frequency response and Dolby noise reduction. Most prerecorded tapes use Dolby B, but if you record your own with Dolby C you may want a deck that offers both B and C. For features, look for auto reverse and auto music search. Choose soft-touch electronic controls if you dislike the feel of mechanical ones. Table 5-5 shows a range of cassette features.

Auto Music Search. Fast-forwards or rewinds to the next song and begins to play automatically. Multitrack auto music search skips forward or backward over multiple songs—hit the fast-forward or rewind button once for each track you want to skip over.

TABLE 5-5

Head Unit Cassette
Features

Performance/ Feature	Comments
Auto music search	Fast-forwards or rewinds to the next song and begins to play automatically.
Auto reverse	Automatically plays the other side of the tape when the end is reached.
Dolby	Noise reduction system to virtually eliminate tape hiss.
Tape eq switch	Selects the best equalization response according to the type of tape—normal, high-bias, or metal.
Tape frequency response	The frequency range a tape deck can reproduce.
Power-off release	Disengages the pinch roller from the capstan when you turn off the tape deck. Prevents a flat spot in the pinch roller.
Radio during rewind	Automatically plays the radio when a tape is fast-forwarding or rewinding.
Tape signal-to-noise ratio	A measure of how well a cassette player silences background noise. Almost purely a function of whether the deck has Dolby, and which type.
Soft-touch controls	More luxurious than the traditional spring-loaded mechanical buttons.
Wow and flutter	How stable the tape playback speed is.

Auto Reverse. Automatically plays the other side of the tape when the end is reached. This feature also lets you switch to the other side of the tape at the push of a button.

Dolby. Noise reduction system to virtually eliminate tape hiss. Head units with this feature decode Dolby-encoded tapes during playback. Dolby B is the most widely used system, but Dolby C offers a greater improvement in signal-to-noise ratio. Dolby is not as important in the relatively noisy automotive listening environment as it is in the home. Note: You have to record with Dolby C to get any benefit from a Dolby C car deck.

Tape EQ Switch. Selects the best equalization response according to the type of tape—normal, high-bias, or metal. In some head units selection is automatic.

Tape Frequency Response. The frequency range a tape deck can faithfully reproduce. Humans can hear sounds as low as 20 Hz and as high as 20 kHz.

Power-Off Release. Disengages the pinch roller from the capstan when you turn off the tape deck or turn off your car without first ejecting the tape. Prevents a flat spot from forming on the pinch roller, as well as a crease in the tape.

Radio During Rewind. Automatically plays the radio when a tape is fast-forwarding or rewinding. On some head units this feature is automatic; on others it's selectable.

Tape Signal-To-Noise Ratio. A measure of how well a cassette player silences background noise. Ratings are in decibels; higher ratings indicate less noise. This spec is almost purely a function of whether the deck has Dolby noise reduction and which type. Don't be swayed by better specs on decks with Dolby C if you only listen to Dolby B tapes: Chances are the performance with Dolby B tapes is the same as for decks with only Dolby B. In other words, you have to record with Dolby C to get any benefit from a Dolby C car deck.

Soft-Touch Controls. Soft-touch electronic controls are more luxurious than the traditional spring-loaded mechanical buttons. When you insert or eject a cassette, the deck automatically loads or smoothly unloads the tape. Soft-touch controls also make possible a number of advanced features, such as multi-track auto music search and blank skip.

Wow and Flutter. This spec indicates how stable the cassette deck's playback speed is. The lower the percentage, the better.

CD Features

A CD player in the dash is now considered standard equipment. Excellent frequency response and signal-to-noise ratio are the norm, and features like intro scan, random play, and track repeat are found on almost all models. A model with electronic shock protection can help reduce skipping on bad roads. The most important differentiating CD feature is MP3/WMA playback—some head units support neither, some MP3 only, others MP3 and WMA. If you're a competitor or plan on using super-high-power amps, you'll want to shop for a unit with higher signal-to-noise ratio. Table 5-6 provides an overview of CD features.

Number of Discs. Single-disc capacity is standard for CD head units. An exception is the Nakamichi MB-VI (Fig. 5-6), a head unit with a built-

TABLE 5-6

Head Unit CD
Features

Performance/ Feature	Comments
Number of discs	Single-disc capacity is standard, six-disc capacity is available.
CD-R, CD-RW compatibility	Can play audio CD-Rs and/or CD-RWs as well as prerecorded CDs.
CD text display	CD players with this feature will display the song title, album name, and artist for CDs having CD text information encoded on them.
MP3/WMA playback	Allows you to listen to CDs with MP3- or WMA-compressed music files.
ID3 tag display	Similar to CD text display, but for MP3/WMA files.
CD frequency response	The frequency range a CD player can reproduce.
Electronic shock protection	A buffer memory used as a reserve against skipping.
Intro scan	Lets you hear the first few seconds of each track. Hit the button again when you hear the song you want.
Random play/shuffle	Mixes up the order of songs for variety during playback.
CD signal-to-noise ratio	A measure of how well a CD player silences background noise.
Zero-bit detect	Mutes the output whenever a series of zeros is detected in the digital bitstream, for complete silence between songs.

in six-disc CD changer. The MB-VI is a DIN-compatible unit, so it will easily fit in most dash openings.

CD-R, CD-RW Compatibility. CD players with this capability can play audio CD-Rs and/or CD-RWs as well as prerecorded CDs. Most CD players will play CD-Rs, but some will not play CD-RWs (rewriteable discs). This is an important feature if you record your own CD-RW discs.

FIGURE 5-6

Nakamichi MB-VI six-disc head unit. (*Courtesy of Nakamichi.*)

CD Text Display. CD players with this feature will display the song title, album name, and artist for CDs having CD text information encoded on them.

MP3/WMA Playback. Allows you to listen to CDs with MP3 or WMA compressed music files. Some players support MP3 only, others support MP3 and WMA. With this feature, you'll also want ID3/WMA tag display.

ID3/WMA Tag Display. Similar to CD text display, but for MP3/WMA files. CD players with this feature will display the song title, album, artist, year, genre, and comments for MP3 files having ID3 tags and for WMA files having WMA tags. Later versions of ID3 (ID3v1.1, ID3v2) add even more information capabilities. This is a very useful feature if you play MP3s, because so many of them fit on a CD.

CD Frequency Response. The frequency range a CD player can faithfully reproduce. Humans can hear sounds as low as 20 Hz and as high as 20 kHz. Virtually every CD player exceeds this range.

Electronic Shock Protection. Electronic shock protection is a buffer memory used to store music as a reserve against skipping. It can significantly reduce skipping on bumpy roads or off road.

Intro Scan. Lets you hear the first few seconds of each track. Hit the button again when you hear the song you want.

Random Play/Shuffle. Mixes up the order of songs for variety during playback.

CD Signal-to-Noise Ratio. A measure of how well a CD player silences background noise. Ratings are in decibels; higher ratings indicate less noise. The signal-to-noise ratio of CD players is generally so good that noise picked up by other means determines the system noise level. Unless you're a competitor or plan on using super-high-power amps, don't place too much emphasis on this spec.

Zero-Bit Detect. Mutes the output whenever a series of zeros is detected in the digital bitstream. The result is complete silence between songs. This is important if you're a competitor, but otherwise you'll never hear the difference.

MP3, WMA, and WAV Digital Audio Formats

MP3 compression revolutionized the audio industry by allowing music files to be small enough to transfer over the Internet and efficiently stored in computers and music players. This revolution has changed the way people exchange and listen to music, and has spawned many exciting new products and features in car stereo.

Even though MP3 started it all, it's not the only game in town. Newer compression schemes such as WMA outperform MP3 and are gaining in popularity. Table 5-7 shows a comparison of MP3 and WMA compression at near-CD quality to the uncompressed WAV format. More details on each of these formats is below.

TABLE 5-7

Compression Comparison of Digital Audio Formats

Format	Bitrate	Sound Quality	MB per minute
WAV		CD	10
MP3	128 kbps	near-CD	1
WMA	64 kbps	near-CD	0.5

WAV

Standard audio format for Windows, used for storing high-quality, uncompressed sound. WAV files can contain CD-quality (44.1 KHz/16-bit) audio signals. However, CD-quality WAV files require relatively large amounts of memory, roughly 10 MB per minute of music.

MP3 (MPEG1, Audio Layer 3)

The most popular compression method for storing and transferring music. Although it uses a "lossy" compression system, MP3 delivers near-CD sound quality in a file that's only about a tenth the size of a corresponding WAV file. When creating an MP3 file, varying amounts of compression can be selected, depending on the desired file size and sound quality.

WMA (Windows Media Audio)

Developed by Microsoft, WMA is one of today's most popular Internet audio formats. Though not as popular as MP3, WMA outperforms MP3 when it comes to compression for a given sound quality. WMA produces a file that's about half the size of an MP3 file for near-CD quality sound. This performance advantage makes it handy for applications like portable digital audio players, where total play time is limited by the amount of internal memory. Like MP3, varying amounts of compression can be selected, depending on the desired file size and sound quality.

Satellite Radio

Satellite radio provides unparalleled musical variety (over **65** channels of commercial-free music per service), news, sports, and entertainment.

There's also continuously updated traffic and weather for major metropolitan areas. The sound is near-CD quality and the programming is available from coast to coast. To receive satellite radio, you'll need a suitable receiver. You'll also need to subscribe to one of the two satellite radio providers, XM or SIRIUS.

There are three factors in deciding which satellite radio service is right for you: the equipment, the fees, and the programming. Once you've studied your equipment options, you may have a strong incentive for choosing one service over the other. But if your equipment options are open, your decision should be about the programming. Look at the websites of XM and SIRIUS to learn about the music, sports, news, and entertainment channels they offer. Better yet, talk with people you know who subscribe and share your taste in music. All commercial-free music channels are not created equal.

You've got a number of equipment options when it comes to receiving satellite radio in your car. These are shown in Table 5-8. Head units with built-in satellite radio or that are satellite-ready will give you top-notch sound, put all your controls in one place, and provide a clean installation. The plug-and-play approach has the advantages of working with any head unit and letting you use your satellite radio receiver in your car and at home with a single subscription.

Head unit with built-in satellite radio. Choosing a head unit with built-in satellite radio (Fig. 5-7) simplifies installation and can reduce overall cost, since there are no extra tuner boxes, adapters, or cable assemblies to deal with. The sound quality is guaranteed to be high quality, since there's no FM modulator involved. But since head units with built-in satellite radio only support a single service, you're locked in to that service.

Satellite-ready head unit and satellite radio tuner. This approach offers the flexibility to add satellite radio later, if you're not quite ready to take the plunge now. If you buy a head unit that supports both XM and SIRIUS, you'll be able to choose either service, or even change services down the road by purchasing the appropriate satellite radio tuner module. With this approach, the tuner module must match the brand and vintage of head unit. The sound quality is guaranteed to be high quality, since there's no FM modulator involved.

Satellite-ready head unit and universal tuner with head unit adapter. This is identical to the previous configuration, except that it uses a universal tuner with head unit adapter instead of a head unit specific tuner. The XMDirect XMD1000 (Fig. 5-8) is an example of an XM

TABLE 5-8

Satellite Radio
Receiver Config-
urations

Configuration	Diagram	Comments
Head unit with built-in satellite radio	satellite radio head unit	Head units only support one satellite radio service.
Satellite-ready head unit and satellite radio tuner	satellite radio tuner — satellite ready head unit	Some head units support both satellite radio services. Tuner module must match brand and vintage of head unit.
Satellite-ready head unit and universal tuner with head unit adapter	universal satellite radio tuner — adapter — satellite ready head unit	Lets you use same tuner for many brands of head unit. Adapter must match brand and vintage of head unit.
Plug-and-play satellite radio tuner with FM modulator	satellite radio tuner + fm modulator — head unit / optional boombox docking station	Works with any head unit. Optional home kits and boombox docking stations let you enjoy satellite radio anywhere with a single subscription.
Plug-and-play tuner with docking adapter and satellite-ready head unit	satellite radio tuner / docking adapter — satellite ready head unit	Eliminates having a plug-and-play tuner cluttering your dash and puts all your controls in one place. Enjoy satellite radio anywhere with a single subscription.

satellite radio universal tuner. With this approach, the same XM tuner works for many head unit brands. Head unit specific adapters are used between the universal tuner and the head unit. If you switch brand of head unit, you'll only have to get a new adapter instead of a whole new tuner. The biggest benefit of this approach will occur if adapters allowing you to use XM universal tuners with SIRIUS-ready head units (and vice versa) become widespread.

Plug-and-play satellite radio tuner with FM modulator. Plug-and-play receivers let you listen to satellite radio with any head unit by using an FM modulator (either built-in or included in the car kit). If your head unit has an aux input, you can use a direct connection for better sound.

FIGURE 5-7

Alpine CDA-9820XM head unit with built-in XM satellite radio.
(*Courtesy of Alpine Electronics, Inc.*)

An optional home kit lets you connect the receiver to your home stereo and an optional boombox docking station lets you enjoy satellite radio wherever you go. With plug-and-play, you pay only one subscription for the ability to have satellite radio anywhere. The Delphi XM2Go MyFi (Fig. 5-9) takes this convenience even further. This hand-held receiver has a built-in FM modulator, built-in satellite radio antenna, ear buds, and a rechargeable integrated battery. If that weren't enough, it lets you record five hours of your favorite shows (even when the unit's not in use), then go back and listen later.

Plug-and-play tuner with docking adapter and satellite-ready head unit. Docking adapters, such as Blitz Safe's SkyLink Direct, allow your plug-and-play satellite radio to be installed anywhere in the vehicle and controlled directly by your satellite-ready head unit. This eliminates having a plug-and-play tuner cluttering your dash and it puts all your controls in one place. The sound quality is guaranteed to be high quality, since there's no FM modulator involved. Best of all, you pay only one subscription for the ability to have satellite radio anywhere.

FIGURE 5-8

XMDirect XMD1000 universal tuner and head unit adapter.
(*Courtesy of XM.*)

FIGURE 5-9

Delphi XM2Go MyFi hand-held satellite radio. (*Courtesy of XM.*)

HD Radio

HD (high-definition) radio technology provides the best-sounding AM/FM ever. It produces near-CD quality FM and near-FM quality AM broadcasts, without a subscription. All you need is a suitable receiver. The digital signals that make HD Radio possible share the same frequencies as normal FM and AM broadcasts, but the HD signal is designed not to interfere with the regular broadcast signal, so old radios aren't adversely affected. HD Radio receivers automatically detect the presence of the HD signal and switch to it, providing improved sound quality and displaying program information such as song title and artist.

HD Radio signals aren't available in all areas, but more radio stations are upgrading to digital every day. Two thousand U.S. stations have com-

TABLE 5-9

HD Radio Receiver Configurations

Configuration	Diagram	Comments
Head unit with built-in HD Radio	hd head unit	Simplifies installation and can reduce overall cost.
HD-ready head unit and HD Radio tuner	hd radio tuner — hd-ready head unit	Offers the flexibility to add HD Radio later. Tuner module must match brand and vintage of head unit.

FIGURE 5-10

Panasonic CQ-
CB8901U head unit
with built-in HD
radio. (*Courtesy of Matsushita Electric Corporation of America.*)

FIGURE 5-11

Kenwood KDC-
MP228 HD Radio-
ready head unit.
(*Courtesy of Kenwood.*)

mitted to HD Radio, meaning multiple stations in top 100 markets and reception available to more than 90 percent of the U.S. population.

You've got two equipment options when it comes to receiving HD Radio in your car: head units with built-in HD Radio, or HD-ready head units with a separate HD tuner box. Table 5-9 shows the details.

Head unit with built-in HD Radio. Choosing a head unit with built-in HD radio (Fig. 5-10) simplifies installation and can reduce overall cost, since there are no extra tuner boxes, adapters, or cable assemblies to deal with. The Panasonic CQ-CB8901U (Fig. 5-10) is a head unit with this feature. It also plays CDs, MP3, and WMA files and has an aux input.

HD-ready head unit and HD Radio tuner. This approach offers the flexibility to add HD Radio reception later, if you're not quite ready to take the plunge now. The Kenwood KDC-MP228 (Fig. 5-11) is an example of an HD Radio-ready head unit, to be used with an optional Kenwood HD Radio tuner. With this approach, the HD Radio tuner module must match the brand and vintage of head unit.

Installation

Once you've determined what size, mounting method, and depth your vehicle can accommodate and what features and performance you want, you're almost ready to buy and install your head unit.

The key to making head unit installation go smoothly is having the necessary mechanical and electrical adapters, supplies, and tools on hand. For vehicles with integrated radio/climate controls, premium factory sound systems, OnStar, steering wheel head unit controls, or 2000 and up GM vehicles with the Class 2 data bus, more sophisticated mechanical or electrical adapters are usually required. Details are covered later in this chapter. The best time to buy adapters and supplies is when you buy your head unit, so it's best to understand what you'll need beforehand. For guidance on the supplies and tools you'll need, check out Chap. 2.

Installing a head unit is really two projects in one—a mechanical mounting project and an electrical wiring project. Each of these is explained next.

Mechanical Mounting

For many installations, an aftermarket head unit will directly fit the factory mounting system and dash opening. For these, you don't need a special mounting kit or faceplate. For other installations, the key to mechanical mounting is using the right mounting kit.

Mounting Kits.   Mounting kits are available to make a DIN head unit fit in virtually any late-model dash. (For vintage vehicles, a shafted head unit must be used, and no kit is required.) Different kits are designed to remedy different mounting problems. For shallow mounting depths, kits with extended faces can give you additional depth to work with. Some kits have a half-DIN equalizer opening built in.

The Metra *Pocket with a Purpose* GM installation kit (Fig. 5-12) will hold an AM/FM/CD player and a CD jewel case. This solves the problem of where to stash a CD case and is a great way to take advantage of the extra space available with a DIN head unit in a GM slot.

Kits for some vehicles require a lot of exposed plastic. For these, it's important to match the factory appearance as much as possible. The Scosche GM1482 kit for Chevy and GMC full-size trucks (Fig. 5-13) is available in six colors to match the dash.

Some vehicles present special challenges. Starting in 2003, Honda decided to integrate the climate controls and head unit controls into the same dashboard panel in their Accords. This made aftermarket head unit installation an extremely difficult proposition. That same year Metra responded with the TURBO2 integrated control panel kit (Fig. 5-14). This kit made it possible to install an aftermarket head unit in an Accord dash while retaining the factory climate controls.

The point of all this is that not all mounting kits are created equal. Ask about your options when shopping.

Removing and Installing in an Oversize GM or Chrysler Dash Opening.   The oversize dash openings found in many GM and Chrysler vehicles give you lots of options because they have extra space to work with. You can choose an adapter kit that lets you install a Euro DIN or ISO-DIN head unit plus a half-DIN equalizer. You can choose a kit that centers the head unit in a plain panel or one with a storage pocket below the head unit. If you prefer the look of a head unit face that fills the entire dash opening, GM- and Chrysler-style aftermarket head units are available. These are designed to fill the large factory openings in many GM and Chrysler vehicles, and eliminate the need for a mounting adapter kit.

Before you can install your new head unit, you'll need to remove the old one. Normally a factory trim panel will need to be removed first. This might be attached with screws or spring clips, or a combination of the

FIGURE 5-13
Scosche GM1482 kit. (*Courtesy of Scosche.*)

FIGURE 5-14

Metra 2003/4
TURBO2 Accord kit.
(*Courtesy of Metra.*)

two. Often, screw heads are hidden by the ashtray or the glove compartment door. After you've removed all visible screws, gently try to pry the panel off. Sometimes a putty knife is helpful here. If you find a spot that doesn't budge, you've either missed a screw or there's a spring clip behind it. Don't use too much force or you'll break the trim panel. Crutchfield MasterSheets can really come in handy here because they show you the locations of hidden clips and screws unique to your vehicle.

After you've taken off the trim panel, remove all the screws attaching the factory head unit to the dash and gently try to pull it out. If it seems

Tip: Always try to find a way to provide rear support for a head unit. The bumps and vibrations in the automotive environment can reduce the life of an unsecured unit and increase skipping in a CD deck or wow and flutter in a cassette deck. Abuse from potholes and railroad crossings can also put stress on the installation kit and surrounding dash panels.

A backstrap (strip of metal perforated with a series of holes) is often supplied with a head unit for rear support (Fig. 5-15). One end of the strap attaches to a stud on the back of the head unit, the other to an existing bolt or screw under the dash. The multiple holes give you a choice of attachment points. You will normally need to bend or twist the backstrap to reach the point of attachment.

FIGURE 5-15

Backstrap. (*Courtesy of MCM Electronics.*)

stuck, there may be some type of rear support. Once you slide the old head unit out, disconnect the antenna plug and factory wiring harness.

If you're installing a GM- or Chrysler-style aftermarket head unit, the installation process is exactly the reverse of the removal process.

If you're installing a Euro DIN or ISO-DIN head unit, you'll need a mounting adapter kit. Most adapter kits are combination Euro DIN and shaft style or combination ISO-DIN and shaft style, where pieces are cut away or omitted for nonshafted applications.

For a Euro DIN head unit, the first step is to screw the adapter to the dash. It should mount the same way the original head unit did. Next, slide the metal mounting sleeve supplied with the head unit (Fig. 5-16) into the adapter opening until the small outer lip makes contact with the edges of the opening. Once you put the sleeve in position, bend the tabs on the sleeve out to secure it in place. Connect the wires to the head unit and test it. Now push the head unit into the sleeve—it should click into place. Install the trim ring, factory trim panel, and backstrap.

For an ISO-DIN head unit, you'll first need to mount the head unit to the adapter. This is achieved by using screws in matching holes in the adapter and sides of the head unit. Next mount the adapter to the dash. Install the factory trim panel and backstrap.

Removing and Installing in a Euro DIN Dash Opening. Euro DIN installations are usually quick and easy. Removal and installation is done from the front, and no dash panels need to be removed.

The factory head unit is secured in a sleeve by spring clips, which you release using a pair of DIN removal tools (Fig. 5-17). These look like U-shaped pieces of bent coat hanger and are often included with a new head unit. Most receivers also have some type of rear support that needs to be detached before the old head unit is pulled out. Once you slide the old head unit out, disconnect the antenna plug and factory wiring harness.

FIGURE 5-16

Tabs on Euro DIN sleeve. (*Courtesy of Crutchfield.*)

FIGURE 5-17
DIN removal tools in
action. (*Courtesy of
Crutchfield.*)

Your new Euro DIN head unit will come with a metal mounting
sleeve. You may be able to use the sleeve already in place in the dash, or
you may need to replace it with the new one. See if your new head unit
slides in properly and whether it locks into place securely in the old sleeve.
If not, remove the original sleeve by bending back the metal tabs holding
it in place and sliding it out. Slide the new sleeve into position until the
outer lip makes contact with the edges of the opening. Make sure the top
of the sleeve is facing up, then bend the tabs on the sleeve out to secure it
in place.

After you make the appropriate wiring connections and plug in the
antenna, slide the new head unit into the sleeve. Try the head unit to
make sure it's functioning properly. If everything is OK, push it all the
way in until it clicks into place.

Removing and Installing in an ISO-DIN Dash Opening. ISO-DIN
dash openings are common among Toyotas and Nissans. The ISO-DIN
mounting method uses factory side support brackets, so no mounting
adapter is needed for ISO-DIN head units.

Before you can install your new head unit, you'll need to remove the
old one. Normally a factory trim panel will need to be removed first. This
might be attached with screws or spring clips or a combination of the two.
Often, screw heads are hidden by the ashtray or the glove compartment
door. After you've removed all visible screws, gently try to pry the panel
off. Sometimes a putty knife is helpful here. If you find a spot that
doesn't budge, you've either missed a screw or there's a spring clip behind
it. Don't use too much force or you'll break the trim panel.

After you've taken off the trim panel, remove all the screws attaching
the factory head unit assembly to the dash and gently try to pull it out.

Tip: Many cassette
and CD head units are
shipped with a plastic
or metal locking screw
that you'll need to
remove before instal-
lation. The owner's
manual will tell you
whether this is the
case.

If it seems stuck, there may be some type of rear support. Once you slide the old head unit assembly out, disconnect the antenna plug and factory wiring harness.

For an ISO-DIN head unit, remove the ISO-DIN brackets from the sides of the factory head unit and install them to the sides of the new head unit in the same way (Fig. 5-18). The plastic trim ring included with the new head unit for Euro DIN installations will not be used here. From this point, the installation process is exactly the reverse of the removal process. Install the head unit assembly in the dash, then install the factory trim panel and backstrap.

Electrical Wiring

The key to making the electrical wiring part of head unit installation easy is to use the proper wiring harness and, if necessary, original equipment manufacturer (OEM) integration and antenna adapters.

Wiring Harness. Snapped into the back of your factory head unit, you will find one or more rectangular wiring plugs. This is called the *factory wiring harness,* and it contains power, speaker, and various other wires such as a power antenna turn-on.

Unfortunately, the factory wiring harness will not directly connect to an aftermarket head unit. For most vehicles, however, you can purchase a wiring harness (Fig. 5-19) to mate with the existing car harness, so you don't need to splice into any of the factory wires. (Crutchfield includes

FIGURE 5-18
Mounted ISO-DIN brackets. (*Courtesy of Crutchfield.*)

FIGURE 5-19

World of wiring har-
nesses. (*Courtesy of
Scosche.*)

one of these harnesses with the purchase of a head unit.) The wires of this
mating harness are first connected to the appropriate wires of the aftermarket head unit. The other end of the harness then snaps right into
your car's factory wiring harness.

There are a number of good reasons to use the mating wiring harness
approach (Fig. 5-20). With a mating harness, you can do the job of connecting wires on a well-lit workbench rather than underneath a dashboard. Leaving the factory wiring harness intact makes it easy if you ever
decide to reinstall the factory radio. And when you buy a mating wiring
harness, the job of identifying each of the factory wires is done for you.

Use butt-splice or closed-end-splice crimp connectors to attach the
wiring harness wires to your new head unit's wires. If you prefer, you can
solder the wire ends together and use heat-shrink tubing. Some harnesses
come with bullet connectors already attached, to mate with those on the
head unit's wires. The most important factor is getting a tight connection
that won't come loose over time. Harnesses are supplied with a color code
reference chart identifying all the wires (or each of the wires is labeled), so
you don't need to figure them out yourself.

If a wiring harness isn't available, Scotchlok connectors can be used to
connect an aftermarket head unit to a factory wiring harness without
cutting off the end of the harness. This makes it easy if you ever decide
to reinstall the factory radio.

OEM Integration Adapters.   In most cases, a wiring harness is all you
need to properly connect an aftermarket head unit to a vehicle's power

FIGURE 5-20

Use a wiring harness
adapter!

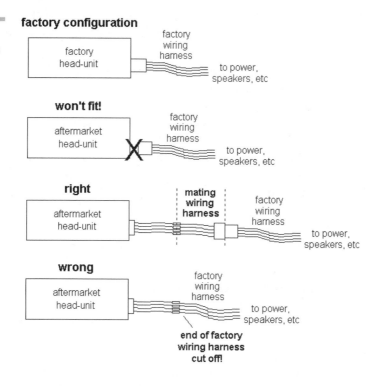

and speaker wires. However, there are many cases where you need to use an OEM integration adapter between the head unit and wiring harness. These include:

- Vehicles with chassis-grounded speakers

- Vehicles with common-grounded speakers

- Vehicles with steering wheel head unit controls

- Premium factory sound systems

- 2000 and up GM vehicles with the Class 2 data bus

- Vehicles with OnStar

How do you know if you're a candidate for an OEM integration adapter? The easiest and most reliable method is to consult with the pros—stop by your favorite local car stereo shop or call Crutchfield. They should each have access to an up-to-date database containing the information. You may be able to scope it out yourself. It should be obvious if your car has steering wheel head unit controls or OnStar. If you have a 2000 and up GM vehicle, listen to see if the door chime comes through the stereo—if so, you have the Class 2 data bus. Check for evidence of a premium factory system by looking for logos on the head unit or speaker grilles. Chassis-grounded and common-grounded speakers can often be detected by inspection of trunk speaker wiring.

OEM integration adapters for chassis- and common-grounded speakers are described here. The last four cases are covered separately, in the next sections.

Vehicles with chassis-grounded speakers or common-grounded speakers not connected to chassis ground present a problem for high-power head units. This is because the minus speaker wires from high-power head units cannot be grounded or tied together and are needed to carry music as well as DC voltage to each of the speakers.

With chassis-grounded or common-grounded speakers, you have two options:

- Rewire the system so two independent wires are used for each speaker.
- Use an OEM integration adapter.

Rewiring the system is a lot of work, but has the added benefit of letting you put in speaker wire better than the 22-gauge stuff commonly used for factory speaker wiring. If you're willing to spend the time, this is the best option from a performance standpoint.

OEM integration adapters provide a quick and easy solution to the problem of using high-power head units in many vehicles. Unfortunately, there may be performance sacrifices involved. In the case of OEM integration adapters for chassis-grounded speaker wiring, it is normal to simply AC-couple the plus speaker wires through a capacitor and not use the minus speaker wires from the head unit at all. This results in slashing the

FIGURE 5-21
SoundGate FLT1.
(*Courtesy of SoundGate.*)

TABLE 5-10

Types of Factory
Antenna Connectors

Type	Comments
Standard (Motorola)	Used on all aftermarket equipment.
GM mini	Used on 1988 and up GM.
Ford	Used on some 1995 and up vehicles, usually for radios with DSP controls.
Chrysler	Used on 2002 and up Chrysler/Jeep.
Nissan	Diversity (two-antenna) system.
Volkswagen/Euro	Factory antenna needs 12 volts to turn on impedance-matching circuit.

power to the speakers by a factor of 4—no better than using a low-power head unit!

In the case of OEM integration adapters for common-grounded (but not connected to chassis ground) speaker wiring, it is possible to maintain a high-power output. Although not all units do this, one device that does is the FLT1 by SoundGate (Fig. 5-21). Not all OEM integration adapters of this type maintain a full 20- to 20,000-Hz frequency response, so check before you buy.

Antenna Adapters. Aftermarket head units all use the standard Motorola antenna connector, but many factory antennas do not. That's where antenna adapters come in. Adapters are available to adapt various factory antennas to aftermarket head units (Table 5-10). Adapters are also available to adapt aftermarket antennas to factory head units, so be careful to get the right adapter.

Factory Steering Wheel Control Interfaces

Many late-model vehicles have steering wheel audio controls in addition to the normal controls on the head unit. They make it easier to control your stereo without taking your hands off the wheel or your eyes off the road. When you install an aftermarket head unit, you normally lose use of these auxiliary controls.

SoundGate now offers solutions to this problem with their factory steering wheel control interfaces (Fig. 5-22). These allow you to retain use of auxilliary head unit controls with most popular brands of aftermarket head units. Interfaces are available for many late-model GM, Ford, and Chrysler vehicles.

Premium Factory Sound Systems

If you have a premium factory sound system (such as Delco/Bose or Ford/JBL) and want to replace your head unit with an aftermarket model, you'll need to use a suitable OEM integration adapter between the head unit and wiring harness. The XR4 radio replacement interface from

Premium Factory Sound System Basics

Although the details of Bose and Ford Premium systems differ (as do different Bose systems among themselves) they share the same basic principle. They all use external amplifiers (amplified speakers or an outboard amp) and they all use differential signals between the head unit and amplifiers.

The advantage of using differential signals is noise immunity. The differential outputs of the head unit provide two equal but opposite versions of the music signal (an inverted version and a noninverted version). At the differential inputs of the amplifier, the two versions of the signal are subtracted. Since any externally induced noise presumably affects both versions of the signal the same, subtraction causes cancellation of the noise. Because one of the music signals was inverted, subtraction also results in a music signal that is twice the original signal.

The differential outputs of the head unit have a DC offset to eliminate the need for coupling capacitors in the head unit and amplifiers. DC offset is also used in Bose systems to "wake up" the amplifiers.

Bose systems often incorporate speakers with impedances much less than the usual 4 ohms (0.4 ohms is common!). This allows the Bose amplifiers to achieve much higher power levels without having to incorporate expensive DC-to-DC converters to provide a higher supply voltage.

GM's Class 2 Data Bus

In 2002, GM added a new twist to some of its premium factory sound systems—Class 2 data bus control. GM's Premium/Smart Bose system is used in 2002 and later full-size trucks and SUVs. With this system, the head unit provides fixed-level audio signals to the factory amplifiers. The head unit issues commands to each amp via the Class 2 data bus to control volume, fader, and balance. This approach provides improved noise immunity, but makes adding an amp to your head unit more challenging.

Chrysler/Infinity Systems

Like Bose and Ford Premium systems, Chrysler/Infinity systems use external amplifiers (amplified speakers). Unlike Bose and Ford, Chrysler/Infinity systems use standard head unit technology. This approach allows upgrading to the premium system in the assembly plant by simply using amplified speaker assemblies instead of normal ones.

Some earlier Chrysler/Infinity systems (prior to 1995) use low-power head units; the rest use high-power head units. If you want to replace a high-power factory head unit with a high-power aftermarket model (and keep the amplified speakers), no OEM integration adapter is required. If the factory head unit is low power, you will need to use an OEM integration adapter of the type normally used for chassis-grounded speaker wiring.

If you're replacing the factory head unit, be sure to connect the remote turn-on wire from the aftermarket head unit to the remote turn-on wire in the factory harness. Chrysler/Infinity systems use this wire to "wake up" the amplifiers.

Another approach you can use when replacing the factory head unit is to bypass the amplifiers at the amplified speakers. This is feasible in Chrysler/Infinity systems because standard-impedance speakers are used. (This is not the case for Bose systems, which commonly use ultra-low-impedance speakers.) By bypassing, you will lose the benefit of custom equalization built into the factory amps, but you will gain the ability to boost the head unit with your own amp.

Tip: Some interfaces are two-channel units. If this is the case, you will need to buy two units to retain functionality of your head unit fader and balance controls.

SoundGate (Fig. 5-23) converts aftermarket head unit signals to the low-level differential type audio signals used by many GM and Ford premium factory sound systems. For more details on how premium factory sound systems work, see the sidebar.

2000 and Up GM Vehicles with the Class 2 Data Bus

General Motor's Class 2 data bus was designed to reduce the amount of wiring in vehicles by providing serial communication (rather than more wires) between system components. Starting in model year 2000, the Class 2 data bus was connected to factory head units in some vehicles. In some cars, this bus connection to the head unit is used only for the radio anti-theft feature and vehicle warning chimes. In other vehicles, the bus connection to the head unit also allows the factory radio to act as a control center for programming a number of vehicle functions. In either case, simply replacing the factory head unit means a loss of important vehicle functions. But with the proper adapters and harnesses, it's possible to replace a Class 2 data bus head unit and retain full functionality of your vehicle's features.

Chime Module Interfaces

In most of their Class 2 data bus vehicles, GM uses the factory head unit to play warning chimes through the front left speaker. Replacing the factory head unit is a serious issue in these vehicles because warning chimes for high coolant temperature, low oil pressure, and other safety related chimes are lost when the head unit is replaced.

SoundGate's GMCHIME (Fig. 5-24) solves this problem by bringing the chime warnings back into the vehicle via a compact, easy-to-install interface unit. GMCHIME's self-contained speaker and digital electronics

FIGURE 5-24
SoundGate
GMCHIME chime
module interface.
(*Courtesy of SoundGate.*)

duplicate the sound of each of the four chimes used by GM. The GMCHIME interface also provides a Class 2 data bus generated accessory/ignition lead. This lead is needed to shut off the head unit when the ignition is off, and is absent from the wiring harness in some GM vehicles.

Relocation Harnesses

In some vehicles, the head unit is used for programming car functions over the data bus in addition to playing warning chimes. These functions include oil life reset, low tire pressure reset, delayed headlamp illumination, automatic door lock and unlock mode, remote visual verification, content theft operation, remote keyless entry programming, and horn chirp on timer. If the factory head unit is removed, these functions are lost, and there is no OEM integration adapter available to restore them.

For these vehicles, a head unit relocation harness (Fig 5-25) can be used to relocate the factory head unit to the trunk. The relocation harness

FIGURE 5-25
Best Kits BHA2004T
head unit relocation
harness. (*Courtesy of
Best Kits and Harnesses.*)

FIGURE 5-26

SoundGate STAR-MOD2V2 OnStar interface. (*Courtesy of SoundGate.*)

extends the factory wiring, allowing the relocated factory head unit to program car functions as well as play warning chimes through the factory speaker system. The relocation harness also provides power and speaker wires for the dash-mounted aftermarket head unit.

Vehicles with OnStar

The OnStar system is standard equipment in many late-model GM, Acura, Audi, Saab and Subaru vehicles. OnStar uses cell phone and GPS technology to provide emergency and other helpful services to subscribers. The problem for aftermarket audio is that the OnStar system routes information through the factory head unit. Replacing the head unit disables OnStar.

An OnStar interface (Fig. 5-26) can be used to retain your OnStar features while replacing the factory head unit. A variety of models are available, depending on your application. Some are for head unit–only replacement, others for when you're replacing the head unit and adding amps. Some models even include a GM chime interface, so you don't need to add a separate interface to solve your Class 2 data bus problem.

CHAPTER 6

Mobile Video and 5.1 Channel Audio

Mobile video and 5.1 channel audio are two of the most exciting new developments in mobile entertainment. The link between them is the DVD. Although there are other video and 5.1 audio sources, DVDs rule. So when you're planning your mobile video system, it's a great time to think about 5.1 channel audio too.

Mobile Video Configurations

There are numerous ways to add mobile video to your vehicle. Which is best depends on whether you're planning on entertaining the kids in the backseat or yourself, what type of vehicle you have, and, of course, your budget.

Table 6-1 lists the most common mobile video configurations. Keep in mind that you can add an additional monitor or monitors, DVD changer, and other video sources like TV tuner, VCR, satellite TV receiver, or digital video player to most of the configurations.

Even if you're not planning on adding any additional monitors, check out the section "Monitor Performance and Features" for what to look for in the built-in monitor of your DVD player.

DVD Head Unit with Built-In Monitor

A DVD head unit with built-in monitor is the ultimate in front-seat entertainment. But the benefits go way beyond being able to watch movies. Having a big up-front display is perfect for wading through folders of MP3 titles, monitoring a rearview camera, or as a navigation system display. If you have a touch-screen monitor, it's even better. Touch screens give you a graphical user interface rather than lots of tiny buttons to command your system. A DVD head unit can also serve as the centerpiece of a 5.1 channel audio system.

Most DVD head units with built-in monitor have motorized retractable displays that let you fit a 6.5- or 7-inch monitor in a single DIN head unit (Fig. 6-1). This is a clever solution to the problem of where to fit a monitor in the dash, and provides stealth when you're out of your car, to help deter theft. But with a retractable monitor, you need to be sure that the extended display doesn't block important dashboard controls or air vents, or interfere with the shift lever or stick shift as it's extending/retracting.

If you have a double-DIN dash opening, you can use a DVD head unit with a non-retracting display. This provides an attractive flush mount

TABLE 6-1

Mobile Video Con-
figurations

Configuration	Comments
DVD head unit with built-in monitor	Ultimate in front-seat entertainment. An in-dash monitor is also ideal for wading through folders of MP3 titles, monitoring a rearview camera, or as a navigation system display.
DVD head unit with separate monitor	Best option if you want a DVD player in the dash but prefer a monitor elsewhere. This configuration also makes sense if your main interest is audio—a DVD player in the dash gives you 5.1 channel sound capabilities, and a recordable DVD can hold over a thousand MP3 songs.
CD head unit controlling DVD changer	Requires a head unit with changer controls, DVD changer, and monitor. Provides a great way to add video and audio functionality in situations where replacing the head unit is difficult or impossible.
Separate DVD player with separate monitor	Requires considerably more installation effort than overhead or headrest DVD players with built-in monitors. Can make sense if you want a monitor in a size or location not feasible with an overhead or headrest player/monitor.
Overhead/headrest DVD player with built-in monitor	Simplest way to provide permanent backseat entertainment.
Portable DVD player with built-in monitor	Easiest and cheapest way to provide backseat entertainment. Downside: cable clutter, lost space, and rigging and unrigging hassles.

and reduces the chances of any clearance problems. The Kenwood Excelon DD7015 (Fig. 6-2) is an example of this approach and features a 6.5-inch touch-screen monitor. The monitor motors down for access to the DVD/CD slot.

DVD Head Unit with Separate Monitor

A DVD head unit with separate monitor is the best option if you want a DVD player in the dash but prefer a monitor (or monitors) elsewhere. This configuration also makes sense if your main interest is audio. A DVD player in the dash gives you 5.1 channel sound capabilities (see the section

FIGURE 6-1

Pioneer AVIC-N2 DVD head unit with retractable display.

(Courtesy of Pioneer.)

FIGURE 6-2

Kenwood Excelon DD7015 DVD head unit with flush-mount display.

(Courtesy of Kenwood.)

FIGURE 6-3

Alpine DVA-9965 DVD head unit.

(Courtesy of Alpine Electronics, Inc.)

on 5.1 Channel Audio Sources in this chapter), and a recordable DVD can hold well over a thousand MP3 songs—a digital jukebox in itself. The Alpine DVA-9965 DVD head unit (Fig. 6-3) is an example of this approach and is packed with features. With the addition of a compatible touch-control monitor, backseat passengers can control the video source.

CD Head Unit Controlling DVD Changer

DVD changers (covered in detail in Chap. 10) play DVDs as well as CDs, and can be controlled using the changer controls of compatible CD head units. In this configuration, the DVD changer acts as the main video source and provides video to one or more monitors. This setup gives you the benefits of a video system with DVD changer and a CD changer with MP3 playback, all controlled by a CD head unit that you may already have in your dash.

This approach can be used with a factory head unit having CD changer controls, by using an appropriate OEM interface changer converter or a factory compatible DVD changer. Overall, it provides a great way to add front- or backseat video plus audio functionality in many situations where replacing the head unit is difficult or impossible.

Separate DVD Player with Separate Monitor

Separate DIN or near-DIN sized DVD players are available inexpensively, for under-seat, under-dash, in-dash, or custom console mounting. You'll need to provide a separate monitor or monitors. For sound, you can buy a set of wireless headphones, or listen through the car's sound system using your head unit's aux inputs.

Installing separate components requires considerably more installation effort than the combined solution offered by overhead or headrest DVD players with built-in monitors. But using separates can make sense if you want a monitor in a size or location that's not feasible with an overhead or headrest player/monitor.

Overhead/Headrest DVD Player with Built-In Monitor

An overhead or headrest DVD player with integrated monitor is the simplest way to provide permanent backseat entertainment. Compared to using a portable DVD player, overhead and headrest players are always ready to play and eliminate the cable clutter, lost passenger compartment space, and rigging and unrigging hassles of a portable player.

With an overhead or headrest player system, you'll need to provide a 12-volt power connection to the player. Beyond that, it depends on whether you want the player's audio output wired to your car's sound system and whether you want to connect a second video source or monitor. Many players include wireless headphones. Some have a wireless FM transmitter for listening over the car's sound system without an A/V connection to the head unit.

Overhead players provide viewing that's good for both sides of the backseat or viewing in second and third rows of seats in vans and large SUVs. The Panasonic CY-VHD9500U overhead DVD system (Fig. 6-4) is an example of this approach. It has two sets of wireless headphones, so you don't need to connect it to your car's audio system.

Vehicle-specific overhead players are available for many popular SUVs. These replace the factory overhead console and provide a factory-installed appearance, plus simplify installation. Overhead players for the Railport Vehicle Personalization System (see sidebar) are also becoming available, and further simplify installation. Both vehicle-specific and Railport overhead players offer the advantage of being able to cleanly remove the player when it comes time to sell or return your vehicle.

A disadvantage of overhead mounting is that the monitor can block the rearview mirror of the driver, especially with large monitors and low-roofed vehicles. Mounting an overhead monitor offset from center may provide a good solution in some vehicles. Some models feature rotatable displays, an asset for offset mounting.

FIGURE 6-4

Panasonic CY-VHD9500U overhead DVD system. *(Courtesy of Matsushita Electric Corporation of America.)*

FIGURE 6-5

Audiovox headrest DVD system. *(Courtesy of Audiovox Electronics Corp.)*

Headrest players provide optimum viewing for individual backseat passengers, but are difficult to share, so you'll want to install a second headrest player or auxiliary monitor. This is more expensive than sharing a single overhead player/monitor, but provides superior viewing—and if you choose dual headrest players, each passenger can watch his own DVD.

The Audiovox headrest DVD system (Fig. 6-5) provides dual vehicle-specific replacement headrests with DVD player/monitors. You simply replace the factory headrests with the player headrests and connect them to 12-volt power.

A big advantage of headrest players is restorability. If you have a leased vehicle or want to sell your car without the system, you remove the player/monitor headrests and reinstall the factory headrests.

Railport Vehicle Personalization System

The Railport Vehicle Personalization System by Johnson Controls (JCI) consists of two parallel overhead rails that run from the front to the rear of a vehicle, down the center of the headliner. The vehicle owner can equip the system with various electronic and non-electronic modules, such as DVD players, flip-down monitors, and storage devices.

This standardized overhead rail is used in Ford minivans, SUVs, and larger pickup trucks, and is being adopted by Chrysler and General Motors. It's estimated that there will be over 1 million vehicles in 2005 with the JCI Railport, projected to grow to 10 million vehicles by 2008.

The Railport rails aren't electrified; wires are run through the channels so that electrical devices can be powered at predetermined positions along the rails. Although the modules can be removed and replaced, you can't slide the modules from one row of seats to another, for crash reasons.

TABLE 6-2

What To Look for in
a Portable DVD
Player

Performance/Feature	Comments
Screen size	6 or 7 inch standard, up to 10 inches available.
Mounting	Choose seat back, center console, or both.
Wireless headphones	Avoids cable clutter and snapped wires.
FM modulator	Lets you listen through the car's sound system.
TV tuner	Lets you watch TV through antenna or cable TV jack.
A/V inputs	Lets you connect video games to the player.
A/V outputs	Lets you connect to a larger TV to watch DVDs.
Rechargeable battery	Use player where there is no power available. Battery life often limited to one movie.

Portable DVD Player with Built-In Monitor

A portable DVD player with built-in monitor is the easiest and cheapest way to keep the kids in the backseat entertained on long drives. You can also share a portable player between multiple vehicles and use it at home, in your hotel room, or cabin.

Some players are designed to hang from the backs of front seats, some are designed to sit on the front or rear center console, and others can be used in either spot. Regardless of where they're located, they must be secured with straps to prevent them from becoming a projectile in a crash. A DC adapter plugs into the cigarette lighter for power in your car, and an AC adapter is used at home. Table 6-2 tells you what to look for in a portable DVD player.

The disadvantages of portable players are the cable clutter of power and headphone wires, the lost passenger compartment space, and the rigging and unrigging hassles of strapping it down. Theft is also a concern if the player is left in the vehicle. If you like the thought of backseat entertainment without these problems, consider an overhead or headrest DVD player with integrated monitor.

Monitor Locations

Adding monitors is a great way to improve your mobile video system. Since off-axis viewing of LCD displays is limited, it's sometimes difficult to share a single (or even two) monitors. Designing your system with multiple monitors gives you more placement flexibility. You don't have to compromise obstructing the rearview mirror or distracting the driver in an attempt to find a single location that all the passengers can enjoy.

Monitor products are available that let you put a monitor just about anywhere in a vehicle. Housed LCD panels can be attached to any surface, LCD modules from 2 to 30 inches can be used for custom installations, and a variety of flip-down, retracting, and pivoting displays designed for specific vehicle locations are available. The most popular locations for monitors are shown in Table 6-3.

Dashboard.   The most common dashboard displays are retractable DIN or 1/2 DIN monitors, 6.5 or 7 inches in size. This is a clever solution to the problem of where to fit a monitor in the dash, and provides stealth when you're out of your car, to help deter theft. But with a retractable monitor, you need to be sure that the extended display doesn't block important dashboard controls or air vents, or interfere with the shift lever or stick shift as it's extending/retracting.

Visor.   There are two types of visor monitors: visor mount and visor replacement. *Visor mount* monitors are attached to your existing visor with screws or straps. *Visor replacement* monitors (Fig. 6-6) replace the primary or secondary factory visor and have the display embedded in them. Size is limited to about 7 inches for both types. Visor monitors provide good front-passenger viewing, and stealth when not in use.

Driver Distraction and Video Monitors

A factor to consider when choosing monitor locations is driver distraction. Most states have laws prohibiting video displays that are visible to the driver in a moving vehicle for this reason. Some states are more strict, prohibiting displays forward of the driver's seat, whether the vehicle is moving or not. Screens for navigation systems are often exempt. But navigation systems and backseat displays can cause distractions too.

According to a study by the AAA Foundation for Traffic Safety, 25 percent of the 6.3 million U.S. auto crashes each year are caused by drivers distracted by "other activities."

To help reduce the problem, many navigation systems will not allow a driver to enter a destination while the vehicle is in motion. Others use voice commands and guidance, so you can keep your eyes on the road while navigating.

Before installing monitors, check your state laws, and choose monitor locations that minimize driver distraction.

TABLE 6-3

Monitor Locations

Location	Comments
Dashboard	Retractable DIN or 1/2 DIN monitors. Size limited to 7 inches. Useful for rearview camera and navigation. Driver distraction for video.
Visor	Visor mount and visor replacement types. Size limited to about 7 inches. Provides good front-passenger viewing, and stealth when not in use.
Center console	Factory replacement lower consoles are available to accommodate a DIN retractable monitor. A housed LCD panel can also be used on the factory console.
Overhead	Provides viewing that's good for both sides of the backseat. Universal, vehicle-specific, and Railport models available. Can block the rearview mirror view of the driver.
Headrest	Provides optimum viewing for individual backseat passengers, but is difficult to share, so you'll want one for each side. Available in factory-replacement, custom-installed, or bracket-mount types. Housed LCD panels may also be used.

Center Console.   The center console was initially a popular monitor location but is losing favor to overhead and headrest locations. Factory replacement lower consoles with DIN slots in the back are available for popular SUVs. This can accommodate a DIN retractable monitor or a DVD head unit with built-in monitor. A housed LCD panel can also be installed at the back of the factory center console.

Overhead.   Overhead monitors provide viewing that's good for both sides of the backseat or viewing in second and third rows of seats in vans and large SUVs. Universal models (Fig. 6-7) fit any vehicle. Vehicle-specific overhead monitors are available for many popular SUVs. These replace the factory overhead console and provide a factory-installed appearance, plus

FIGURE 6-6

Vizualogic visor replacement monitor. *(Courtesy of Vizualogic.)*

simplify installation. Overhead monitors for the Railport Vehicle Person-alization System are also available, and further simplify installation. Both vehicle-specific and Railport overhead monitors offer the advantage of being able to cleanly remove the monitor when it comes time to sell or return your vehicle. A disadvantage of overhead mounting is that they can block the rearview mirror view of the driver, especially with large monitors and low-roofed vehicles.

Headrest.   Headrest monitors provide optimum viewing for individual backseat passengers, but are difficult to share, so you'll want one for each side. This is more expensive than sharing a single overhead monitor, but provides superior viewing. Headrest monitors are available in factory-replacement, custom-installed, or bracket-mount types. Housed LCD panels may also be used. *Factory-replacement* headrest monitors (Fig. 6-8) replace the factory headrests, providing easy installation, a factory look, and restor-ability when it comes time to sell your car. *Custom-installed* headrest moni-tors require cutting and installation, but provide the most professional appearance in vehicles where factory-replacement headrest monitors aren't available. *Bracket-mount* monitors provide easy installation and restorability, but lack a factory appearance.

Monitor Performance and Features

Whether it's a housed LCD panel or the display of a DVD player with built-in monitor, monitor performance is a key factor in your video

FIGURE 6-7

Audiovox VOH1012 10.2-inch overhead monitor. *(Courtesy of Audiovox Electronics Corp.)*

FIGURE 6-8
Vizualogic factory-
replacement head-
rest monitor.
(Courtesy of Vizualogic.)

enjoyment. Aside from the obvious size and aspect ratio differences, all monitors are not created equal. Nowadays, all mobile video LCD monitors are TFT (Thin Film Transistor) Active Matrix displays. But display performance is all over the map. Compare resolution, viewing angle, and brightness when choosing a monitor or player with monitor. Some specifications are hard to find, especially in players and head units, but it pays to compare the specs you can find. Table 6-4 shows what to look for.

Diagonal Size.   Housed LCD panels are available from 3 to over 15 inches. LCD modules are available from 2 to 30 inches.

Aspect Ratio.   Aspect ratio is the ratio of the picture width to height. A 4:3 aspect ratio is often called "standard" and 16:9 is called "widescreen." Most monitors are 16:9, but there are some 4:3 monitors, especially in the smaller screen sizes.

Aspect ratio refers to video sources as well as monitors. Displaying 4:3 sources on 16:9 monitors (and vice versa) means the picture will need to be displayed using some combination of cropping, letterboxing, or stretching (see display modes).

Display Modes.   16:9 monitors generally offer multiple display modes to accommodate the different aspect ratios of video sources:

- Normal: This mode is suited for watching *full screen DVDs* or any standard 4:3 video source, such as terrestrial television or VCRs. 4:3 images are displayed with black bars on the left and right sides.

- Wide: This mode is suited for watching *anamorphic widescreen DVDs*, and will completely fill the display with widescreen video. If you don't mind a horizontally stretched picture, this mode lets you fill the screen with a standard 4:3 image.

- Cinema: This mode is suited for watching *widescreen DVDs*, and will completely fill the display with widescreen video. If you don't mind cutting off the top and bottom of the picture, this mode lets you fill the screen with a standard 4:3 image.

TABLE 6-4

Monitor Performance and Features

Performance/Feature	Comments
Diagonal size	Available in sizes from 2 to 30 inches, depending on application.
Aspect ratio	Ratio of the picture width to height. Most monitors are 16:9, but some are 4:3, especially in smaller screen sizes.
Display modes	16:9 monitors generally offer multiple display modes to accommodate the different aspect ratios of video sources. Normal, wide, and cinema are the most important.
Video inputs	A second input is useful for selecting from multiple video sources at the monitor itself, such as between a DVD player and video game.
Resolution	A measure of the amount of detail that a monitor can display, given in pixels. Many manufacturers count red, green, and blue pixels individually, which inflates the specified resolution by a factor of three.
Viewing angle	With LCD displays, the image brightness and colors change as your viewing angle changes. A reasonable goal for a shared monitor is 120 degrees.
Brightness	When you're trying to view a display in bright sunlight, you'll appreciate having extra brightness. Specified in units of cd/m², also called nits. A reasonable goal is 300 nits.
Contrast ratio	A measure of "how black is black." Most important for nighttime viewing quality. Look for a monitor with 300 or higher.

Some monitors provide additional display modes, but normal, wide, and cinema are the most important.

Video Inputs.   Some monitors provide a single composite video input, others provide two. A second input is useful for selecting from multiple video sources at the monitor itself, such as between a DVD player and video game.

Resolution.   Resolution is a measure of the amount of detail that a monitor can display, given in pixels. Some manufacturers give the total number of pixels, others give the number of horizontal pixels times the number of vertical pixels. Many (but not all) manufacturers count red, green, and blue pixels individually, which inflates the specified resolution by a factor of 3. For example, a monitor that has

$$3 \text{ (red, green, blue)} \times 480 \text{ (horizontal)} \times 234 \text{ (vertical) pixels}$$

would be advertised as having $1440 \times 234 = 336{,}960$ pixel resolution. How much resolution do you need? Counting pixels the inflated way, a widescreen DVD (displayed in cinema mode) has $3 \times 720 \times 360 = 777{,}600$ displayed pixels' worth of resolution. That means a 336,960 pixel display isn't able to display a widescreen DVD in its "full glory." For small screen sizes and normal viewing distances, your eyes are the limiting factor and lower resolution is perfectly acceptable. For larger screen sizes, you'll start to appreciate being able to display the video source to its full resolution.

Viewing Angle.   With LCD displays, the image brightness and colors change as your viewing angle changes. For tilting headrest displays viewed by a single passenger, this isn't a problem. But for shared overhead displays, you need to have a monitor with viewing angles (horizontal and vertical) satisfactory for all viewers. Viewing angle can be specified in each direction (up, down, left, right) or as a total horizontal range. Some monitors have horizontal viewing angles as narrow as 90° (45° left and right). Viewing angle in high-end displays can be 170°. A reasonable goal for a shared monitor is 120°. Unfortunately, viewing angle is not always specified, so you're often forced to take your chances, contact the manufacturer, or look at monitors in a showroom.

Brightness.   When you're trying to view a display in bright sunlight, you'll appreciate having extra brightness. Brightness for LCD monitors is specified in units of cd/m², also called nits. LCD monitors can have brightness levels as low as 140 nits to as high as 450 nits. A reasonable goal is 300 nits. As with viewing angle, brightness is not always specified, so you're often forced to take your chances or contact the manufacturer.

Contrast Ratio.   In practical terms, contrast ratio is a measure of "how black is black." Technically, it's the ratio of the amount of light of the brightest white to the darkest black. In daylight viewing, contrast ratio isn't likely to be an issue. But at night, the importance of contrast ratio becomes more apparent. Monitors with a poor contrast ratio will have blacks that look illuminated—more like dark gray. The contrast ratio of LCD monitors generally ranges from 150 to over 400 (higher is better). Look for a monitor with 300 or higher. But be warned: contrast ratio specifications are rarely provided.

Other Video Sources

For mobile video, DVD is king. But there are plenty of other video sources you can add to your system to take advantage of the monitors and sound system you've installed. Table 6-5 lists the most popular of them. For systems incorporating multiple video sources and monitors, you'll want to consider using an A/V switcher to wire everything together. These are described at the end of the section.

TV Tuner

A TV tuner adds local VHF and UHF analog television programming to your mobile video system. Most TV tuner packages include the tuner, a diversity antenna system, and remote control. Diversity antenna systems use up to four separate antennas to improve reception in a moving vehicle. Most systems can operate as stand-alone units with any brand of head unit as well as be directly controlled by compatible head units.

The problem with adding a TV tuner to your system is that analog television broadcasting will soon end. The FCC has mandated that analog NTSC broadcasts cease and the frequency bands used for them be turned

TABLE 6-5

Other Mobile Video Sources

Source	Comments
TV tuner	Adds local VHF and UHF analog television programming to your mobile video system.
	Analog television broadcasting will eventually cease.
Satellite TV receiver	Lets you watch DIRECTV in your vehicle, even while it's moving. DIRECTV subscription required.
VCR	Lets you play your existing library of VHS tapes in the car.
DVD changer	Convenient way to have a collection of discs (DVDs and CDs) on-tap for any trip. See Chap. 10, "Changer and Player Projects."
Digital A/V player	Hard-drive-based system that lets you store and play back a combination of songs and movies. The hard-drive cartridge is removable for connection to your home computer, to transfer content for playback in the vehicle.
Rearview camera	Available in a number of mounting configurations. Be sure to choose a model with a reversed image.

over to the FCC on December 31, 2006. It's likely that this deadline will be extended to 2008 or later, but analog television's days are numbered.

Satellite TV Receiver

A mobile satellite TV receiver lets you watch DIRECTV in your vehicle, even while it's moving. If you've ever installed a home satellite TV system, you know that the dish antenna needs to be precisely aimed to work, so a mobile system is an amazing feat.

Mobile HDTV

Since HDTV is being broadcast across the country, and analog television broadcasting will soon end, it would seem natural to add an HDTV tuner to your mobile video system. The problem is, nobody is selling one.

Although cost is a factor (HDTV technology is considerably more expensive than analog TV technology), the main hurdle is technical. In a moving vehicle, it's difficult to readjust to the rapidly changing signal strength and multipath that's encountered. A diversity antenna system helps, but the HDTV system is less forgiving of these problems than analog television. A mobile HDTV tuner will require a considerable development effort to bring to market.

The KVH TracVision A5 mobile DIRECTV package (Fig. 6-9) consists of a TracVision antenna, compact receiver, and wireless remote control. The 5-inch tall, 32-inch diameter antenna mounts to the roof rack (either factory-installed or aftermarket) on your vehicle. It has a rugged plastic housing to withstand the elements and trips to the car wash. The antenna uses phased-array, satellite-tracking technology to provide superb reception in a moving vehicle. The antenna does require an unimpeded view of the southern sky for DIRECTV reception; reception can be blocked temporarily by very large obstacles such as bridges or tall buildings. Once installed, you'll receive DIRECTV's hundreds of satellite TV channels (and over 50 commercial-free music channels) anywhere in the lower 48 states. A DIRECTV subscription is required.

VCR

A mobile VCR (or VCP, video cassette player, if you don't need to record) may not wow your friends, but it will let you play your existing library of VHS tapes in the car.

Although mobile VCRs are more compact than their at-home counterparts, they still require some ingenuity when it comes to finding a good spot to stash them. Some units allow horizontal and vertical mounting, which helps. Under a seat is a popular location. Factory replacement center consoles with a compact VCR slot and DIN slot in the back are available for popular SUVs. This can accommodate the VCR along with a DIN DVD player, retractable monitor, or DVD head unit with built-in monitor.

Models with a TV tuner provide the additional benefit of local VHF and UHF analog television programming, but without a diversity antenna system, don't expect great reception. An important feature not usually

FIGURE 6-9

TracVision A5 Mobile Satellite System. *(Courtesy of KVH Industries.)*

found on home VCRs is dew/heat protection. This checks for condensation and high internal temperature and prevents operation under conditions that would damage the tape or VCR.

DVD Changer

A DVD changer is a convenient way to have a collection of discs (DVDs and CDs) on-tap for any trip—long or short. Chapter 10, "Changer and Player Projects," tells you what to look for in a DVD changer and how to connect it to your system.

Digital A/V Player

A digital A/V player is a hard-drive-based system that lets you store and play back a combination of songs and movies. The hard-drive cartridge is removable for connection to your home computer, to transfer content for playback in the vehicle.

GM's 2005 crossover sports vans offer a digital A/V player by PhatNoise. Its 40 GB cartridge holds approximately 10,000 songs, 40 movies, or any combination of the two. Songs can be stored using MP3, WMA, or WAV formats. Movies and video are stored in MPEG format. The system has a voice-browsing interface so you can find the song you want and keep your eyes on the road.

A digital A/V player not only gives you instant access to a sizable personal library of movies and music on the road, you don't need to mess with discs in the car and you can keep the originals at home.

Watch for aftermarket digital A/V players to become available.

Rearview Camera

The view from the back of your SUV probably wouldn't score a high Nielsen rating, but when you're backing up or pulling a trailer, it may be the most valuable use of your in-dash monitor.

Rearview cameras (also called backup cameras) are available in a number of mounting configurations including surface mount, under-bumper, through-bumper, license plate frame, and brake light replacement. Brake light replacement cameras replace the third brake light assembly of specific vehicles and have a brake light built in.

Be sure to choose a model with a reversed image so that what you see on your monitor looks like what you would see in a mirror. The viewing angle of rearview cameras can range from 85° to 150°—choose a model that suits your needs. The SAVV VAC-RV2000NC (Fig. 6-10) provides a reversed image and has a wide 150° viewing angle.

Color cameras usually have a light sensitivity of about 2 lux. Black-and-white cameras are better—a light sensitivity of 0.2 lux is common. For the best of both worlds, choose a color/B&W auto switching camera—it switches to B&W under low light conditions for improved sensitivity. If you need to see in the dark, choose a rearview camera with IR night vision. These use built-in LEDs for illumination of objects up to 30 feet away.

Wiring Up Your System Using an A/V Switcher

Once you've added all those monitors and extra video sources to your system, you've got to figure out how to hook them all together. You'd like to be able to watch any video source on any monitor, regardless of what's going on with the other monitors. An A/V switcher makes this possible.

The Kenwood KVA-S300 A/V switcher (Fig. 6-11) has three sets of A/V (stereo audio and video) inputs and three sets of A/V outputs. You can connect up to three A/V sources to the inputs, and connect up to three monitors (and corresponding audio devices, such as wireless headphones) to the outputs. Each output channel is controlled by its own wired remote control. The KVA-S300 also has special provisions for a rearview camera.

I'll use an example to show how this works. Suppose you've got a DVD head unit with built-in monitor, left and right headrest monitors, a VCR, and a rearview camera. The head unit A/V outputs, VCR, and rearview

FIGURE 6-10

SAVV VAC-RV2000NC rearview camera. *(Courtesy of SAVV.)*

FIGURE 6-11

Kenwood KVA-S300
A/V switcher. *(Courtesy
of Kenwood.)*

camera are connected to the three A/V inputs of the switcher. The head unit A/V inputs, and left and right headrest monitors are connected to three A/V outputs of the switcher. For this example, we'll forgo wireless headphones and use the volume controls and headphone jacks provided on the wired remote controls.

Now each of the backseat passengers can independently watch the DVD head unit, the VCR, or even the rearview camera. The driver can manually select the rearview camera when backing up, or take advantage of the automatic switching feature of the KVA-S300 that connects the camera to the head unit monitor when the vehicle is put in reverse.

For simple systems, you probably don't need a switcher. But for complex systems, switchers provide a convenient and flexible solution for wiring up your equipment.

5.1 Channel Audio Formats

5.1 channel surround sound uses five full-range speakers (right, left and center front, right and left rear) plus a subwoofer to bring a new level of realism to your listening experience. It's already popular for home theater systems, and is becoming a reality in factory and aftermarket car audio. Not only is it great for watching DVDs, 5.1 channel sound provides the ultimate imaging performance for music.

Before thinking about equipment for 5.1 channel mobile audio, it's important to understand the various 5.1 channel audio formats. These are shown in Table 6-6.

TABLE 6-6

5.1 Channel Audio
Formats

Format	Comments
Dolby Pro Logic II	Produces 5.1 channel audio from encoded or non-encoded stereo (two-channel) recordings. Provides an indispensable role in 5.1 channel sound systems by providing surround sound from all your non-DVD audio sources.
Dolby Digital/DTS	Similar but competing formats for 5.1 channel DVD movie soundtracks. Both use compression to fit audio plus video on a DVD. Provide true 5.1 channel surround sound.
DVD-Audio	5.1 channel audio format specifically designed to provide the highest possible audio fidelity on DVD. The audio fidelity exceeds that of conventional CDs and Dolby Digital/DTS.
	DVD-Audio discs generally include a Dolby Digital/DTS version of the music for backwards compatibility with standard DVD players.

Dolby Pro Logic II

Dolby Pro Logic II produces 5.1 channel audio from stereo (two-channel) recordings. The stereo recording may have been produced from a 5.1 channel source that was converted to two channels using Dolby Pro Logic II encoding. This is the method used by SIRIUS satellite radio for its 5.1 channel programming. If you have a mobile VCR, many VHS tapes contain Dolby Pro Logic II encoded audio as well.

Dolby Pro Logic II is also able to create 5.1 channel audio from ordinary stereo recordings (like regular audio CDs and FM radio), giving them a more spacious and enveloping feel.

To experience the real impact of what 5.1 channels brings to car audio, you'll need Dolby Digital/DTS or DVD-Audio. But Dolby Pro Logic II provides an indispensable role in 5.1 channel sound systems by providing convincing surround sound from all your non-DVD audio sources.

Dolby Digital/DTS

Dolby Digital and DTS provide similar but competing formats for 5.1 channel DVD movie soundtracks. Both use compression to fit audio plus video on a DVD. But unlike Dolby Pro Logic II, they provide discrete 5.1 channel sound. This means individually recorded information for left, center, and right front channels, left and right rear surround channels, and a mono subwoofer channel. The advantage is accuracy and sound quality. With discrete channels, you hear multichannel sound as it was intended by the artist who made the soundtrack or audio recording.

Since both formats are popular, you'll want equipment that can handle Dolby Digital and DTS.

The good news for audio enthusiasts is that most DVD-Audio discs also contain a Dolby Digital/DTS version of the music for backwards compatibility with standard DVD players.

DVD-Audio

DVD-Audio (also called DVD-A) is a 5.1 channel audio format specifically designed to provide the highest possible audio fidelity on DVD. The audio fidelity of DVD-Audio exceeds that of conventional CDs and Dolby Digital/DTS audio on DVD-Video.

DVD-Audio has improved on the PCM audio technology used in CDs by taking advantage of higher sampling rates—96 kHz, compared to 44.1 kHz for standard CDs. DVD-Audio also uses 24 bits of resolution compared to 16 for CDs. The result is richer, more detailed sound.

In addition to audio, a DVD-Audio disc can contain a limited number of video stills, which can be used to display lyrics, album art, or a photo album. Up to 16 graphic stills can be associated with each track and on-screen displays can be used for lyrics and disc navigation. DVD-Audio discs generally include a Dolby Digital/DTS version of the music for backwards compatibility with standard DVD players.

5.1 Channel Audio Sources

In many ways 5.1 channel sound is a natural for vehicles. Much of the hardware you need is already in place. Car systems already have four channels of amplified sound, and many have a subwoofer. Upgrading to 5.1 requires a 5.1 channel audio source and a center channel speaker. Table 6-7 lists four possible sources of 5.1 channel audio. Adding a center channel is discussed in the section on center channel speakers in Chap. 3.

TABLE 6-7

5.1 Channel Audio Sources

Source	Comments
CD head unit with Dolby Pro Logic II	Capable of improving your sound stage, and works with all your two-channel sources like CDs and FM radio. Without a DVD player, this is your only option for 5.1 channel sound.
DVD head unit with Dolby Digital/DTS optical output and separate surround-sound processor	Produces 5.1 channel surround signals from any DVD. Since most DVD-Audio discs also contain a Dolby Digital/DTS version of the music, you can listen to them too.
	Processors with Dolby Pro Logic II let you produce surround signals from two-channel inputs, giving you 5.1 channels from every possible source.
DVD head unit with built-in Dolby Digital/DTS surround-sound processor	Produces 5.1 channel surround signals from any DVD. Since most DVD-Audio discs also contain a Dolby Digital/DTS version of the music, you can listen to them too.
	Processors with Dolby Pro Logic II let you produce surround signals from two-channel inputs, giving you 5.1 channels from every possible source.
	Simplifies installation and can reduce overall cost.
DVD head unit with built-in Dolby Digital/DTS surround-sound processor and DVD-Audio	The ultimate in surround-sound source units—provides the best possible 5.1 channel output for every conceivable source: DVD-Audio, DVD-Video, and any two-channel signal.

CD Head Unit with Dolby Pro Logic II

To experience the real impact of what 5.1 channels brings to car audio, you'll need Dolby Digital/DTS or DVD-Audio. But a CD head unit with Dolby Pro Logic II is capable of improving your sound stage, and works with all your two-channel sources like CDs and FM radio. For sources produced from a 5.1 channel source using Dolby Pro Logic II encoding (like SIRIUS surround programming and some VHS tapes), the results are even better. Without a DVD player, this is your only option for 5.1 channel sound.

DVD Head Unit with Dolby Digital/ DTS Optical Output and Separate Surround-Sound Processor

Virtually all DVD head units (and DVD changers) provide an optical output with Dolby Digital/DTS. By connecting this output to a Dolby Digital/DTS surround-sound processor, you're able to produce 5.1 channel surround signals from any DVD. Since most DVD-Audio discs also contain a Dolby Digital/DTS version of the music, you can listen to them too. You won't be getting the benefits of DVD-Audio's extended resolution and sampling rate, but the sound is CD-quality.

The Clarion DVH940 Dolby Digital/DTS surround-sound processor (Fig. 6-12) also includes Dolby Pro Logic II circuitry. This lets you produce surround signals from any two-channel input, giving you 5.1 channels from every possible source.

DVD Head Unit with Built-In Dolby Digital/DTS Surround-Sound Processor

Some DVD head units have a built-in Dolby Digital/DTS surround-sound processor. These usually include Dolby Pro Logic II processing as well. This provides the same capabilities as the previous configuration, but simplifies installation and can reduce overall cost, since there are no extra boxes or cable assemblies to deal with.

FIGURE 6-12

Clarion DVH940 surround-sound processor. *(Courtesy of Clarion.)*

FIGURE 6-13

Kenwood Excelon
KVT-915DVD DVD-
Audio head unit.
(Courtesy of Kenwood.)

DVD Head Unit with Built-In Dolby Digital/DTS Surround-Sound Processor and DVD-Audio

A DVD head unit with built-in Dolby Digital/DTS, Dolby Pro Logic II, and DVD-Audio processing is the ultimate in surround-sound source units. It provides the best possible 5.1 channel output for every conceivable source: DVD-Audio, DVD-Video, and any two-channel signal. The Kenwood Excelon KVT-915DVD head unit/monitor (Fig. 6-13) does all that, and more. It includes other advanced audio features, like DSP sound-fields, digital time correction, and a four-band parametric equalizer.

CHAPTER 7

Amplifiers and Amplifier Projects

TABLE 7-1

Amplifier Projects

Project	Comments
Boosting head units with front and rear preamp outputs	
Boosting head units with one set of preamp outputs	
Boosting head units with no preamp outputs and four speaker outputs	
Boosting head units with no preamp outputs and two speaker outputs	
Boosting premium factory sound system head units	
Adding a subwoofer	See Chap. 4
Biamping	See Chap. 9

With today's high-power (13 watts per channel and up) head units, you may not need separate amps to provide the volume levels you want. But if you have a low-power head unit you want to keep or want to play extra loud, then separate amps are what you need.

In addition to boosting head units, separate amps are used for adding subwoofers and biamping. Because of their complexity, the latter projects are given their own chapters, but be sure to read this chapter for important information on choosing and using amps.

The project sections in this chapter focus on using amps to boost all types of head units. Head units are categorized according to their available outputs, and fall into one of the first five project classes shown in Table 7-1.

Before jumping into the head unit boosting projects, there are a few things you should know about amplifiers.

What to Look for in an Amp

The first thing to consider when buying an amp is the application. Is it for a full-range application, a subwoofer, or for biamping? How many channels do you need? What impedance will the amp need to drive? Once you've answered these questions, you'll need to decide how much power you need and which specs and features are important to you.

Amps for Subwoofers

If you're looking for an amp to drive a mono subwoofer, you can use a two-channel amp in bridged mode or a mono amp that specializes in low-frequency reproduction. Mono sub amps include features useful for driving subs, such as subsonic filters, bass equalization and steep-slope subwoofer crossovers. Many of these amps are Class D, providing higher efficiency. Consult the subwoofer chapter for additional info on choosing an amp for your subwoofer.

Performance and Features

Table 7-2 lists the most important specs and features to consider when buying an amp. Read the next few sections of this chapter to understand what the power specs mean and to figure out how much power you need. Which features are important depends mostly on your application.

CEA Compliant Power.   The amount of power the amp can deliver into a 4-ohm load with a 14.4-volt supply and 1 percent distortion. This provides a uniform method for determining an amplifier's power for the car stereo industry. (See sidebar, "CEA-2006 Compliance.")

Bridged Power.   The amount of power the amp can deliver in the bridged mode. Bridging combines two channels into one bridged channel. See "Bridging" in the "More Power for Your Money" section.

2-Ohm Power.   The amount of power the amp can deliver per channel into a 2-ohm load. You get a 2-ohm load by wiring two 4-ohm speakers in parallel. See "Running 2-Ohm Loads" in the "More Power for Your Money" section.

Signal-to-Noise Ratio.   A measure of how well an amplifier silences background noise. Ratings are in decibels; higher ratings indicate less noise. Prior to CEA-2006 (see sidebar, "CEA-2006 Compliance") it was common to reference noise to rated power. With CEA-2006, noise is referenced to 1 watt. The difference between the two methods can be substantial. For a 100-watt amp, the CEA-2006 spec would be 20 dB lower. For a 1000-watt amp, the CEA-2006 spec would be 30 dB lower. When comparing amps for SNR, make sure you're comparing apples to apples.

TABLE 7-2

What to Look for in an Amp

Performance/Feature	Comments
CEA compliant power	The power the amp can deliver into a 4-ohm load with a 14.4-volt supply and 1 percent distortion.
Bridged power	The power the amp can deliver in the bridged mode.
2-ohm power	The power the amp can deliver per channel into a 2-ohm load.
Signal-to-noise ratio	A measure of how well an amplifier silences background noise. Spec strongly depends on measurement method (see text).
Class D	Provides higher efficiency than Class AB. Produces less heat. Can save you money in power wiring.
Crossover	Saves the expense and inconvenience of an external crossover. Important for subs, full-range speakers, and biamping. Look carefully at specs for filter slope and cutoff frequency range.
Bass boost	Useful for improving bass of subwoofers.
Speaker-level inputs	Important if your head unit lacks preamp-level outputs.
Preamp outputs	Let you feed signals to a second amp.
Remote gain controls	Let you adjust the amp from the comfort of the driver's seat.

Class D. Already popular for mono sub amps, Class D may eventually make its way into mainstream full-range amps. The big benefit is high efficiency. This translates to less heat, and higher reliability. It also means that the amount of current drawn is about half that of an equivalently rated class AB amp. This can save you money in power wiring and power line capacitors. (See sidebar, "Power Wiring for Class D Amps.")

Crossover. A built-in crossover saves the expense and inconvenience of adding an external crossover. A low-pass crossover filter blocks unwanted high frequencies to a subwoofer (or to a woofer, if you're biamping). A high-pass filter blocks low frequencies. This is useful for a tweeter in the case of biamping. It's also useful for keeping deep bass out of small full-range speakers, allowing them to play louder with less distortion. All built-in crossovers are not created equal, so look at the specs for crossover filter slope and cutoff frequency range carefully. See "What to Look for in a Subwoofer Crossover" in the subwoofers chapter and "Choosing a Crossover" in the biamping and crossovers chapter for specifics on what to look for in crossovers.

Bass Boost.   Five to 10 dB of bass boost at 40 or 45 Hz extends the low-frequency response of most subwoofer systems without overdriving them.

Speaker-Level Inputs.   If your head unit lacks preamp-level outputs, then speaker-level inputs are an important feature. This saves you from having to buy a line output converter to convert your head unit's speaker-level signals to preamp-level.

Preamp Outputs.   Preamp outputs let you feed signals to a second amp. If you're planning on having a multi-amp system, these are very handy.

Remote Gain Controls.   Some amps provide remote gain controls that let you adjust the amp from the comfort of the driver's seat. These are usually in the form of wired remote controls. Kenwood takes this idea to the next level with its A.M.S. (Amplifier Management System). Kenwood Excelon amps with A.M.S. (Fig. 7-1) allow you to adjust the bass and treble EQ, bass extension and gain of up to 8 amps from a connected Excelon head unit. The system also lets you monitor amplifier source voltage, current consumption, internal temperature, and fan speed.

Advertised Power versus Honest Power

Unlike the home stereo industry, the car stereo industry has not fully adopted a uniform standard of power measurement. By fudging the

FIGURE 7-1

Kenwood Excelon KAC-X521 with A.M.S. (*Courtesy of Kenwood.*)

power supply voltage and distortion limit of the measurement, car stereo manufacturers are able to claim inflated power ratings. Table 7-3 shows how this works, rating an amplifier using various methods. The amplifier is an 18-watt per channel amplifier made by a reputable manufacturer.

Honest power (my terminology) uses 13.8 volts for the supply voltage, a typical value for most cars when the engine is running. It also uses an audibly acceptable distortion limit of 0.1 percent. This limit is similar to that used by the home stereo industry. For this amplifier, the power rating using this method is 13 watts per channel.

RMS power uses a 14.4 volt supply and allows 1 percent distortion. This is identical to the method specified by the CEA-2006 standard (see sidebar). This allows manufacturers to claim higher power levels than the honest power method. For the example amplifier, the power rating by this method is 18 watts per channel. The adoption of CEA-2006 will solidify this method as the standard power specification for the reputable segment of the industry.

Maximum power uses a 14.4-volt supply and allows 10 percent distortion. This allows manufacturers to claim even higher power levels than with the RMS power method. For this amplifier, the power rating using the maximum power method is 25 watts per channel.

An even more inflated method of specifying power is the peak power method. This method measures the instantaneous power at the peak output voltage of the amplifier. For this amplifier, the power rating using this method would be 35 watts per channel—almost 3 times the honest power value!

The point of all this is that you should make sure you are comparing apples to apples when you are shopping for amps or head units. Look at the measurement conditions specified. If none are specified, assume the worst. I have seen flea market amps use 15-volt supply voltages and 3.2-ohm loads in addition to the peak power measurement method to achieve spectacular power ratings for low-power amps.

TABLE 7-3

Amplifier Power Rating Methods

Measurement Method	Load	Supply Voltage	THD	Power Rating
Honest power	4 ohms	13.8 volts	0.1%	13 watts per channel
RMS power-CEA 2006	4 ohms	14.4 volts	1%	18 watts per channel
Maximum power	4 ohms	14.4 volts	10%	25 watts per channel
Peak power	4 ohms	14.4 volts		35 watts per channel

CEA-2006 Compliance

In May 2003, the Consumer Electronics Association published standard CEA-2006, "Testing & Measurement Methods for Mobile Audio Amplifiers." This voluntary standard advocates a uniform method for determining an amplifier's power and signal-to-noise ratio for the car stereo industry. Power is measured using a 4-ohm load with 14.4 volt supply and allows 1 percent distortion. Signal-to-noise ratio is measured in weighted absolute decibels (dBA) at a reference of 1 watt into 4 ohms. This standard applies to both external amps and the amps within head units.

CEA-2006 allows consumers to compare car amps and head units on an equal basis. Manufacturers who choose to abide by the new standard are able to stamp their products with the CEA-2006 logo that reads: "Amplifier Power Standard CEA-2006 Compliant."

How Much Power Do You Need?

Two good rules of thumb regarding amplifier power are:

- Doubling the volume level requires 10 times more amplifier power.
- A just noticeable increase in volume level requires a 10 percent increase in amp power.

This can be good news or bad news depending on how you look at it. If you have 50 watts per channel now and want to be able to play twice as loud, you'll need 500 watts per channel. On the other hand, you can have half the volume level of a 500-watt per channel amp by buying a 50-watt per channel model.

The bottom line is, achieving high volume levels becomes increasingly expensive in terms of amplifier power.

How much power you need depends on how loud you want to play your music. Calibrate yourself by listening to a high-powered head unit in your vehicle or a similar one. Drive at highway speeds with the window cracked for the worst-case situation. High-powered head units are normally rated at 13 to 18 watts per channel, so adjust this figure according to the rules of thumb. If you need a little less than twice the volume, then 100 watts per channel would be about right. Speaker sensitivity also comes into play here; you'll need more power for inefficient speakers and less for efficient ones. Remember, 3 dB lower speaker sensitivity translates to needing twice the amplifier power to provide the same volume level.

More Power for Your Money

Table 7-4 shows two tricks you can sometimes use to get more watts per dollar from separate amplifiers.

Running 2-Ohm Loads

The formula for power (from your amp to your speakers) is:

$$\text{Power} = \frac{\text{Amplifier Output Voltage}^2}{\text{Speaker Impedance}}$$

Virtually all car speakers are 4 ohms. By using 2-ohm speakers, you can double the power from the amp! It sounds too good to be true. It is. There are three limitations to this scheme:

- You must use an amp that is 2-ohm stable.
- You don't actually double the power—a factor of 1.5 is more typical. This is because the amplifier output voltage drops when driving a 2-ohm load.
- Two-ohm speakers are almost impossible to come by—you must use two 4-ohm speakers wired in parallel or a dual voice coil subwoofer.

The unavailability of 2-ohm speakers is the big problem with this idea for most installations. Using two speakers in parallel does make sense if

TABLE 7-4

Methods of Getting More Watts per Dollar from Amps

Technique	Comments
Run 2-ohm loads	Must use two 4-ohm speakers wired in parallel or a dual voice coil subwoofer
Run bridged amps	Bridging with four-channel amps usually provides the best value

FIGURE 7-2

Using two speakers
in parallel.

from amp

Tip: An amp driving
2-ohm loads runs
hotter, so be sure to
mount it where it will
have good air circu-
lation.

you need multiple speakers per channel to handle unusually high power
levels. Parallel front/rear speaker configurations also take advantage of
this trick. This wiring is shown in Fig. 7-2.

A more common situation for running 2-ohm loads occurs with dual
voice coil subwoofers. Subwoofers are commonly available with dual
4-ohm voice coils. There is little or no cost premium for the additional
voice coil. These can be wired in parallel to create a 2-ohm subwoofer as
shown in Fig. 7-3.

Bridging

Another method that can sometimes give you more watts per dollar is
called *bridging*.

Bridging converts a stereo amp into a mono amp, which gives you more
power than the sum of the two stereo channels. Bridging typically provides 3 times the power of a single amplifier channel (which is 1.5 times
the combined power of two stereo channels). As an example, a 50-watt per
channel stereo amp might be bridgeable to a 150-watt mono configuration. Similarly, a 50-watt per channel four-channel amp might be bridgeable to a 150-watt per channel stereo configuration.

There are four limitations to this scheme:

- You must use an amp that is bridgeable.
- You need twice as many amplifier channels.

FIGURE 7-3

Parallel-wired DVC
subwoofer.

from amp

TABLE 7-5
Bridging Cost
Comparison

Model	Power	Bridged Power	Price Each	Total
A	50W × 2 channels	150W × 1 channel	$140	$280
B	150W × 2 channels		$230	$230
C	50W × 4 channels	150W × 2 channels	$200	$200

- A bridged amp cannot normally drive less than 4 ohms.
- The lowest bridged power is about 75 watts per channel.

Whether or not bridging can give you more watts per dollar depends on several factors. Suppose you need two channels of 150 watts for a set of 4-ohm speakers. Table 7-5 shows what you might find.

By bridging model A, you get 150 watts, but you would need to buy two amps for a grand total of $280. Model B is the conventional solution—a two-channel, 150-watt per channel amp for $230. This is usually cheaper than buying two model As. The third option is to bridge model C—for this example, this ends up being the cheapest solution. Any of these options could have been the most cost effective, depending on what's on sale. But in general, four-channel amps not only start out as a cheaper approach, they are more aggressively marked down when clearance time comes around!

You must normally use a 4-ohm or higher speaker load when bridging. This means you can't run two 4-ohm woofers wired in parallel, for example. This is because a bridged amplifier "sees" a speaker load of half the actual value, so a 4-ohm speaker looks like a 2-ohm equivalent load. Very few amps can handle using anything less than 4 ohms in the bridged mode. So if you were thinking of saving big money by running 2-ohm loads *and* bridging with the same amplifier, forget it.

Be sure to follow the instructions included with the amp for the correct bridging procedure and connections—not all amps are alike.

Tip: An amp running in the bridged mode runs hotter, so be sure to mount it where it will have good air circulation.

Where to Put Your Amps

Where to put your amps is more a matter of convenience than performance, but you should always mount amps away from noise sources and in a spot with good air circulation. This means avoiding locations like underneath the driver's side of the dash and near the blower motor. Because interference from the amp may affect your radio reception, try to

Important: When mounting a power amp (or any car stereo component), secure it in such a way that the metal case does not make electrical contact with the car chassis. This guarantees that the amplifier's ground wire is the exclusive connection between the amp's internal ground and the system ground.

NOTE   A few components have electrically isolated cases—these should be electrically connected to the car chassis to provide shielding to the internal circuitry. When in doubt, use an ohmmeter to measure the resistance between the case and ground wire of the component.

Use rubber grommets inside metal mounting bracket holes to prevent screws from making an electrical connection with the chassis. Alternately, you can mount your components on a board, then mount the board to the car chassis.

Electrical isolation is important to prevent ground loops, which are a major source of noise problems in car audio. See Chap. 12 for more on this subject.

mount it at least 3 feet away from the head unit. The most popular mounting locations are shown in Table 7-6.

If you plan to use a four-channel amp to drive both front and back speakers, then the best location is probably under the passenger side of the dash—if it will fit. Many four-channel amps are too big for this location.

TABLE 7-6
Popular Amplifier Mounting Locations

	Mounting Location	Comments
BEST FOR FRONT SPEAKER AMPS	Under dash (passenger side only)	Short wires and patch cords can be used
		Space is tight
		Moderate electrical noise
BEST FOR REAR SPEAKER AMPS	Trunk or hatch area	Plenty of space, near rear speakers
		Low electrical noise location
		Long patch cords from head unit may be needed
		Subject to damage from sliding cargo
	Under seat	Short wires and patch cords can be used
		Space is very tight
		Subject to dirt and spills

Power and Ground Wiring

Power and ground wiring is one of those subjects a lot of people don't pay much attention to. But improper wiring can easily rob your amplifiers of 25 percent or more of their rated power—or, worse yet, cause a fire.

Wire Gauge

There are two factors that determine the recommended wire gauge for amplifier power and ground wires:

- Voltage drop
- Wire overheating

Voltage drop is determined by the resistance of the power wire multiplied by the current. It results in the amplifier getting less than the full battery voltage for power. A drop of just 1 volt can result in a 15 percent loss of maximum power to the speakers. Because of the high currents consumed by power amps, voltage drops can be significant.

Take a 100W × 2 amp, for example. It can provide 200 watts of power to a pair of speakers, but draws about 30 amps to do so, because of efficiency losses in the amp. Suppose you need to run 20 feet of power wire to the amp in the trunk. Using 10-gauge wire (1.0 milliohms per foot), the wire resistance is 20 milliohms. With 30 amps of current, you would get a voltage drop of 0.60 volts, resulting in roughly a 10 percent loss of maximum power to the speakers. Using 8-gauge wire (0.64 milliohms per foot) reduces this to a more acceptable 6 percent loss of maximum power.

Wire overheating is a concern because of the high currents drawn by amplifiers. The current-carrying capacity of a wire is determined by its resistance per foot and the acceptable temperature rise in the wire. Exceeding the current rating of a wire will cause melting of the insulation and result in possible short circuits or fire.

Table 7-7 shows the recommended wire gauge, depending on wire length, for various power amps. Choose the amplifier entry in the table that corresponds to how you're actually using the amp. In other words, if you're using an amp to drive 2-ohm loads or in the bridged mode, use the amp power rating for that mode of operation. The wire lengths shown in the table guarantee a drop of less than 0.5 volts in the power wire. This should result in less than 8 percent loss of maximum amplifier power.

Voltage, Current, Resistance, and Power

The best way to understand the four basic electrical quantities is by thinking about water and plumbing:

voltage (volts) = water pressure (pounds per square inch)

current (amps) = water flow (gallons per minute)

resistance (ohms) = pipe resistance

power (watts) = pressure × flow

Voltage and current are easy to understand—voltage is like water pressure and current is like water flow.

Electrical resistance is analogous to a pipe's resistance to flow. Imagine trying to fill a swimming pool with a regular garden hose. Then think about how much longer it would take if the hose were the diameter of spaghetti. This is because of the higher resistance of the spaghetti-sized hose. In both cases the water pressure is the same, but in the case of the higher resistance, the flow is reduced. With electricity, this same relationship holds true. It's called Ohm's law:

current = voltage/resistance

This says that you can double the current (water flow) by doubling the voltage (water pressure) or by halving the resistance (pipe resistance). Ohm's law can be rearranged to calculate any of the three quantities if you know the other two.

In electricity, power is calculated using this equation:

power = voltage × current

In terms of water, this means that you need both water pressure and water flow to hose the mud off your car. Having lots of pressure but little flow is like trying to wash the car with a squirt gun. Having lots of flow but little pressure is like gently pouring buckets of water over the car.

This equation can be rearranged and combined with Ohm's law to let you calculate any of the four quantities if you know two of them.

Using a thicker wire (lower gauge) and shorter length will always give you better performance. The wire gauges shown in Table 7-7 also guarantee a temperature rise of less than 35°C in the wire at maximum current. NEVER use thinner wire (higher gauge) than that shown in Table 7-7, even for short wires, or you risk a meltdown. For example, #10 is the thinnest wire you should use with a 100W × 2 amp, even for a 1-foot length of wire.

If you are running multiple amps on the same power wire, just add their power ratings together. For example, a pair of 50W × 2 amps should use the 100W × 2 row of the table.

TABLE 7-7

Recommended Wire Gauge for Power Amps

Amplifier	Power Wire		Amplifier	Power Wire	
35W × 2	Up to 12'	#16	100W × 2	Up to 17'	#10
	Up to 18'	#14		Up to 26'	#8
	Up to 30'	#12	150W × 2	Up to 17'	#8
50W × 2	Up to 13'	#14		Up to 28'	#6
	Up to 21'	#12	200W × 2	Up to 21'	#6
	Up to 33'	#10		Up to 33'	#4
75W × 2	Up to 14'	#12	350W × 2	Up to 19'	#4
	Up to 22'	#10		Up to 30'	#2
	Up to 35'	#8	500W × 2	Up to 21'	#2
				Up to 26'	#1/0

Power Wire Hookup

If you are only adding a single 35W × 2 amp, then you can get away with using the factory distribution/fuse block for power. Otherwise, because of the high currents drawn by power amps, you will need to provide

Power Wiring for Class D Amps

Class D amplification is already popular for mono sub amps and may eventually make its way into mainstream full-range amps. The big benefit of Class D amps is their high efficiency, as compared to traditional Class AB amps. Efficiency is how much of the power consumed by the amp is provided to the speakers. Class AB amps have a typical efficiency of 50 percent. Class D provides close to 90 percent efficiency. This translates to less heat (less likely to need a fan, and higher reliability). It also means that the amount of current drawn by a Class D amp is about half that of an equivalently rated Class AB amp. This can save you money in power wiring and power line capacitors.

For a Class D amp, a conservative rule-of-thumb would allow you to go with a wire gauge that's two numbers higher (smaller wire diameter) than that shown in Table 7-7. (Equivalently, you can use the table for an amp that's one power level lower.) For example, a traditional (Class AB) 100W x 2 amp should use #10 wire for a short run. A 200W mono amp would have the same requirement. If the amp were Class D, you could safely use #12 wire instead.

your own power supply wiring directly to the battery. Figures 7-4 and 7-5 show two methods of doing this.

Figure 7-4 is a diagram of a single wire running through the firewall. A fuse block is located very close to the battery to protect against shorts on the battery side of the distribution/fuse block. The distribution/fuse block may be located under the dash, in the trunk, or in any other convenient location.

Important: The wire from the battery to the distribution/fuse block must have a current rating high enough for the total current drawn by all the amps.

To determine the proper wire gauge for this wire, add together the power ratings of all the amps, then refer to the previous table. For example, a 100W × 2 amp plus a 50W × 2 amp should use the 150W × 2 row of the table.

For a pair of identical amps, you may simply choose a wire gauge 4 less than the highest gauge (smallest wire) recommended for a single amp. For example, if you have a pair of 50W × 2 amps, use #10 wire to the battery since #14 wire is the highest gauge recommended for a 50W × 2 amp.

Figure 7-5 is a diagram of multiple wires running through the firewall. The distribution/fuse block is located very close to the battery to protect against shorts. This approach eliminates the need for a separate fuse block, but you have to run multiple wires through the firewall.

You may be able to use an existing hole in the firewall to run wires from the engine compartment to the passenger compartment. Otherwise, you'll need to drill a hole in a strategic location. Always protect the wires from the sharp metal edges of the hole by using a rubber grommet or split loom tubing.

FIGURE 7-4

Single wire through the firewall.

FIGURE 7-5

Multiple wires through the firewall.

Fuses

Even choosing the right fuse requires some thought. In addition to the standard AGC glass tube and ATO/ATC blade styles, there are giant versions of each of these for high-current applications (called AGU and MAXI, respectively). For ultra-high-current applications, there are two types of wafer-style fuses. Figure 7-6 shows a variety of fuse styles.

The main factor in deciding which style of fuse to use is the current rating. For applications up to 35 or 40 amps, use AGC or ATO/ATC. For up to 60 or 80 amps, use AGU or MAXI. Above 80 amps, you must use a wafer-type fuse. Table 7-8 provides further comparison of the different fuse types.

Choose a fuse holder that accommodates the wire gauge you plan to use. High-amperage fuse blocks are generally designed for 8-gauge or 4-gauge wire. Distribution fuse blocks usually have a 4-gauge input and multiple 8-gauge outputs.

> **Important:** Make sure the fuse holder is rated to handle the current of the fuse you plan to use, or you can melt or burn the holder. Do not assume a fuse holder is designed to work safely with any fuse that will fit in it. For example, many AGC fuse holders are only rated at 10 amps, even though AGC fuses can go up to 35 amps.

FIGURE 7-6

(a) AGC fuse; (b) ATO/ATC fuses; (c) AGU fuse; (d) MAXI fuses; (e) MIDI fuses; (f) ANL fuses. (*Courtesy of Littelfuse.*)

For high-current situations, using circuit breakers instead of fuses is attractive because of the high cost and hassle of replacement fuses. In many cases, the cost of a circuit breaker is actually less than the cost of a fuse plus fuse holder. Since circuit breakers do not require holders, you can actually save money even if you never overload a circuit. (MAXI circuit breakers are a plug-in replacement for MAXI fuses, and do require a holder.)

Some circuit breakers incorporate a "valet" feature that lets you turn off power to the amplifiers for valet parking or work on your system without disconnecting wires or a battery cable. A disadvantage with circuit breakers is that if you need to change the current rating, it is more difficult than just popping in a different fuse.

TABLE 7-8

Fuse Types for
Auto Sound

Fuse Type	Description	Current	Pricing	Comments
AGC	Glass tube $1\frac{1}{4} \times \frac{1}{4}$	up to 35 amps	Fuse $.50 Holder $2	Standard automotive fuse of the seventies
ATO/ATC	Blade	up to 40 amps	Fuse $.50 Holder $2	Standard automotive fuse of the eighties
AGU	Glass tube $1\frac{1}{2} \times \frac{13}{32}$	up to 60 amps	Fuse $1 Holder $7—16	Large version of AGC type
MAXI	Blade	20—80 amps	Fuse $1 Holder $4—11	Large version of ATO/ATC
MIDI	Wafer (bolt-on)	30—200 amps	Fuse $3—5 Holder $7—16	Same as AFS and mini KF. Required for very high current applications
ANL	Wafer (bolt-on)	60—250 amps	Fuse $6—14 Holder $8—40	Required for very high-current applications

Calculating Fuse Current Rating

The simplest method to determine the correct current rating for a fuse is to add together the maximum currents of everything on that circuit. The owner's manuals should list the maximum current; otherwise, look at the equipment fuses.

An alternate rule-of-thumb method is to add the rated power of all amplifier channels together and divide by 6. For example, for a pair of 30W × 2 amps (four channels altogether):

$$(30 + 30 + 30 + 30)/6 = 20$$

In this case you would use a 20-amp fuse.

Wiring for Automatic Turn-On

Most amps have a remote turn-on lead—the amp turns on when 12 volts is applied to this lead. Normally, you connect this lead to the power antenna lead of your head unit (or amp turn-on lead, if your head unit provides one). Such a connection will turn your amp on and off with your head unit.

If your head unit doesn't have a wire suitable for amplifier turn-on (some vehicles provide a low-voltage turn-on signal, some power antenna leads only work when you actually use the radio, other head units may have no wire at all), you'll have to consider your options. For the case of low-voltage turn-on signals, you can buy a low-voltage turn-on adapter to convert the low-voltage trigger signal to 12 volts.

Another option is to buy a remote power adapter. This device monitors the DC voltage on a convenient speaker wire (5–7 volts for a high-powered head unit), and provides a 12-volt amp turn-on signal to the amp. Even if your head unit has a suitable turn-on wire, this device can save you from having to run a wire from the head unit to the trunk.

As a last resort, you can use the ignition/accessory 12 volts as a turn-on signal. This will turn on your amps whenever the car is running. The downside is that you'll be more likely to hear turn-on and turn-off pops from your head unit (because the amps will be on during these times). You may also notice some low-level noise from your speakers when the head unit is off, that would otherwise be concealed by music.

If you have multiple amplifiers in your system, you can usually tie the turn-on leads together. If you have four or more amps in your system, the power turn-on lead of the head unit may not be able to provide enough current, and you risk damaging the head unit.

A relay can solve this problem. It's connected to your system as shown in Fig. 7-7.

The head unit turn-on lead energizes the magnetic coil inside the relay, which activates the internal switch. The switch connects the amp remote turn-on leads to 12 volts. Here are the key points for success:

■ Use a 12-volt automotive relay or relay with 12VDC coil. The coil rating should be 100 mA or less to prevent damaging the head unit. The contact rating should be 2 amps or higher.

■ Connect the relay coil terminals to the head unit turn-on lead and ground as shown. The two coil terminals may or may not be interchangeable—the relay case will show + and – if they are not.

FIGURE 7-7

Using a relay for more current drive.

■ Connect the relay switch terminals as shown. Use ignition/accessory 12 volts or battery 12 volts. Some relays have both NO (normally open) and NC (normally closed) switch terminals in addition to COM (common). Use the NO and COM terminals. They may be interchanged.

Ground Wire Hookup

The metal chassis of a car forms a huge, low-impedance ground plane. The basic grounding strategy is to ground each amplifier (or other component) at the nearest chassis ground location.

The ground wire should be the same gauge as the power wire and must make direct contact with bare metal of the car. Not all metal in a car is electrically connected to the chassis, so use a multimeter to confirm a low-resistance connection to a known good ground.

Important: Some cars (Audi, Porsche) have galvanized bodies. In these cars, you must find one of the manufacturers' grounding points or else some noise can result.

Look for an existing bolt or screw that makes contact with the car body near the amp. Remove the bolt or screw and scrape away any paint or dirt. A star washer will help your ground wire maintain good contact with the car body. Crimp and solder a ring terminal onto the end of the ground wire, slip it underneath the washer, and replace the bolt or screw. If you can't find a convenient ground screw or bolt, drill a hole for one. Be careful not to drill into the gas tank or a gas or brake line.

If you're installing several components, ground the amps separately. This prevents the high currents drawn by an amp from modulating the ground voltage of any of the other components. It's okay for low-current components to share a common ground point.

Connectors

Using the proper wire gauge is an important factor in getting the power you paid for from your amps. Another equally important factor is connectors.

After about six months, a properly crimped connection has an impedance of roughly 0.03 ohms, due to oxidation (it gets even worse as time goes on). This doesn't sound like much, but consider the fact that from the battery to the amp there can easily be five or more crimped connections through distribution blocks and so forth.

Let's assume five connections of 0.03 ohms, for a grand total of 0.15 ohms. For a 50W × 2 amp, the maximum current is approximately 17 amps. This results in a maximum voltage drop of 2.5 volts, and a reduction in maximum power of over 30 percent. Remember, this is due to the connectors alone, and is on top of any additional losses in the wires themselves.

Crimping and then soldering results in an impedance of 0.01 ohms per connection. This number does not degrade over time. For our example, this would limit the maximum voltage drop to 0.85 volts, and the reduction in maximum power to 10 percent.

The point of this is:

- Solder crimped connectors where high currents are involved. This means power supply and ground wires for all power amps. While you're at it, soldering crimped speaker wire connectors is a good idea too.
- Eliminate unnecessary connections.

Soldering crimped spade lugs and quick disconnects is simple because the end of the wire is exposed. For high-current butt splices, don't use crimp connectors. Solder the ends directly and insulate with heat-shrink tubing.

Eliminating unnecessary connections favors using the "multiple wires through the firewall" power wire hookup approach explained previously.

Speaker Wiring

For speaker wiring, the dominating consideration in selecting wire gauge is damping factor. Damping factor is the ratio of speaker impedance to driving impedance, where driving impedance is usually dominated by the speaker wires. For 4-ohm speakers, the speaker wires should have an impedance of less than 0.1 ohms for best performance. Impedance values higher than this will result in damping factors less than 40, which can start to affect bass response.

Table 7-9 provides minimum recommended wire gauges, depending on wire length, for all power amps. The wire lengths shown in Table 7-9 guarantee damping factors greater than 40. Using thicker wire (smaller gauge) and shorter lengths will give you higher damping factors.

TABLE 7-9

Minimum Recommended Gauge for Speaker Wire

Amplifier	Speaker Wire	
All wattages	up to 12′	#16-2
	up to 20′	#14-2
	up to 30′	#12-2

If you are running 2-ohm loads, subtract 2 from the recommended wire gauge in the chart. For example, use #10-2 up to 30 feet.

Boosting Head Units with Front and Rear Preamp Outputs

Head units with front and rear preamp outputs provide the most flexibility for boosting with amplifiers. The preamp outputs provide a low-noise, low-distortion interface to any amplifier. Having front and rear preamp outputs means the head unit fader control can remain functional for all but one of the configurations.

There are five configurations with this type of head unit. The first two configurations let you provide as much power as you want to each of two pairs of speakers. The third configuration lets you save an amp when equal power to front and rear speakers is acceptable. The last two configurations let you save an amp when high power is needed for only one pair of speakers. This may seem like a strange idea at first, but it actually can make a lot of sense. Table 7-10 shows the five configurations.

Standard Configuration

The standard configuration boosts all four channels. Two stereo amps or a single four-channel amp may be used. In this configuration, the speaker outputs of the head unit are unused.

You may choose to use two stereo amps with different power ratings if more power is needed for one pair of speakers. One example of this is for rear fill applications, where the rear speakers are operated at a reduced volume level to improve imaging (see the "Imaging Overhaul" section in Chap. 3). Another example is where the front speakers have much lower

TABLE 7-10

Configurations for
Boosting Head Units
with Front and Rear
Preamp Outputs

Configuration	Diagram	Comments
Standard		Lets you provide as much power as you want to two pairs of speakers. Head unit fader control is functional.
Cable-saving		Lets you provide as much power as you want to two pairs of speakers. Saves having to run patch cord to trunk-mounted amp. Head unit fader control is functional.
Parallel front/rear speakers		Saves one amp when equal power to front and rear speakers is acceptable. (No relative front/rear level adjustment is possible.)
Amp-saving		Saves one amp when high power is needed for one pair only: ■ Rear fill applications ■ Low-power front/high-power rear applications Head unit fader control is functional.
Cable-saving amp-saving		Saves one amp when higher power is needed for one pair only. Saves having to run patch cord to trunk-mounted amp. Head unit fader control is functional.

power handling capacity than the rear speakers. In this case, you might want to run a more powerful amp in back and put bass blocking filters at the preamp-level inputs of the front amp. Use 100- or 200-Hz, 12-dB/octave filters for best results. (Many amps now include built-in 100-Hz high-pass filters.) These prevent deep bass frequencies from wasting amplifier power and distorting your front speakers, so you can run a high volume level up front. Since deep bass is nondirectional, the back speakers will fill in the missing deep bass in front.

Cable-Saving Configuration

This configuration lets you provide as much power as you want to two pairs of speakers.

If you choose to use a trunk-mounted amp for the rear speakers, this configuration saves having to run a patch cord to the trunk-mounted amp since the speaker wires already in place are used to carry the signal to the amp. Either the trunk amp will need to be a model that accepts speaker-level inputs or you will need to use a line output converter to convert the speaker-level signals to preamp level (see the box on line out put converters on p. 224).

You may choose to use two stereo amps with different power ratings if more power is needed for one pair of speakers. One example of this is for rear fill applications, where the rear speakers are operated at a reduced volume level to improve imaging (see the "Imaging Overhaul" section in Chap. 3). Another example is where the front speakers have much lower power handling capacity than the rear speakers. In this case, you might want to run a more powerful amp in back and put bass blocking filters at the preamp-level inputs of the front amp. Use 100- or 200-Hz, 12-dB/octave filters for best results. (Many amps now include built-in 100-Hz high-pass filters.) These prevent deep bass frequencies from wasting amplifier power and distorting your front speakers, so you can run a high volume level up front. Since deep bass is nondirectional, the back speakers will fill in the missing deep bass in front.

For proper fader operation, be sure to use the correct set of head unit speaker outputs.

Parallel Front/Rear Speakers Configuration

The parallel front/rear speakers configuration shares a single amp for front and rear channels. This gives you almost the same power per speaker as having identical separate amps for front and rear. The drawback with this configuration is that you are stuck with having equal power for front and back speakers.

Since the amplifier used in this configuration will see a parallel speaker load, it must be 2-ohm stable. An amp driving 2-ohm loads runs hotter, so be sure to mount it where it will have good air circulation.

Amplifier-Saving Configuration

The amplifier-saving configuration is the same as the standard configuration, except that one amplifier is eliminated by using an existing amp in the head unit. This can be useful in applications where more power is needed for one pair of speakers than the other.

One example of this is for rear fill applications, where the rear speakers are operated at a reduced volume level to improve imaging (see the "Imaging Overhaul" section in Chap. 3). Another example is where the front speakers have much lower power handling capacity than the rear speakers. In this case, you could use the head unit speaker outputs in front.

Be sure to use the correct set of preamp outputs for this configuration. The fader control will work properly for one set and oppositely for the other set.

Cable-Saving Amplifier-Saving Configuration

This configuration is useful when higher power is needed for only the rear pair of speakers and you want to mount the amp in the trunk. Either the amp will need to be a model that accepts speaker-level inputs, or you will need to use a line output converter to convert the speaker-level signals to preamp level.

As with the previous configuration, this one lets you save an amp and maintain fader functionality. By using the existing rear speaker wires to carry the signal to the amp, you save having to run a patch cord from the head unit to the trunk-mounted amp.

Boosting Head Units with One Set of Preamp Outputs

There are five configurations with this type of head unit. The first two let you provide as much power as you want to each of two pairs of speakers. The third lets you save an amp when equal power to front and rear speakers is acceptable. The last two configurations let you save an amp when high power is needed for only one pair of speakers. The cable-saving version of the amp-saving configuration saves having to run a patch cord to a trunk-mounted amp when you are boosting the rear speakers. Table 7-11 shows the five configurations.

Standard Configuration

In this configuration, Y cables are used to feed the preamp-level outputs from the head unit to two stereo amps (or a single four-channel amp). The speaker outputs of the head unit are unused. You may choose to use two stereo amps with different power ratings if more power is needed for one pair of speakers. One example of this is for rear fill applications, where the rear speakers are operated at a reduced volume level to improve imaging (see the "Imaging Overhaul" section in Chap. 3). Another example is where the front speakers have much lower power handling capacity than the rear speakers. In this case, you might want to run a more powerful amp in back and put bass blocking filters at the preamp-level inputs of the front amp. Use 100- or 200-Hz, 12-dB/octave filters for best results. (Many amps now include built-in 100-Hz high-pass filters.) These prevent deep bass frequencies from wasting amplifier power and distorting your front speakers, but still let you run a high volume level up front. Since deep bass is nondirectional, the back speakers will fill in the missing deep bass in front.

Set the relative front/rear level by using the gain controls on the amps.

Fader-Restoring Configuration

This configuration lets you provide as much power as you want to two pairs of speakers, and restores use of the fader. This is accomplished by using speaker-level outputs from the head unit as the inputs to the second amp. Either the second amp will need to be a model that accepts speaker-level inputs, or you will need to use a line output converter to convert the speaker-level signals to preamp level.

If you choose to use a trunk-mounted amp for the rear speakers, this configuration saves having to run a patch cord to the trunk-mounted amp since the speaker wires already in place are used to carry the signal to the amp.

TABLE 7-11

Configurations for
Boosting Head Units
with One Set of
Preamp Outputs

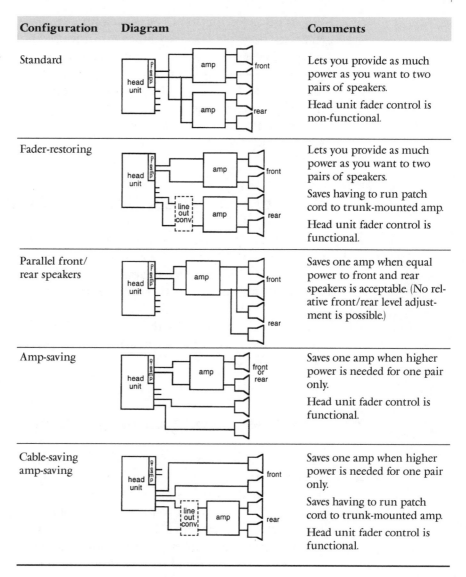

Configuration	Diagram	Comments
Standard		Lets you provide as much power as you want to two pairs of speakers. Head unit fader control is non-functional.
Fader-restoring		Lets you provide as much power as you want to two pairs of speakers. Saves having to run patch cord to trunk-mounted amp. Head unit fader control is functional.
Parallel front/ rear speakers		Saves one amp when equal power to front and rear speakers is acceptable. (No relative front/rear level adjustment is possible.)
Amp-saving		Saves one amp when higher power is needed for one pair only. Head unit fader control is functional.
Cable-saving amp-saving		Saves one amp when higher power is needed for one pair only. Saves having to run patch cord to trunk-mounted amp. Head unit fader control is functional.

You may choose to use two stereo amps with different power ratings if more power is needed for one pair of speakers. One example of this is for rear fill applications, where the rear speakers are operated at a reduced volume level to improve imaging (see the "Imaging Overhaul" section in Chap. 3). Another example is where the front speakers have much lower power handling capacity than the rear speakers. In this case, you might want to run a more powerful amp in back and put bass blocking filters at the preamp-level inputs of the front amp. Use 100- or 200-Hz, 12-dB/octave filters for best results. (Many amps now include built-in 100-Hz high-pass filters.) These prevent deep bass frequencies from wasting amplifier power and distorting your front speakers, but still let you run a high volume level up front. Since deep bass is nondirectional, the back speakers will fill in the missing deep bass in front.

For proper fader operation, be sure to use the correct set of head unit speaker outputs.

Parallel Front/Rear Speakers Configuration

The parallel front/rear speakers configuration shares a single amp for front and rear channels. This gives you almost the same power per speaker as having identical separate amps for front and rear. The drawback with this configuration is that you are stuck with having equal power for front and back speakers.

Since the amplifier used in this configuration will see a parallel speaker load, it must be 2-ohm stable. An amp driving 2-ohm loads runs hotter, so be sure to mount it where it will have good air circulation.

Amplifier-Saving Configuration

This configuration lets you save an amp when higher power is needed for only one pair of speakers.

One example of this is for rear fill applications, where the rear speakers are operated at a reduced volume level to improve imaging (see the "Imaging Overhaul" section in Chap. 3). Another example is where the front speakers have much lower power handling capacity than the rear speakers. In this case, you could use the head unit speaker outputs in front.

For proper fader operation, be sure to use the correct set of head unit speaker outputs.

Cable-Saving Amplifier-Saving Configuration

This configuration is useful when higher power is needed for only the rear pair of speakers and you want to mount the amp in the trunk. Either the amp will need to be a model that accepts speaker-level inputs, or you will need to use a line output converter to convert the speaker-level signals to preamp level.

As with the previous configuration, this one lets you save an amp and maintain fader functionality. By using the existing rear speaker wires to carry the signal to the amp, you save having to run a patch cord from the head unit to the trunk-mounted amp.

Boosting Head Units with No Preamp Outputs and Four Speaker Outputs

Head units without preamp outputs can be boosted by choosing amplifiers that accept speaker-level inputs. Alternately, line output converters can be used to convert a head unit's speaker-level signals to preamp level for use with any amp.

There are four configurations for head units with no preamp outputs and four speaker outputs. The standard configuration provides the most flexibility, and lets you provide as much power as you want to each of two pairs of speakers. The converter-saving configuration can eliminate the need for a second line output converter (at the expense of losing fader control). The parallel front/rear speaker configuration lets you save an amp when equal power to front and rear speakers is acceptable. The amp-saving configuration lets you save an amp when high power is needed for only one pair of speakers. This may seem like a strange idea at first, but it actually can make a lot of sense. Table 7-13 shows the four configurations.

Standard Configuration

The standard configuration boosts all four channels and retains the functionality of the head unit fader control. If you use amps without speaker-level inputs, two line output converters are required for this configuration. Two stereo amps or a single four-channel amp may be used.

You may choose to use two stereo amps with different power ratings if more power is needed for one pair of speakers. One example of this is for

Line Output Converters

Line output converters reduce the signal amplitude from speaker level to preamp level. Better models also eliminate common-mode noise and break ground loops.

Table 7-12 shows the three basic types of line output converters.

TABLE 7-12

Types of Line Output Converters

Type	Price	Active or Passive	Comments
Resistive	$2–$30	Passive	*Does not* eliminate common-mode noise or break ground loops.
			Typically very small.
Transformer	$15–$30	Passive	Eliminates common-mode noise and breaks ground loops.
			Typically palm-sized case.
Differential amp	$15–$30	Active	Eliminates common-mode noise and breaks ground loops.
			Typically palm-sized case.

⟨BEST⟩ marks the Differential amp row.

Resistive converters are the least expensive, but do not provide ground isolation. Transformer and differential amplifier converters do provide ground isolation, but cost more. Differential amp converters provide better frequency response and are less susceptible to magnetic fields than transformer converters.

Ground isolation helps reduce system noise problems caused by ground loops. Some amplifiers provide ground isolation at their preamp-level inputs, in which case there is no additional benefit to having isolation in the line output converter. The level of benefit provided by ground isolation also depends on the ground structure of your installation. Trunk-mounted amps usually benefit the most from ground isolation.

When deciding what to buy, either buy a differential amp model right off the bat or start with a $2 resistive converter and upgrade if necessary.

rear fill applications, where the rear speakers are operated at a reduced volume level to improve imaging (see the "Imaging Overhaul" section in Chap. 3). Another example is where the front speakers have much lower power handling capacity than the rear speakers. In this case, you might want to run a more powerful amp in back and put bass blocking filters at the preamp-level inputs of the front amp. Use 100- or 200-Hz, 12-dB/octave filters for best results. (Many amps now include built-in 100-Hz high-pass filters.) These prevent deep bass frequencies from wasting amplifier

TABLE 7-13

Configurations for
Boosting Head Units
with No Preamp
Outputs and Four
Speaker Outputs

Configuration	Diagram	Comments
Standard	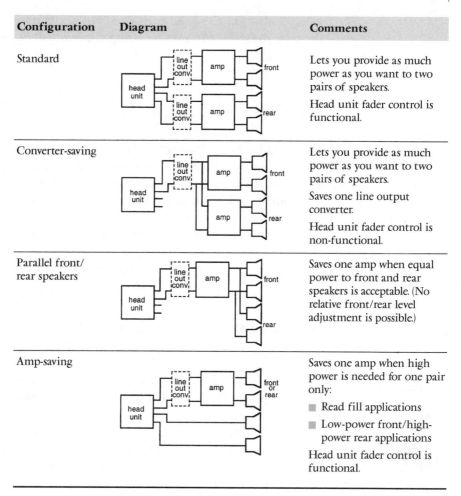	Lets you provide as much power as you want to two pairs of speakers. Head unit fader control is functional.
Converter-saving		Lets you provide as much power as you want to two pairs of speakers. Saves one line output converter. Head unit fader control is non-functional.
Parallel front/ rear speakers		Saves one amp when equal power to front and rear speakers is acceptable. (No relative front/rear level adjustment is possible.)
Amp-saving		Saves one amp when high power is needed for one pair only: ▪ Read fill applications ▪ Low-power front/high-power rear applications Head unit fader control is functional.

power and distorting your front speakers, but still let you run a high volume level up front. Since deep bass is nondirectional, the back speakers will fill in the missing deep bass in front.

Converter-Saving Configuration

The converter-saving configuration is similar to the standard configuration, except that a line output converter is eliminated by sharing a single converter for both amps. If you use amps with speaker-level inputs, then there's no advantage to this configuration. The disadvantage is that the fader control on the head unit becomes nonfunctional. You can still set the relative front/rear level by using the controls on the amps themselves, but you lose the convenience of head unit control.

Parallel Front/Rear Speakers Configuration

The parallel front/rear speakers configuration shares a single amp for front and rear channels. This gives you almost the same power per speaker as having identical separate amps for front and rear. The drawback with this configuration is that you are stuck with having equal power for front and back speakers.

Since the amplifier used in this configuration will see a parallel speaker load, it must be 2-ohm stable. An amp driving 2-ohm loads runs hotter, so be sure to mount it where it will have good air circulation.

Amplifier-Saving Configuration

The amplifier-saving configuration is similar to the standard configuration, except that one amplifier is eliminated by using an existing amp in the head unit. This can be useful in applications where more power is needed for one pair of speakers than the other.

One example of this is for rear fill applications, where the rear speakers are operated at a reduced volume level to improve imaging (see the "Imaging Overhaul" section in Chap. 3). Another example is where the front speakers have much lower power handling capacity than the rear speakers. In this case, you could use the external amp in back.

Boosting Head Units with No Preamp Outputs and Two Speaker Outputs

There are four configurations for head units with no preamp outputs and two speaker outputs (Table 7-14). The first simply boosts two speakers. The last three allow you to add a set of speakers.

Standard Configuration

The standard configuration boosts two channels. If you use an amp without speaker-level inputs, a line output converter is required for this configuration.

Two- to Four-Speaker Upgrade Configuration

This configuration lets you boost the original speakers as well as add a second pair of boosted speakers.

You may choose to use two stereo amps with different power ratings if more power is needed for one pair of speakers. One example of this is for

TABLE 7-14

Configurations for Boosting Head Units with No Preamp Outputs and Two Speaker Outputs

Configuration	Diagram	Comments
Standard		
Two-to-four upgrade		Most flexible configuration for adding two channels to head units with two speaker outputs.
Parallel front/rear speakers two-to-four upgrade		For adding two channels to head units with two speaker outputs. Saves one amp when equal power to front and rear speakers is acceptable. (No relative front/rear level adjustment is possible.)
Amp-saving two-to-four upgrade		For adding two channels to head units with two speaker outputs. Saves one amp when high power is needed for one pair only.

rear fill applications, where the rear speakers are operated at a reduced volume level to improve imaging (see the "Imaging Overhaul" section in Chap. 3). Another example is where the front speakers have much lower power handling capacity than the rear speakers. In this case, you might want to run a more powerful amp in back and put bass blocking filters at the preamp-level inputs of the front amp. Use 100- or 200-Hz, 12-dB/octave filters for best results. (Many amps now include built-in 100-Hz high-pass filters.) These prevent deep bass frequencies from wasting amplifier power and distorting your front speakers, but still let you run a high volume level up front. Since deep bass is nondirectional, the back speakers will fill in the missing deep bass in front.

Set the relative front/rear level by using the controls on the amps.

Parallel Front/Rear Speakers Configuration

The parallel front/rear speakers configuration lets you add a pair of speakers by sharing a single amp for front and rear channels. This gives you almost the same power per speaker as having identical separate amps for front and rear. The drawback with this configuration is that you are stuck with having equal power for front and back speakers.

Since the amplifier used in this configuration will see a parallel speaker load, it must be 2-ohm stable. An amp driving 2-ohm loads runs hotter, so be sure to mount it where it will have good air circulation.

Amplifier-Saving Two- to Four-Speaker Upgrade Configuration

This configuration lets you add a pair of speakers and takes advantage of the existing amp in the head unit to drive the other, lower-power pair of speakers. This is useful for rear fill applications, where the rear speakers are operated at a reduced volume level to improve imaging (see the "Imaging Overhaul" section in Chap. 3). Another example is where the front speakers have much lower power handling capacity than the rear speakers. In this case, you could use the external amp in back.

Because the head unit lacks a fader control, the proper front/rear level balance must be set by adjusting the level control on the amp.

Boosting Premium Factory Sound System Head Units

If you have a premium factory sound system (such as Delco/Bose or Ford/JBL) and want to boost your head unit with an amp, the situation is more complicated than with standard systems. You'll need to bypass the factory amps plus use a line output converter designed specifically for Bose or Ford Premium systems. Depending on the system, you may need to replace the factory speakers as well.

Premium Factory Sound System Basics

Although the details of Bose and Ford Premium systems differ (as do different Bose systems among themselves), they share the same basic principle. All use external amplifiers (amplified speakers or an outboard amp) and all use differential signals between the head unit and amplifiers.

Chrysler/Infinity Systems

Like Bose and Ford Premium systems, Chrysler/Infinity systems use external amplifiers (in the form of amplified speakers). Unlike Bose and Ford, Chrysler/Infinity systems use standard head unit technology. This approach allows upgrading of the premium system in the assembly plant by simply using amplified speaker assemblies instead of normal ones.

If you want to boost a Chrysler/Infinity head unit with an aftermarket amp, you will need to bypass the factory amps. By bypassing, however, you will lose the benefit of custom equalization built into the factory amps. Chrysler/Infinity systems use standard-impedance speakers, so you will not need to replace the speakers if you decide to drive them with an aftermarket amp.

Some earlier Chrysler/Infinity systems (prior to 1995) used low-power head units; the rest use high-power head units. In either case, a standard line output converter will do the job of interfacing a Chrysler/Infinity head unit to an amp lacking speaker-level inputs.

The advantage of using differential signals is noise immunity. The differential outputs of the head unit provide two equal but opposite versions of the music signal (an inverted version and a noninverted version). At the differential inputs of the amplifier, the two versions of the signal are subtracted. Since any noise presumably affects both versions of the signal the same, subtraction causes cancellation of the noise. Because one of the music signals was inverted, subtraction also results in a music signal that is twice the original signal.

The differential outputs of the head unit have a DC offset to eliminate the need for coupling capacitors in the head unit and amplifiers. DC offset is also used in Bose systems to "wake up" the amplifiers.

Bose systems often incorporate speakers with impedances much less than the usual 4 ohms (0.4 ohms is common!). This allows the Bose amplifiers to achieve much higher power levels without having to incorporate expensive DC-to-DC converters to provide a higher supply voltage.

GM's Class 2 Data Bus.   In 2002, GM added a new twist to some of its premium factory sound systems—Class 2 data bus control. GM's Premium/Smart Bose system is used in 2002 and later full-size trucks and SUVs. With this system, the head unit provides fixed-level audio signals to the factory amplifiers. The head unit issues commands to each amp via the Class 2 data bus to control volume, fader, and balance. This approach provides improved noise immunity, but makes adding an amp to your head unit more challenging.

Do You Need to Replace Your Factory Speakers?

Most Bose systems use speakers that are only 0.4 ohms (instead of the usual 4 ohms). Aftermarket amps can't handle driving this low of an impedance. If your vehicle uses low-impedance speakers, you'll need to replace them if you want to boost your head unit with an aftermarket amp.

It's smart to scope this out beforehand, so you know what you're getting into. Remove one of the factory speaker assemblies. Disconnect the wires going to the driver itself, then use a multimeter to measure the resistance of the driver. If it's less than 3.2 ohms, you'll need to replace the speakers with aftermarket ones.

An easier alternative is to call Crutchfield. They can tell you what you've got and how to proceed. They also stock a wide selection of adapters and harnesses for interfacing to premium factory sound systems.

Bypassing Factory Amps

Bose and Ford Premium sound systems use external amplifiers (in the form of amplified speaker assemblies or outboard amps). These amplifiers need to be bypassed in order to use an aftermarket amp.

In the case of amplified speaker assemblies, the aftermarket amp should be located near the head unit to make best use of the factory wiring. Each speaker assembly will need to be removed and modified to bypass its amp. For amplified speaker assemblies with low-impedance factory speakers (less than 4 ohms), replace the entire amplified speaker with a 4-ohm aftermarket speaker. For amplified speaker assemblies with 4-ohm factory speakers, bypass the signal wires feeding each amplifier to the speaker itself.

For outboard factory amp systems, the aftermarket amp can be located near the head unit or at the factory amp location, to make best use of the factory wiring. In either case, the wiring harness from the output of the factory amp will need to be unplugged from the factory amp and driven by the aftermarket amp.

Line Output Converters for Bose/Ford Premium Head Units

Tip: Most line output converters are two-channel units. If this is the case, you will need to buy two converters to retain functionality of your head unit fader and balance controls.

Line output converters are commonly used to convert head unit speaker-level outputs to levels suitable for the preamp-level inputs of amps.

If you're dealing with a Bose or Ford Premium Sound factory head unit, you'll want to use a line output converter specifically designed for interfacing to those units. Using a standard LOC having low-input impedance may damage the output circuit of a Bose or Ford Premium Sound head unit. Using a standard LOC with a Bose or Ford system can also result in extremely low output from the LOC because of the relatively low signal levels of many premium factory system head units.

The LOCB.2 by SoundGate (Fig. 7-8) will accept any input signal from 350 mV to 6.6 volts and convert it to a 2.5-volt audio output suitable for

FIGURE 7-8
SoundGate LOCB.2.
(*Courtesy of SoundGate.*)

aftermarket crossovers and amps. It also has a noise-blanking circuit that activates the audio path after turn-on noises have subsided.

Line Output Converters for Systems Using GM's Class 2 Data Bus. As described earlier, some of GM's Premium/Smart Bose sound systems provide fixed-level audio signals from the head unit to the factory amps. Data bus commands from the head unit are used to control volume, fader, and balance. This makes adding an amp to your head unit more challenging—but not impossible.

Peripheral's GMAA (Fig. 7-9) line output converter decodes GM's Class 2 data bus commands and uses them to provide varying output levels to an aftermarket amp. The GMAA can be set to provide front, rear, or subwoofer outputs. Additionally, the GMAA reads the data bus and generates an amplifier remote turn-on signal so the aftermarket amp turns on and off with the head unit, not with the ignition.

System Configurations

There are four configurations for boosting premium factory sound system head units. The standard configuration provides the most flexibility, and lets you provide as much power as you want to each of two pairs of speakers. The converter-saving configuration can eliminate the need for a second line output converter (at the expense of losing fader control). The parallel front/rear speaker configuration lets you save an amp when equal power to front and rear speakers is acceptable. The amp-saving con-

FIGURE 7-9

Peripheral GMAA LOC for GM Class 2 data bus systems. (*Courtesy of Peripheral Electronics.*)

figuration lets you save an amp when high power is needed for only one pair of speakers. This may seem like a strange idea at first, but it actually can make a lot of sense. Table 7-15 shows the four configurations.

Standard Configuration.   The standard configuration boosts all four channels and retains the functionality of the head unit fader control. Two line output converters are required for this configuration. Two stereo amps or a single four-channel amp may be used.

You may choose to use two stereo amps with different power ratings if more power is needed for one pair of speakers. One example of this is for rear fill applications, where the rear speakers are operated at a reduced volume level to improve imaging (see the "Imaging Overhaul" section in Chap. 3). Another example is where the front speakers have much lower power handling capacity than the rear speakers. In this case, you might want to run a more powerful amp in back and put bass blocking filters at the preamp-level inputs of the front amp. Use 100- or 200-Hz, 12-dB/octave filters for best results. (Many amps now include built-in 100-Hz high-pass filters.) These prevent deep bass frequencies from wasting amplifier power and distorting your front speakers, but still let you run a high volume level up front. Since deep bass is nondirectional, the back speakers will fill in the missing deep bass in front.

TABLE 7-15

Configurations for
Boosting Premium
Factory Sound
System Head Units

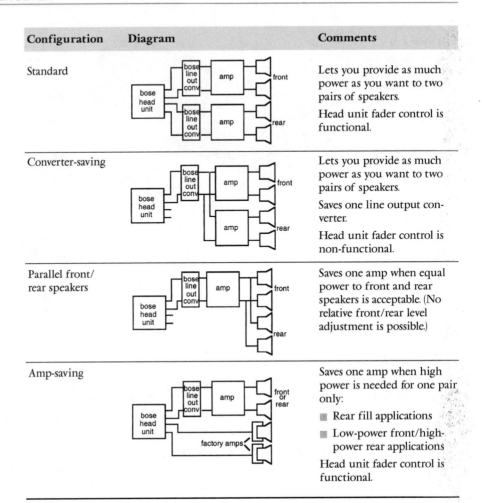

Configuration	Diagram	Comments
Standard		Lets you provide as much power as you want to two pairs of speakers. Head unit fader control is functional.
Converter-saving		Lets you provide as much power as you want to two pairs of speakers. Saves one line output converter. Head unit fader control is non-functional.
Parallel front/ rear speakers		Saves one amp when equal power to front and rear speakers is acceptable. (No relative front/rear level adjustment is possible.)
Amp-saving		Saves one amp when high power is needed for one pair only: ■ Rear fill applications ■ Low-power front/high-power rear applications Head unit fader control is functional.

Converter-Saving Configuration. The converter-saving configuration is similar to the standard configuration, except that a line output converter is eliminated by sharing a single converter for both amps. The disadvantage is that the fader control on the head unit becomes non-functional. You can still set the relative front/rear level by using the controls on the amps themselves, but you lose the convenience of head unit control.

Parallel Front/Rear Speakers Configuration. The parallel front/rear speakers configuration shares a single amp for front and rear channels. This gives you almost the same power per speaker as having identical separate amps for front and rear. The drawback with this configuration is that you are stuck with having equal power for front and back speakers.

Since the amplifier used in this configuration will see a parallel speaker load, it must be 2-ohm stable. An amp driving 2-ohm loads runs hotter, so be sure to mount it where it will have good air circulation.

Amplifier-Saving Configuration. The amplifier-saving configuration is similar to the standard configuration, except that an aftermarket amplifier is eliminated by retaining use of factory amps for one pair of speakers. This can be useful in applications where more power is needed for one pair of speakers than the other.

One example of this is for rear fill applications, where the rear speakers are operated at a reduced volume level to improve imaging (see the "Imaging Overhaul" section in Chap. 3). Another example is where the front speakers have much lower power handling capacity than the rear speakers. In this case, you could use the aftermarket amp in back.

Adjusting Amp Gain Settings

Once you've installed your amp or amps, you'll need to set the level controls for optimum performance. If you set the level too low, you'll have noise problems. If you set the level too high, you'll have distortion problems. The goal is to find the level that maximizes the signal-to-noise ratio while avoiding of distortion.

Follow these steps, depending on the configuration of your system.

Procedure for Two-Amp Configurations

1. Set the amp level controls to minimum and the head unit fader control to its center detent position. If you're using any line output converters with their own level controls, set them to minimum.

2. With music, turn up the head unit volume control (you should barely be able to hear the music). When you reach the point where you start to hear distortion from any speaker, turn the volume control down

slightly until the distortion disappears. Leave the volume control at this setting.

NOTE *If the sound from the speakers is so low that you cannot clearly hear the onset of distortion, turn up the amp's level controls a bit.*

3. If you're using any line output converters with their own level controls, return all amp level control settings to minimum, then turn up each LOC level control until you reach a point where you start to hear distortion. Back the LOC level controls down slightly until the distortion disappears. (If you never reach a point where you hear distortion, the LOC level controls should be set to max.)

4. Turn up your front amp level control until the system is as loud as you'll ever play it or you begin to hear distortion. If you hear distortion, slightly decrease the amp level control.

5. Turn down the head unit volume to a normal listening level.

6. Turn up the rear amp level until the desired front/rear balance is achieved.

Procedure for Amp-Saving Configurations

If you're not using a line output converter with its own level controls, skip to Step 4.

1. Set the amp level controls and LOC level controls to minimum. Set the head unit fader control all the way toward the channels with the amp.

2. With music, turn up the head unit volume control (you should barely be able to hear the music). When you reach the point where you start to hear distortion from a speaker (on an amplified channel), turn the volume control down slightly until the distortion disappears. Leave the volume control at this setting.

NOTE *If the sound from the speakers is so low that you cannot clearly hear the onset of distortion, turn up the amp's level controls a bit.*

3. Return all amp level control settings to minimum, then turn up each LOC level control until you reach a point where you start to hear distortion. Back the LOC level controls down slightly until the distortion disappears. (If you never reach a point where you hear distortion, the LOC level controls should be set to max.) Turn down the head unit volume control before proceeding to step 4.

4. Set the head unit fader control to its center detent position.

5. With music, adjust the head unit volume to a normal listening level.

6. Adjust the amp level controls until the desired front/rear balance is achieved.

Eliminating Turn-On and Turn-Off Pops

Turn-on and turn-off pops (or in extreme cases, thumps) are a fairly common problem when amplifiers have been added to a system. The problem stems from power supply imbalances, bias problems in amplifier output stages, or component tolerances.

Using the proper amplifier turn-on signal goes a long way toward solving most turn-on and turn-off pop problems. Ideally, an amplifier is turned on a fraction of a second after the head unit, to allow time for the head unit's outputs to stabilize. If an amp turns on before this, you can hear a pop. The reverse is true at turn-off; you want the amp to turn off a fraction of a second before the head unit, to prevent head unit transients from being amplified.

The first thing to do when you have a turn-on or turn-off pop problem is to make sure the amplifier itself doesn't have a problem. Unplug all input cables to the amp and replace them with shorting plugs. Use the remote turn-on signal of the amp to turn it off and on, listening for pops or thumps at the speakers. If you hear objectionable pops, the problem is with the design of the amp, or the amp itself is defective. If the amp is acceptably quiet for this test, the problem is due to the turn-on/turn-off order of your system.

If this is the case, first make sure you're using the best possible amp turn-on signal. If your head unit doesn't have a suitable turn-on signal, adapters are available to convert the low-voltage turn-on signals of some head units to 12 volts or to generate turn-on signals from the speaker signals. If these don't solve the problem, the next line of defense is to use a specialty trigger device.

FIGURE 7-10

(a) TRIGDLA turn-on delay; (b) TRIG-RCA turn-off pop eliminator. (*Courtesy of SoundGate.*)

(a)   (b)

A turn-on delay trigger (Fig. 7-10a) is useful for turn-on pops. It allows you to delay the amplifier turn-on until the transients from the head unit have subsided. A turn-off pop eliminator (Fig. 7-10b) is useful for turn-off problems. It installs in the preamp-level signal path to the amp, and mutes the signal before the head unit transients have a chance to affect the amp.

CHAPTER 8

Equalizers and Equalizer Projects

To Equalize or Not?

Although equalizers were once thought of as the savior of great sound quality for high-end systems, the trend for their use is down. The philosophy of many seems to be that less is more. In other words, the fewer the number of components, the better the guard against the introduction of noise and distortion. Better-quality speakers, good speaker placement, and subwoofers have alleviated much of the need for equalizers.

On the other hand, the acoustics of cars are notorious for introducing frequency response peaks and valleys. Even if your speakers are perfect, your overall frequency response will be bumpy. Boomy-sounding bass due to resonances, as well as irregularities in the mid-range and treble due to window reflections, are typical. Equalization still offers the best solution to these problems.

How Many Bands Do You Need?

It's important to differentiate between the different classes of equalizers (see Fig. 8-1).

Five- and seven-band graphic equalizers are essentially sophisticated tone controls, and don't give you the control you need to correct the narrow peaks and valleys of your car's acoustic response. On the positive side, these definitely give you more flexibility than just bass and treble controls, and can be set reasonably well by ear. For this reason they are best mounted within easy reach.

Fifteen- through thirty-band graphic equalizers, and most parametric equalizers, can be considered tools. They give you the control you need to correct real-world response problems. Unfortunately, they are more expensive, and cannot reliably be set by ear—a ⅓-octave real-time ana-

FIGURE 8-1

Classes of equalizers.

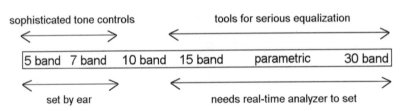

lyzer (RTA) is required to set them properly. The good news is that any serious car stereo shop should have one of these, and should be willing to help you set your equalizer for a reasonable fee. Equalizers falling into the tools category are normally set once, then left alone. For this reason, they are best mounted out of sight and out of reach of curious fingers. Be sure to write down the settings of each control or use a marker on the face to indicate the proper setting.

Ten-band graphic equalizers fall in the transition region between sophisticated tone controls and tools. Table 8-1 shows a summary of the performance levels for various equalizers.

The Pioneer DEQ-7600 (Fig. 8-2) is a fifteen-band dash-mount digital equalizer and sound processor. It allows you to create and store three eq curves. A nuance control lets you fine-tune the setting for a particular song without losing the stored curve. This solves the "curious fingers" problem, and provides the convenience of dash access.

The DQT by AudioControl (Fig. 8-3) is a thirty-band ($^1/_3$ octave) stereo digital equalizer. It's a favorite among competitors. The DQS is a six-channel version of the DQT, perfect for 5.1 channel installations or simply to let you retain the use of your head unit fader control in four-channel systems.

Parametric equalizers have been around a long time, but have never enjoyed the popularity of graphic equalizers. Instead of the familiar slider controls at each frequency band, parametric equalizers have center, bandwidth, and gain controls. This provides plenty of flexibility to combat response peaks and valleys, but makes setting these equalizers quite difficult without a real-time analyzer.

TABLE 8-1

Performance Levels for Various Equalizer Types

Type	Comments
Five-band	Better than tone controls, but inadequate for serious equalization.
Seven-band	Better than tone controls, but inadequate for serious equalization.
Ten-band (octave)	Can correct broad response problems.
Fifteen-band	Can correct most response problems
Thirty-band ($^1/_3$-octave)	The ultimate!
Parametric	Can correct most response problems, depending on number of stages.

FIGURE 8-2

Pioneer DEQ-7600
15-band dash-
mount equalizer.
(*Courtesy of Pioneer.*)

FIGURE 8-3

AudioControl DQT
30-band equalizer.
(*Courtesy of AudioControl.*)

What About Equalizer Boosters?

Equalizer boosters typically combine a seven-band graphic equalizer with a power amp, and have speaker-level inputs. This was a popular package in the eighties, but is dying out. The decrease in popularity of equalizers in general combined with the high power of most modern head units is one reason. Another is the deservedly poor reputation of these units for high noise and distortion.

The prices of equalizer boosters are amazingly low, but they're a good example of "you get what you pay for."

Connecting Your Equalizer

Figure 8-4 shows the standard connection for a preamp-level (often incorrectly called passive) equalizer.

FIGURE 8-4

Standard connection for a preamp-level equalizer.

Some models provide speaker-level as well as preamp-level inputs. Since equalizers are normally two-channel devices, the head unit fader control is rendered inoperative. Dash-mounted equalizers often provide their own fader controls and separate front and rear outputs to remedy this problem. When using an equalizer without a fader, the relative front/rear level will need to be set by adjusting the amp level controls.

How to Set Your Equalizer

You can set equalizers of ten bands or less fairly well by ear, but you need a real-time analyzer to set thirteen- to thirty-band or parametric equalizers properly. Note: If you do have access to an RTA, it can improve the quality of your five- to ten-band equalizer settings as well.

Setting by Ear

Initial Preparation. Start by setting your head unit bass and treble controls flat, and your equalizer sliders to their center detent positions. The fader control should be in the position you normally use when listening. Pick a CD or tape that you like and that sounds good on your home stereo. Choose one that covers the entire audio spectrum—something with bass drums, voice, and cymbals. Acoustic instruments such as piano, sax, and so on are better than synthesized ones because you know what they should sound like. Play your selection at a normal listening level.

Familiarize yourself with how each of the frequency bands sounds. One by one, slide a control to the max position and listen to the effect, then return it to the center position. Try to characterize each frequency band in your head, for example, "solid bass," "boomy bass," "female vocals," and so on. This will help you later as you try to compensate for things like bass that is too boomy or weak female vocals.

Setting the Bass.   The area that normally benefits the most from equalization is the bass. Car acoustics tend to overemphasize mid-bass, so start by reducing the level in the 200-Hz region. For a seven-band equalizer, this means moving the 150-Hz slider down a third of the way. For a ten-band equalizer, move the 120- and 250-Hz sliders down a fourth of the way. You will probably want to boost the bass in the 60-Hz region to provide a more solid bottom end. This will also help overcome the masking effects of road noise. Don't overdo it—maybe a third of the way up is good.

What Is Road Noise Masking?

First of all, what is road noise? *Road noise* refers to all the sounds associated with driving your car—the roar of your engine, the sound of your tires rolling on the pavement, and wind noise. Of course, road noise depends on the vehicle you're driving, how fast you're going, whether the windows are rolled up, and so forth. The important point is that, in general, road noise is dominated by deep bass frequencies.

Road noise masking means that you can't hear the deep bass of your music until it is loud enough to overcome the road noise. This isn't just interference—your ears actually reduce their sensitivity to deep bass in response to road noise! This means that to provide correct-sounding bass for normal listening levels, you need to boost your deep bass a bit. About 5 dB in the 45- to 100-Hz region is a good start, but let your ears have a vote.

Leave the 30-Hz slider of a ten-band equalizer set to its center detent position. Boosting 30 Hz will not give you much benefit (few speaker systems can reproduce this range effectively): It will instead dramatically reduce your amp headroom and cause your woofers to distort on those passages that have energy in this frequency range.

Adjusting by Ear.   Now the fun part. One by one, slide each control up and down a little bit and listen to the effect. Ask yourself if the music sounds more accurate. Listen to specific instruments or vocalists, then to the overall mix. Be aware that to the human ear, louder always sounds better. If you aren't careful, all your sliders will be set to the top of their range! Your goal should be to keep most of the sliders at (or very near) their center detent positions.

Once you are fairly satisfied with your settings, try another cassette or CD and permit yourself minor touchups. Eventually you will find settings that sound right for most material. Use a marker to make a dot on the face of the equalizer next to each slider to show the preferred position. Now you (or your passengers) can make temporary changes without having to worry about setting the sliders back.

From now on, you may want to use the bass and treble controls to compensate for specific tapes or songs that need an extra dose of bass or treble. The broad characteristics of the tone controls are well suited for this type of compensation.

Setting by RTA

You would think that having an RTA would make setting an equalizer a snap. Unfortunately, that's not the case. Using an RTA properly requires skill and patience.

The reason for this becomes apparent once you try to use one. You hook up the pink noise generator, turn on the stereo, and hold the calibrated test microphone about where your head would be. Now you move the microphone about 6 inches to the left and notice that the frequency response curve now looks nothing like the previous one. What happened?

The problem is that direct and reflected sound add together to create a highly spatially dependent response. This means that you can't simply pick a spot to hold the microphone, then adjust the equalizer until you get a flat response.

One strategy is to use spatial averaging. This means that you use the average response from half a dozen strategically chosen microphone locations to set your equalizer. Easier said than done. Furthermore, this strategy glosses over the fact that the human ear is able to separate the direct response (the sound straight from the speakers) from the reflected response (the sound after it has reflected around inside your car). What sounds best is somewhere between a flat direct response and a flat total response. What the RTA measures is the total response.

The audio engineers at Ford, AudioControl, Pioneer, and other places have been trying for years to figure out how to automate setting an equalizer by using frequency response measurements from a microphone. One thing they agree on—it isn't simple.

The method I recommend for setting an equalizer with an RTA is explained below. It tries to achieve the desired blend between flat direct response and flat total response. It also relies on a tool that is impossible to automate—your ears! Note: This method is designed to provide optimized sound—it is not the method you would use if you were trying to win the ruler-flat frequency response portion of a sound-off competition.

Initial Preparation.   Start by setting your head unit bass and treble controls flat, and your equalizer sliders or knobs to their center detent positions. The fader control should be in the position you normally use when listening. Connect the pink noise output of the RTA to the inputs of the equalizer.

What Is a Real-Time Analyzer?

A real-time analyzer provides a graphic display of the frequency response of a stereo system. Its calibrated pink noise* output is connected to the equalizer input of the system under evaluation, and then a calibrated microphone is used to monitor the sound output of the system. It's an invaluable tool for setting equalizers and for general frequency response evaluation and improvement.

The RTA of choice for car stereo work is the AudioControl SA-3055 (see Fig. 8-5; suggested retail price for the basic version is $1599). It's a ⅓-octave real time analyzer with calibrated mike and printer interface. The term *⅓ octave* means the audio spectrum is broken into thirty bands. This resolution is necessary to display the narrowest peaks and valleys the human ear can readily perceive.

Audio analysis software for PCs often provides ⅓-octave real-time analysis in addition to other useful tools such as speaker parameter measurement. The software uses your computer's sound card to provide a pink noise output and microphone input. You'll need a suitable measurement microphone with this approach. Prices for software and microphone range from less than $100, to thousands of dollars for professional packages.

FIGURE 8-5
AudioControl
SA-3055 RTA.
(*Courtesy of
AudioControl.*)

* Pink noise is random noise that has been filtered to provide equal energy per octave. This makes it ideal for use with RTAs because it produces a flat frequency response display for flat frequency responses. It's called pink noise because it's generated from white noise with a filter that emphasizes low frequencies, and red corresponds to the low-frequency end of the visible light spectrum.

Presetting the Mid-Bass and Mid-Range.   Turn up the volume to a normal listening level. Set the balance control all the way to the left, so only the left speakers are playing. Position the microphone about 6 to 12 inches directly in front of the front left speaker, pointing right at it. This position strongly emphasizes the direct response over the reflected response. Now adjust the equalizer for flat response from 150 Hz to 1.5 kHz, trying to keep most of the sliders or knobs centered at their detent positions.

Setting the Deep Bass.   Position the mike in the driver's head position, pointing upward. Adjust the equalizer for flat response from 45 to 150 Hz. Leave the controls below 45 Hz set to their center detent positions. Boosting these ultra-low frequencies will not give you much benefit (few speaker systems can reproduce this range effectively)—it will instead dramatically reduce your amp headroom and cause your woofers to distort on those passages that have energy in this frequency range. To overcome the masking effects of road noise, you should now boost the response in the 45- to 100-Hz region by 5 dB or so.

Setting the Mid-Range and Treble.   Position the mike in the driver's head position, pointing toward the front left speaker. Adjust the equalizer for flat response from 1.5 kHz on up. Now move the microphone a foot to the right. Adjust the equalizer (1.5 kHz and up) to find a good compromise setting between the two positions. Try more mike positions in the vicinity of the driver's head to improve the blend further. In general, ignore frequency response valleys that do not occur for all mike positions. If you see a consistent strong peak or valley below 1.5 kHz, you should correct it as well, but for the most part, try to leave the lower frequency settings alone.

Touchup By Ear.   Return the balance control to the center detent position. Reconnect the equalizer to the head unit. Pick a CD or tape that you like and that sounds good on your home stereo. Choose one that covers the entire audio spectrum—something with bass drums, voice, and cymbals. Acoustic instruments such as piano, sax, and so on are better than synthesized ones because you know what they should sound like. Play your selection at a normal listening level.

Touch up the high-frequency (5 kHz and up) equalizer settings by ear. Maintain the general shape established previously, but add a gentle downward ramp as your ear dictates. It's normal to reduce the response at 16 kHz by 6 dB.

Look over the settings you have made. Any control above 150 Hz with more than 6 dB of boost compared to its neighbors should be checked by ear. Try reducing it by 3 dB and listening to decide which sounds better. Similarly, any control above 150 Hz with more than 10 dB of attenuation compared to its neighbors should be checked. (Response peaks sound worse than valleys, so the criteria are different.)

Use a marker to make a dot on the face of the equalizer next to each slider or knob to show the preferred position. Now you can make temporary changes without having to worry about setting the controls back right.

From now on, you will want to use the bass and treble controls to compensate for specific tapes or songs that need an extra dose of bass or treble. The broad characteristics of the tone controls are well suited for this type of compensation.

CHAPTER 9

Biamping and Crossovers

Biamping refers to using two amplifiers per channel (rather than the usual one amp per channel) to separately drive woofers and tweeters. Biamping offers an improvement in sound quality as well as increased tweeter protection, but it can be expensive. Biamping makes the most sense for high-power (50 watts per channel and above), high-performance systems.

More than almost any other subject, biamping requires knowledge of many areas of car stereo as well as subjects unique to itself. Rather than repeat information found in other chapters, I would like to direct your attention to them. Be sure to read Chap. 7 for important information on choosing and using amps. Chapters 3 and 4 contain similarly useful information on speakers and subwoofers, respectively.

Crossover Basics

To understand what biamping is all about, you need to understand the basics of crossovers.

The job of a crossover is to split the music signal into specific frequency bands—for example, low frequencies that go to a woofer, and high frequencies that go to a tweeter. Separate drivers are necessary because it's impractical to make a single driver that can cover the full audio range. Woofers can't effectively reproduce treble because of their large cone mass and high voice coil inductance. Tweeters can't effectively reproduce bass because their radiating surfaces are too small and their lightweight voice coils can't handle much power.

Speaker-Level and Preamp-Level Crossovers

For coax speakers, the crossover network is usually just a single capacitor in series with the tweeter, mounted on the speaker (Fig. 9-1).

FIGURE 9-1

Single-capacitor crossover.

The capacitor prevents low frequencies from going to the tweeter. There is no woofer filter—this low-budget approach relies on the natural high-frequency roll-off of the woofer. For separates, a better crossover (with an actual woofer low-pass filter) is usually provided (Fig. 9-2).

In both of these examples, the crossover is effectively *after* the amp, as represented in Fig. 9-3.

Crossovers after an amp are called *speaker-level crossovers* because the inputs and outputs are at speaker level. (Speaker-level crossovers are often called *passive crossovers* because they require no power, but this can be misleading since preamp-level crossovers can be passive too.) Speaker-level crossovers must handle high power levels and are built using large inductors and capacitors (Fig. 9-4).

Biamping instead puts the crossover *before* the amps, as shown in Fig. 9-5.

FIGURE 9-2

External crossover module.

FIGURE 9-3

Crossover after amp.

FIGURE 9-4

Speaker-level crossover. (*Courtesy of MCM Electronics.*)

This is called biamping because it requires two amplifiers per channel
instead of one. This type of crossover is called a *preamp-level crossover*
because the input and output signals are at preamp level (Fig. 9-6).

Crossover Slopes

One of the most important characteristics of a crossover filter is the slope.
Slope refers to how effectively the crossover filters out the unwanted frequencies.

Figure 9-7 shows the frequency response characteristics of four filters,
each a 5-kHz high-pass filter. This type of filter would be used for a
tweeter. The only difference between the filters is the slope—the shallow-
est slope is for a first-order (6 dB/octave) filter and the steepest slope is for
a fourth-order (24 dB/octave) filter. Second-order (12 dB/octave) and third-
order (18 dB/octave) filter responses are in between.

FIGURE 9-7

First- through
fourth-order
crossover slopes.

Above 5 kHz, all four filters are almost the same—they pass the signal with very little attenuation. This is where the similarity ends. At 2 kHz, the first-order filter is –8 dB. To put that into perspective, –10 dB sounds like half volume. This means that the tweeter is still strongly contributing to the total sound of the system at this frequency. More importantly, it's being subjected to lots of additional power. The fourth-order filter is –32 dB at 2 kHz. Not only will you not hear the tweeter at this level, it won't be subjected to dangerous power levels.

Why do you care if the tweeter is strongly contributing to the total sound below the crossover frequency? Two reasons. One, the frequency response of most tweeters starts to roll off and get bumpy below 2 kHz. This causes the total frequency response of the system to get bumpy as well. Two, where both the woofer and tweeter are trying to reproduce the same frequencies, an interference pattern is created. This causes spatially dependent reinforcement and cancellation of the sound, which degrades imaging. It's beneficial to reduce the range of frequencies where this happens by using sharper filter slopes.

The biggest concern about shallow slopes for tweeters is power handling. A tweeter that is rated at 50 watts (read the fine print: with a 5-kHz, 12-dB/octave crossover) is really only able to handle about 2 watts. This is because most of the power in music is in the bass—very little is in the treble. Table 9-1 shows the normal frequency distribution of power in music.

Using a shallow 6-dB/octave slope means huge amounts of additional mid-range and even bass power are directed to the tweeter. You can get away with this for conservatively powered systems (18 watts per channel or less) by using a high crossover frequency—for example, 8.5 kHz. Unfor-

TABLE 9-1

Normal Frequency
Distribution of
Power in Music

Frequency	Maximum Power Above That Frequency
300 Hz	50%
600 Hz	25%
1200 Hz	10%
2400 Hz	5%

tunately, this tactic usually results in a weak and bumpy system response near 5 kHz due to the high-frequency limitations of the woofer.

The bottom line is to avoid 6-dB/octave crossovers for the tweeter.

Why Biamp?

Everything just said about crossover slopes applies equally to both speaker-level and preamp-level crossovers. The problems with a shallow slope are exactly the same for speaker-level and preamp-level crossovers. You can get the same improvement by using a higher-order crossover, regardless of whether it's speaker level or preamp level.

So why would you want to put the crossover before the amps if you have to buy two amps instead of one? Good question. There are three main advantages to using preamp-level crossovers:

- Increased practicality of high-order slopes
- Driver impedance characteristic doesn't affect frequency response
- Tweeter protection during clipping of bass

Combined, these factors provide an improvement in sound quality as well as increased tweeter protection under a number of circumstances.

Increased Practicality of High-Order Slopes

Speaker-level crossovers must handle the high power levels of the amplifier outputs. This means massive high-power inductors and capacitors are required. The steeper the crossover slope, the more components required. In practice, anything higher than 12 dB/octave is considered cost prohibitive.

Preamp-level crossovers are low-power circuits and eliminate the need for expensive high-power components. With active filters, the cost of implementing a 24-dB/octave slope is not much more than that for a 6-dB/octave slope. Active filters make it simple to provide switch-selectable crossover frequencies. They are also immune to many of the performance problems, caused by inductor resistance and saturation and electrolytic capacitor degradation due to aging, that plague speaker-level crossovers. In short, they act more like ideal filters.

Driver Impedance Characteristic Doesn't Affect Frequency Response

The impedances of woofers and tweeters vary dramatically with frequency. This makes it difficult for speaker-level crossovers to work as intended. The result is frequency response anomalies.

So-called universal speaker-level crossovers that you can buy assume that your speakers are 4 ohms for all frequencies. Crossovers that are custom designed for a specific woofer and tweeter offer some improvement, but there are practical limitations.

Biamping solves this problem because the amplifiers directly drive the speakers. Since the output impedance of the amplifiers is small compared to that of the drivers, driver impedance variations with frequency have no effect on the response.

Tweeter Protection During Clipping of Bass

In a single-amp system, when you turn up the volume of your stereo loud enough to cause distortion, massive amounts of high-frequency energy are produced at the output of the amplifier. This is because distorting amplifiers "clip" the musical peaks. This generates high-frequency harmonics not in the original signal. Tweeters are often unable to handle the additional power, and are damaged or destroyed.

Ironically, using an underpowered amp (in a normal speaker-level crossover situation) risks blowing tweeters more than using an overpowered amp, because of clipping.

Most clipping occurs during loud bass passages, such as drumbeats. Even though a loud drumbeat may only contain bass frequencies, high-power "spikes" are produced at high frequencies when the amp clips. These spikes get to the tweeters with a single-amp system, but not with biamping. Biamping eliminates this problem because the tweeters are powered by their own amp, which is unaffected by the woofer amp. Clipping of the tweeter amp is not a concern because the total power to the tweeters is not increased.

What to Look For in Equipment

Before you start shopping for equipment, study the project sections ("Biamping Head Units with Front and Rear Preamp Outputs," "Biamping Head Units with One Set of Preamp Outputs") to see which configuration best suits your needs. If you're buying a head unit, get one with front and rear preamp outputs so you can be sure to have full use of your fader.

Choosing a Crossover

There are a number of considerations for choosing the best crossover for your application. These include crossover configuration, filter slopes, and choice of crossover frequencies.

A common configuration is shown in Fig. 9-8. All inputs and outputs are preamp level.

There is no standard configuration for crossovers, but this configuration is assumed for the projects section because it's the most prevalent. Other variations exist, and may be better suited to your needs. For example, speaker-level inputs would be important if your head unit doesn't have preamp-level outputs. Manufacturers' "front" and "rear" designations simply

FIGURE 9-8

Common crossover configuration.

front
rear

tweeters (front)
woofers (front)
full-range (rear)
subwoofer (rear)

crossover

indicate which inputs are used for each of the outputs—they may not be accurate for your application. Similarly, manufacturers often refer to the woofer outputs as the mid-band or bandpass outputs, and the subwoofer outputs as low-pass. It is standard for all output pairs to have level controls.

The requirements for crossover filter slopes and frequencies are shown in Table 9-2.

The tweeter crossover slope must be 12 dB/octave minimum for tweeter power handling considerations. Anything less forces you to use a crossover frequency that is too high for good woofer response. The woofer low-pass slope and crossover frequency should match those of the tweeter for best performance.

To enable placement of a subwoofer anywhere in the vehicle, the subwoofer crossover must be 18 dB/octave or higher. Slopes less than 18 dB/octave allow mid-bass and even mid-range to be heard from the subwoofer. Since only deep bass frequencies are nondirectional, this gives away the subwoofer location and degrades imaging. Who wants a bass guitar player under their seat? The only exception to this is for bandpass boxes, where you can successfully use a 12-dB/octave crossover. Either buy a crossover that has a steep enough subwoofer slope or use a separate subwoofer crossover that does.

A continuously variable subwoofer cutoff frequency is a real plus. It gives you the flexibility to seamlessly blend the subwoofer with the rest

TABLE 9-2

Crossover Requirements

Crossover Characteristic	Subwoofer Low-Pass	Woofer High-Pass	Woofer Low-Pass	Tweeter High-Pass
Filter slopes	18 dB/octave minimum	6 dB/octave minimum	12 dB/octave minimum	12 dB/octave minimum
	Need not be the same as woofer high-pass slope	Need not be the same as subwoofer low-pass slope	Should be the same as tweeter high-pass slope	Should be the same as woofer low-pass slope
Crossover frequencies	75 to 150 Hz minimum range	100 to 200 Hz minimum range	2.4 to 5 kHz minimum range	2.4 to 5 kHz minimum range
Other important features	40 or 45 Hz bass boost			
	Subsonic filter			
	Polarity switch			

of your system. Even with high-pass crossovers on your woofers, the natural low-frequency roll-off of woofers makes it difficult to predict the best subwoofer crossover frequency. A continuously variable crossover lets you avoid a gap or peak in your mid-bass.

Five to 10 dB of bass boost at 40 or 45 Hz extends the low-frequency response of most subwoofer systems without overdriving them. A subsonic filter and polarity switch are other important features for a subwoofer crossover. See the chapter on subwoofers for a detailed explanation.

Buying Amps for Biamping

Most of what you should know about buying amps is contained in Chap. 7. For biamping, you also need to know the relative power levels for tweeter amps, woofer amps, and subwoofer amps (if you have them).

This comes down to the normal frequency distribution of power in music. Table 9-3 shows the maximum percentage of power above various frequencies.

How much power a tweeter amp should have depends on the crossover frequency. The higher the crossover frequency, the less the required power. Rarely is a tweeter crossover frequency lower than 2400 Hz, so a tweeter amp having roughly 5 percent of the total system power should be sufficient.

On the subwoofer end, the power requirements also depend on the crossover frequency. The lower the crossover frequency, the less the required power for the sub amp, but the more the required power for the woofer amp.

The rules of thumb in Table 9-4 should help you determine the right power levels for tweeter and subwoofer amps, based on the total system power. The tweeter recommendation applies whether you have a subwoofer or not.

TABLE 9-3

Normal Frequency Distribution of Power in Music

Frequency	Maximum Power Above That Frequency
300 Hz	50%
600 Hz	25%
1200 Hz	10%
2400 Hz	5%

TABLE 9-4

Amplifier Power
Requirements for
Biamping

Amps	Power
Tweeter amps	5% of total system power
Sub amps	40% of total system power

For example, suppose you're biamping in front and back and don't plan to use a subwoofer. If you're using 100-watt per channel woofer amps, then your tweeter amps should have at least 5 watts per channel. (In practice, you'll have to buy 35-watt per channel amps, since they're the smallest available.)

Suppose you plan to have a subwoofer as well as biamp in front and back. Let's say you're shooting for a total system power of around 400 watts (about the same as the last example). Once again, the tweeter amps should have at least 5 watts per channel. (You'll have to buy 35-watt per channel amps.) The total power to the subwoofer should be about 160 watts. The total power to the woofers would be 220 watts or 55 watts per channel.

Speakers

For biamping, you'll either need to use separate woofers and tweeters (component speakers) or biampable coax drivers. Biampable coax drivers are like regular coaxial speakers, but they provide separate terminals for the woofer and tweeter. These save you from having to mount separate tweeters, but you lose the flexibility of being able to put the tweeters wherever you want.

More about selecting and mounting component speakers is contained in Chap. 3. Subwoofers are covered in Chap. 4.

Biamping Head Units with Front and Rear Preamp Outputs

Having front and rear preamp outputs is a big plus for biamping because it lets you retain full use of your head unit fader in most configurations. There are five biamping configurations for head units with front and rear preamp outputs (Table 9-5)—all but the second and third retain use of the

TABLE 9-5

Biamping
Configurations for
Head Units with
Front and Rear
Preamp Outputs

Configuration	Diagram	Comments
Separate rear crossover		Allows you to retain full use of your head unit fader. Lets you choose different crossover frequencies for the front and rear. Crossovers may be purchased as a single combined unit.
Shared crossover		Head unit fader becomes non-functional. Difficult to make front/rear level adjustments since you must also maintain the proper relative tweeter/woofer levels. Not recommended.

TABLE 9-5
(continued)

Configuration	Diagram	Comments
Parallel front/rear speakers		Saves two amps when equal power to front and rear speakers is acceptable. (No relative front/rear level adjustment is possible.)
Full-range rear		Allows you to retain full use of your head unit fader. Saves the cost of an amplifier, and you only need a single crossover. Provides virtually same performance as separate rear crossover configuration.
Amp-saving full-range rear		Allows you to retain full use of your head unit fader. Useful for rear fill applications where high power is needed for front only. Saves the cost of two amplifiers, and you only need a single crossover.

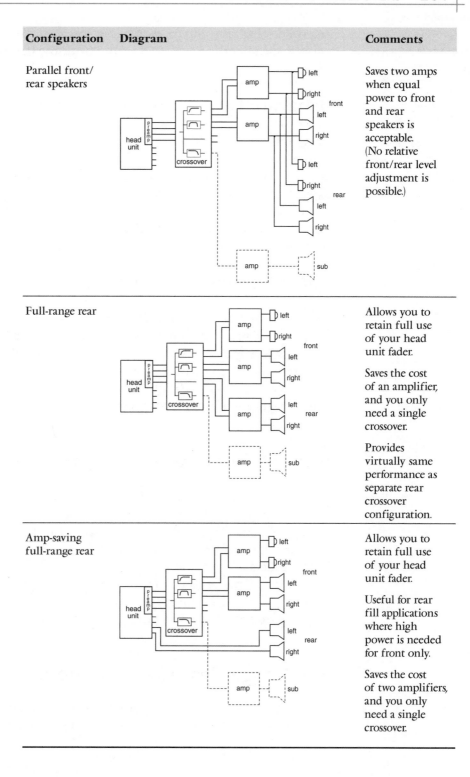

fader. The first configuration provides the most flexibility and highest performance, but the fourth and fifth provide the best performance value.

Separate Rear Crossover Configuration

This configuration provides the most flexibility and highest performance, but is the most expensive. It uses separate crossovers for the front and rear speakers, which allows you to retain full use of your head unit fader. This also lets you choose different crossover frequencies for the front and rear (of limited value). The crossovers may be purchased as two separate units or as a single combined unit.

Shared Crossover Configuration

This configuration shares a single crossover for front and rear component speakers. The main problem is the loss of head unit fader functionality—you must use the amp level controls to set the relative front/rear levels. Since you must also maintain the proper relative tweeter/woofer levels, it becomes a chore to make slight front/rear readjustments. For this reason, this configuration is not recommended.

Parallel Front/Rear Speakers Configuration

The parallel front/rear speakers configuration shares amps for front and rear channels. This gives you almost the same power per speaker as having identical sets of amps for front and rear. The drawback with this configuration is that you are stuck with having equal power for front and back speakers.

Since the amplifiers used in this configuration will see a parallel speaker load, they must be 2-ohm stable. Amps driving 2-ohm loads run hotter, so be sure to mount them where they will have good air circulation.

Full-Range Rear Configuration

This configuration biamps only the front set of speakers—the rear speakers are full-range (usually coaxial) speakers. This saves the cost of an amplifier and you only need a single crossover. This configuration allows you to retain full use of your head unit fader.

Since the performance of the front speakers is the most critical, this configuration provides virtually the same performance as the separate rear crossover configuration, but at a much lower cost.

Amp-Saving Full-Range Rear Configuration

This configuration is identical to the previous one, except it saves an additional amplifier by using the head unit's internal amp to drive the rear speakers. This makes sense if you are using the rear speakers for rear fill and operating them at a reduced volume level to improve imaging (see the "Imaging Overhaul" section in Chap. 3). This configuration allows you to retain full use of your head unit fader as well.

In general, providing rear fill requires one-tenth the power necessary for the front. Assuming an 18-watt per channel head unit, this configuration should work for up to 180 watts per channel in the front.

Biamping Head Units with One Set of Preamp Outputs

Having only one set of preamp outputs is a minus for biamping because you generally lose use of your head unit fader. There are five biamping configurations for head units with one set of preamp outputs (Table 9-6)—only the fifth retains use of the fader. The first configuration provides the most flexibility and highest performance otherwise, but the fourth and fifth provide the best performance value.

Separate Rear Crossover Configuration

This configuration provides the most flexibility (except for the loss of fader) and the highest performance. It is the most expensive as well. It uses separate crossovers for the front and rear speakers. This lets you choose different crossover frequencies for the front and rear (of limited value).

TABLE 9-6

Biamping
Configurations for
Head Units with
One Set of Preamp
Outputs

Configuration	Diagram	Comments
Separate rear crossover		Head unit fader control is non-functional, but setting the relative front/rear level is facilitated by having a common rear level control. Lets you choose different crossover frequencies for the front and rear. Crossovers may be purchased as a single combined unit.
Shared crossover		Head unit fader is non-functional. Difficult to make front/rear level adjustments since you must also maintain the proper relative tweeter/woofer levels. Not recommended.

TABLE 9-6
(continued)

Configuration	Diagram	Comments
Parallel front/ rear speakers		Saves two amps when equal power to front and rear speakers is acceptable. (No relative front/rear level adjustment is possible.)
Full-range rear		Head unit fader control is non-functional, but setting the relative front/ rear level is facilitated by having a common rear level control. Saves the cost of an amplifier, and you only need a single crossover. Provides virtually the same performance as the separate rear crossover configuration.

Configuration	Diagram	Comments
TABLE 9-6 Biamping Configurations for Head Units with One Set of Preamp Outputs (continued)	Amp-saving full-range rear	Allows you to retain full use of your head unit fader. Useful for rear fill applications where high power is needed for front only. Saves the cost of two amplifiers, and you only need a single crossover.

Although the head unit fader control is nonfunctional, setting the relative front/rear level is facilitated by having the level of all rear speakers affected by a single control (the full range output control of the front crossover). The crossovers may be purchased as two separate units or as a single combined unit.

Shared Crossover Configuration

This configuration shares a single crossover for front and rear component speakers. The head unit fader control is nonfunctional. Setting the relative front/rear levels is especially difficult because there is no level control that affects only all front or only all rear speakers. For this reason, this configuration is not recommended.

Parallel Front/Rear Speakers Configuration

The parallel front/rear speakers configuration shares amps for front and rear channels. This gives you almost the same power per speaker as having identical sets of amps for front and rear. The drawback with this configuration is that you are stuck with having equal power for front and back speakers.

Since the amplifiers used in this configuration will see a parallel speaker load, they must be 2-ohm stable. Amps driving 2-ohm loads run hotter, so be sure to mount them where they will have good air circulation.

Full-Range Rear Configuration

This configuration biamps only the front set of speakers—the rear speakers are full-range (usually coaxial) speakers. This saves the cost of an amplifier, and you only need a single crossover. Although the head unit fader control is nonfunctional, setting the relative front/rear level is facilitated by having the level of all rear speakers affected by a single amplifier control.

Since the performance of the front speakers is the most critical, this configuration provides virtually the same performance as the separate rear crossover configuration, but at a much lower cost.

Amp-Saving Full-Range Rear Configuration

This is the only configuration that provides head unit fader control for head units with one set of preamp outputs. Like the previous configuration, this one biamps only the front set of speakers, but it saves an additional amplifier by using the head unit's internal amp to drive the rear speakers. This makes sense if you are using the rear speakers for rear fill and operating them at a reduced volume level to improve imaging (see the "Imaging Overhaul" section in Chap. 3).

In general, providing rear fill requires one-tenth the power necessary for the front. Assuming an 18-watt per channel head unit, this configuration should work for up to 180 watts per channel in the front.

NOTE   *If you're using this configuration and have front preamp outputs, your fader control will operate properly between the front biamped speakers and the rear head unit driven speakers. But if you have rear preamp outputs, you'll want to connect your rear speakers to the front head unit amps to restore fader control. The change is easily made at the head unit wiring harness. This will cause the fader control to operate backwards, but it's a small price to pay for fader control.*

Adjusting Your System

Once you've installed everything, it's time to set all the crossover frequencies and amp levels. Follow the order below for best results.

Setting Tweeter High-Pass and Woofer Low-Pass Crossover Frequencies

Setting the tweeter high-pass and woofer low-pass crossover frequencies should be done prior to the other system adjustments.

The optimum tweeter high-pass and woofer low-pass crossover frequency settings depend on the specific woofer and tweeter involved. If you are fortunate enough to have recommended crossover frequencies or frequency response data for your drivers, you can base your crossover settings on that information. Otherwise, you'll have to make an educated guess.

- *If your component speakers came with speaker-level crossovers:* Component speakers bought as a matched set often come with speaker-level crossovers. Using the same crossover frequencies as the speaker-level crossovers is your best bet.

- *If you have frequency response curves for your speakers:* Ideally, the high-frequency roll-off point of the woofer extends above the low-frequency roll-off point of the tweeter. If so, the woofer and tweeter crossover frequencies should both be set to the same frequency—an equal compromise between woofer and tweeter roll-off points. If the high-frequency roll-off point of the woofer does not extend above the low-frequency roll-off point of the tweeter, you will need to set the woofer crossover frequency higher than the tweeter crossover frequency. This usually means using 5 kHz for the woofer and 3.5 kHz for the tweeter.

- *If you don't have anything (except the chart in Table 9-7):* In general, the smaller the woofer, the more extended its high-frequency response. Table 9-7 is based on that fact.

Regardless of which method you use, don't be afraid to use your ears and experiment with other settings later, after you've made a first pass at all the other system settings.

TABLE 9-7

Crossover
Frequency Settings
Based on Woofer
Diameter

Woofer Diameter	Woofer Crossover Frequency	Tweeter Crossover Frequency
4″	3.5 kHz	3.5 kHz
5¼″	3.5 kHz	3.5 kHz
6½″	5 kHz	3.5 kHz

Setting Woofer High-Pass Crossover Frequencies

If you don't have a subwoofer, and you're using the rear speakers only for fill, then you should not use any woofer high-pass filtering at all. If you don't have a subwoofer, and you play your rear speakers loud enough to provide bass for the whole system, then consider using 150-Hz high-pass filtering for the front woofers. This will let them play louder with less distortion, and will not significantly reduce the total bass of the system. This is especially true for small front woofers.

If you do have a subwoofer, then you should use high-pass filtering for all your woofers. Use 200 Hz for 6-dB/octave woofer high-pass slopes and 150 Hz for 12-dB/octave or higher slopes.

Setting Woofer and Tweeter Amp Levels

Setting woofer and tweeter amp levels is a complicated process. You need to simultaneously set the proper relative tweeter-to-woofer levels, the proper relative front-to-rear levels, and the optimum absolute levels for lowest noise and distortion. On top of that, you probably have level controls on the crossover outputs as well as amplifier inputs to worry about.

Follow the procedure for your specific configuration.

Separate Rear Crossover and Shared Crossover Configurations.

1. Set the head unit fader control to its center detent position. Set all tone controls and equalizer controls flat.

2. Set the level controls of all amps to minimum. Set all crossover level controls to maximum.

3. With music, turn up the head unit volume control (you should barely be able to hear the music). When you reach the point where you start to hear distortion, turn the volume control down slightly until the distortion disappears. Leave the volume control at this setting.

4. Turn up the front woofer amp level control until you the system is as loud as you'll ever play it or you begin to hear distortion. If you hear distortion, slightly decrease the amp level control.

5. Turn down the head unit volume to a normal listening level.

6. Turn up the rear woofer amp level until the desired front/rear balance is achieved.

7. With the fader set all the way to the front, turn up the front tweeter amp to achieve the proper tonal balance.

8. With the fader set all the way to the rear, turn up the rear tweeter amp to achieve the proper tonal balance. Return the fader to its center detent position.

Parallel Front/Rear Speakers Configurations.

1. Set the head unit fader control to its center detent position. Set all tone controls and equalizer controls flat.

2. Set the level controls of all amps to minimum. Set all crossover level controls to maximum.

3. With music, turn up the head unit volume control (you should barely be able to hear the music). When you reach the point where you start to hear distortion, turn the volume control down slightly until the distortion disappears. Leave the volume control at this setting.

4. Turn up the woofer amp level control until you the system is as loud as you'll ever play it or you begin to hear distortion. If you hear distortion, slightly decrease the amp level control.

5. Turn down the head unit volume to a normal listening level.

6. Turn up the tweeter amp to achieve the proper tonal balance.

Full-Range Rear (Not Amp-Saving) Configurations.

1. Set the head unit fader control to its center detent position. Set all tone controls and equalizer controls flat.

2. Set the level controls of all amps to minimum. Set all crossover level controls to maximum.

3. With music, turn up the head unit volume control (you should barely be able to hear the music). When you reach the point where you start to hear distortion, turn the volume control down slightly until the distortion disappears. Leave the volume control at this setting.

4. Turn up the (front) woofer amp level control until you the system is as loud as you'll ever play it or you begin to hear distortion. If you hear distortion, slightly decrease the amp level control.

5. Turn down the head unit volume to a normal listening level.

6. Turn up the (front) tweeter amp to achieve the proper tonal balance.

7. Turn up the (rear) full-range amp level until the desired front/rear balance is achieved.

Amp-Saving Full-Range Rear Configurations.

1. Set the head unit fader control to its center detent position. Set all tone controls and equalizer controls flat.

2. Set the level controls of all amps to minimum. Set all crossover level controls to maximum.

3. With music, set the head unit volume to a normal listening level.

4. Turn up the (front) woofer amp level control until the desired front/rear balance is achieved.

5. Turn up the (front) tweeter amp to achieve the proper tonal balance.

Setting Subwoofer Crossover Frequency and Amp Level

Perform the adjustments in this order for best results. Use your favorite cassette, CD, or radio station. Use several sources to get a good average.

Preset the subwoofer crossover to 100 Hz. If there is a 40- or 45-Hz bass boost feature, turn it off for now. Adjust the subwoofer amp level control to the point that sounds best, erring on the side of too little bass. If there is a subwoofer polarity switch, set it to whichever position gives you the most bass. The effect is usually small.

If you plan to use the 40- or 45-Hz bass boost feature, turn it on now. In general, it will help extend the system bass response and provide tighter-sounding bass. If you later find that your subwoofer sometimes distorts, you should turn the bass boost off.

Now fine-tune the cutoff frequency of the subwoofer crossover and the level control of the subwoofer power amplifier to provide the most natural-sounding bass. You will find that you need more bass when you are driving to overcome the masking effects of road noise. (See the box on road noise masking in the chapter on equalizers.) Try to find a level that is acceptable for all conditions.

CHAPTER 10

Changer and Player Projects

Adding a CD changer, DVD changer, or digital music player to your system will give you hours of audio or video without having to fumble with discs as you drive.

A CD changer is a great way to add CD and/or MP3 capabilities to your system without having to replace your head unit. Even if you have a CD/MP3 head unit, there's nothing better than a changer loaded with your favorite discs for long road trips.

If your system already has a DVD player, a DVD changer can be added to conveniently store the entertainment for your mobile video system. If you don't have a DVD player, a DVD changer can be used as the main DVD player for your system. And since DVD changers also play CDs, you get the benefits of a CD changer included.

Digital music players give you easy access to your entire music collection without the hassle of discs in the car. They connect to your system like a CD changer, but store MP3, WMA, or WAV files of your music rather than discs. Files are transferred to the digital music player using your home computer.

Adding a CD Changer to Your System

Unlike most other car stereo projects, adding a CD changer strongly depends on the type of head unit you have. That's because many head units don't have CD changer controls, and there is no industry standard for those that do. It's important to scope out the interfacing issues before you start choosing features or brands of equipment.

For the purposes of adding an aftermarket CD changer, there are three head unit categories: head units without CD changer controls, aftermarket head units with CD changer controls, and factory head units with CD changer controls. Table 10-1 provides an overview of these head unit categories.

Head Units Without CD Changer Controls

Most older head units (and many new ones) have no provisions for adding a CD changer. Many people deal with this situation by replacing their head unit with one having CD changer controls. If you want to keep the

TABLE 10-1

Head Unit Categories for Adding a CD Changer

Head Unit	Comments
Head unit without CD changer controls	An aftermarket CD changer can be added using an FM modulator.
Aftermarket head unit with CD changer controls	No performance compromises and all your controls are in one place.
	You are generally restricted to choosing the same brand and vintage of equipment for both changer and head unit.
Factory head unit with CD changer controls	Adding an aftermarket CD changer is often possible using a factory-compatible changer or a standard aftermarket changer with an OEM interface CD changer converter.

head unit you have, the aftermarket industry offers a solution: CD changers with FM modulators. Figure 10-1 shows how this type of CD changer connects to your system. The JVC CH-X1500RF (Fig. 10-2) is in this changer category.

With this approach, the CD changer effectively becomes a personal radio station for your FM receiver. The FM modulator converts the audio signals of the CD changer to an FM stereo signal that is injected into your existing antenna wire. This assures good reception. You can choose the frequency of your personal radio station to avoid a conflict with a commercial station.

When you want to listen to the CD changer, you simply tune your FM receiver to your "personal station." Your head unit controls (such as volume, bass, and treble) function normally. The CD changer itself is controlled through a dash-mounted display panel with controls. A wireless remote control is offered with some models.

The weakness of the FM modulator approach is the degradation in the signal quality due to the modulation/demodulation process. Frequency response, signal-to-noise ratio, distortion, and stereo separation all suffer. Because of this, purists often consider the FM modulator approach unac-

Tip: If you travel, choose a model that lets you change the transmitting frequency from the control panel.

FIGURE 10-1

CD changer with FM modulator.

ceptable. But to put this in perspective, consider the sound quality of the most noise-free, best-sounding FM station you've ever heard. That's what you'll get. In fact, because of the heavy compression used by commercial broadcasters to reach the maximum audience, the audio quality can be much better than any FM broadcast.

Aftermarket Head Units with CD Changer Controls

With an aftermarket head unit with CD changer controls, it's easy to add a CD changer. There are no performance compromises and all your controls are in one place. You can even control everything with a single remote. The Sony CDX-757MX (Fig. 10-3) is an example of this type of changer.

It's important to realize that *not all CD changers work with all head units.* In fact, you are generally restricted to choosing the same brand and vintage of equipment for both changer and head unit. This means that you should look closely at CD changers when you're choosing a head unit. It also means that you shouldn't put off buying a CD changer too long after buying a head unit, or incompatibility may become a problem.

Factory Head Units with CD Changer Controls

Adding an aftermarket CD changer to a factory head unit with CD changer controls is often possible using a factory-compatible changer or a standard aftermarket changer with an OEM interface CD changer converter.

Factory-compatible CD changers can be either brand-specific or universal. USA SPEC makes a line of brand-specific factory-compatible changers to cover many popular makes and models of vehicles. Their model SCD-VW44EBU (Fig. 10-4) is compatible with many Volkswagen factory head units. The Neo Changer (Fig. 10-5) is a universal factory-compatible CD changer. It comes with a set of 15 different cables that fit most factory car stereos. You just use the one that fits your car.

OEM interface CD changer converters connect between the factory head unit and the aftermarket CD changer. For some applications, it's simply a matter of converting from one connector type to another. In other cases, the handshaking protocol between the head unit and changer must be digitally converted from one format to another.

FIGURE 10-4
USA SPEC SCD-VW44EBU CD changer for Volkswagen factory stereos. (*Courtesy of USA SPEC.*)

FIGURE 10-5

Neo Changer universal factory-compatible CD changer. (*Courtesy of Neo Car Audio.*)

Precision Interface Electronics (PIE) manufactures OEM interface CD changer converters for many vehicles (Fig. 10-6). Each of these is designed to work with a specific brand and vintage of CD changer, so don't buy a changer until you're sure a suitable converter exists.

CD Changer Performance and Features

If you listen to MP3 or WMA compressed music files, you'll want a changer with MP3/WMA playback. If your head unit doesn't have this feature, it's a great way to add MP3/WMA capabilities to your system without having to replace your head unit.

You can expect excellent frequency response and signal-to-noise ratio with virtually any CD changer. Features like intro scan, random play, and track repeat are found on almost all models. Look to the number of CDs, CD-R/CD-RW compatibility, CD text, and disc naming/track programming features to help you choose the right changer. If you go off road,

FIGURE 10-6

PIE DPX™ OEM interface CD changer converter. (*Courtesy of Precision Interface Electronics.*)

electronic shock protection can help reduce skipping. Don't forget to consider size and mounting angle, especially if you're thinking about a glove compartment or console installation. Table 10-2 provides information on various CD changer features.

Number of CDs.   Most changers hold six, ten, or twelve CDs.

TABLE 10-2

Performance and
Features of CD
Changers

Performance/Feature	Comments
Number of CDs	Choose 6, 10, or 12 discs.
CD-R, CD-RW compatibility	Can play audio CD-Rs and/or CD-RWs as well as prerecorded CDs.
CD text display	CD changers with this feature will display the song title, album name, and artist for CDs having CD text information encoded on them.
MP3/WMA playback	Allows you to listen to CDs with MP3 or WMA compressed music files.
ID3 tag display	Similar to CD text display, but for MP3/WMA files.
Disc naming/track programming	Lets you program disc names to appear on the display and preprogram the songs you want to hear on each disc.
FM modulator	Important for head units lacking CD changer controls. The CD changer effectively becomes a personal radio station for your FM receiver.
Mounting angle	Defines the range of mounting angles for proper operation.
CD frequency response	The frequency range a CD player can faithfully reproduce.
Electronic shock protection	A buffer memory used as a reserve against skipping.
Intro scan	Lets you hear the first few seconds of each track. Hit the button again when you hear the song you want.
Random play/shuffle	Mixes up the order of songs for variety during playback.
CD signal-to-noise ratio	A measure of how well a CD player silences background noise.
Zero-bit detect	Mutes the output whenever a series of zeros is detected in the digital bitstream.

CD-R, CD-RW Compatibility. CD changers with this capability can play audio CD-Rs and/or CD-RWs as well as prerecorded CDs. Most changers will play CD-Rs, but some will not play CD-RWs (rewriteable discs). This is an important feature if you record your own CD-RW discs.

CD Text Display. CD changers with this feature will display the song title, album name, and artist for CDs having CD text information encoded on them.

MP3/WMA Playback. Allows you to listen to CDs with MP3 or WMA compressed music files. Some changers support MP3 only, others support MP3 and WMA. With this feature, you'll also want ID3/WMA tag display. For more information about MP3 and WMA, see the chapter on head unit projects.

ID3/WMA Tag Display. Similar to CD text display, but for MP3/WMA files. CD changers with this feature will display the song title, album, artist, year, genre, and comments for MP3 files having ID3 tags and for WMA files having WMA tags. Later versions of ID3 (ID3v1.1, ID3v2) add even more information capabilities. This is a very useful feature if you play MP3s, because so many of them fit on a single CD—not to mention a whole changer-full!

Disc Naming/Track Programming. Disc naming lets you program disc names to appear on the display. Track programming allows you to preprogram the songs you want to hear on each disc. Most changers with these features will store information for about 100 discs.

FM Modulator. Important for adding a CD changer to a head unit lacking CD changer controls. With this approach, the CD changer effectively becomes a personal radio station for your FM receiver. The FM modulator converts the audio signals of the CD changer to an FM stereo signal that is injected into your existing antenna wire. You can choose the frequency of your personal radio station to avoid a conflict with a commercial station.

Mounting Angle. Defines the range of mounting angles for proper operation. Almost all models allow 0°, 45°, and 90° (90° means "face up"). Some allow mounting over the entire 0- to 90° range or more, important for glove compartment installations.

CD Frequency Response.   The frequency range a CD player can faithfully reproduce. Humans can hear sounds as low as 20 Hz and as high as 20 kHz. Virtually every CD player exceeds this range.

Electronic Shock Protection.   Electronic shock protection is a buffer memory used to store music as a reserve against skipping due to bumps in the road.

Intro Scan.   Lets you hear the first few seconds of each track. Hit the button again when you hear the song you want.

Random Play/Shuffle.   Mixes up the order of songs for variety during playback.

CD Signal-to-Noise Ratio.   A measure of how well a CD player silences background noise. Ratings are given in decibels; higher ratings indicate less noise. The signal-to-noise ratio of CD players is generally so good that noise picked up by other means determines the system noise level. Unless you're a competitor or plan on using super high-power amps, don't rely too heavily on this spec.

Zero-Bit Detect.   Mutes the output whenever a series of zeros is detected in the digital bitstream. The result is complete silence between songs. This is important if you're a competitor, but otherwise you'll never hear the difference.

Adding a DVD Changer to Your System

If your system already has a DVD player, a DVD changer can be added to conveniently store the entertainment for your mobile video system. If you don't have a DVD player, a DVD changer can be used as the main DVD player for your system.

Most DVD changers can be controlled by a compatible head unit of the same manufacturer and vintage as the changer, using the head unit CD changer or DVD changer controls. Most changers can also be used

.without a compatible head unit. This is called stand-alone operation, and utilizes a separate remote control, which may be included with the changer or may be an optional accessory. The Clarion VCZ625 (Fig. 10-7) is a DVD changer that can be controlled by a compatible head unit or used in stand-alone mode.

System Already Has a DVD Player

If you have a head unit that plays DVDs or an overhead DVD player with built-in monitor, a DVD changer is a convenient way to have a collection of discs (DVDs and CDs) on-tap for any trip. You'll need to connect the video output of the changer to a video input on the head unit or monitor. You'll also need to connect the stereo audio outputs of the changer to your head unit or overhead DVD player. If your system is equipped for 5.1 channel sound, you'll want to connect the optical output of the changer to your surround-sound processor.

Using a Changer as the Main DVD Player

It's possible to use a DVD changer as the main DVD player for your system. To complete your video system, you'll need a monitor, and optionally, wireless headphones. If you have a head unit with compatible changer controls, it can conveniently control the changer. This is the best arrangement if you have a head unit with built-in monitor or other type of front-seat viewing monitor. If your head unit doesn't have compatible

FIGURE 10-7

Clarion VCZ625 DVD changer. (*Courtesy of Clarion.*)

controls, control the changer using stand-alone mode with the included (or optional) remote.

To use a changer as your main DVD player, you'll need to connect the video output of the changer to the video input of the monitor, and the stereo audio outputs of the changer to your head unit aux inputs or wireless headphones. If your head unit lacks aux inputs, you can use an FM modulator or auxiliary input converter (see the chapter on accessories) to provide audio to your head unit.

Regardless of whether your system already has a DVD player or you're planning to use a changer as the main DVD player, many mobile video system configurations are possible, depending on the equipment involved. Refer to the chapter on mobile video for more details on the many ways to configure your mobile video system.

DVD Changer Performance and Features

Choosing a DVD changer can be simple or complex, depending on your needs. If you want a changer that can be controlled by a particular head unit (and such a changer exists), then choosing will be simple. If you're just looking to play standard prerecorded DVDs and CDs and don't care about head unit controls, then virtually any DVD changer will meet your needs. But if you're into recordable DVDs and CDs, 5.1 channel sound, or advanced features, then you'll want to look more closely at features and specs.

Table 10-3 shows important performance characteristics and features to consider. Since DVD changers also play CDs, most of the CD changer specs in Table 10-2 also apply. For brevity, only the most important of these are included in Table 10-3. Even though DVD changers play CDs, they may not provide all the features you've come to expect in a CD changer. For example, DVD players may not automatically play the next CD when the current CD is over. And DVD changers are often one step behind in-dash DVD players when it comes to features.

Number of Discs. Most changers hold 6 or 10 discs (DVDs and/or CDs).

Stand-Alone Mode. Can be controlled using its own remote control (rather than a compatible head unit with changer controls). Allows the

TABLE 10-3

Performance and Features of DVD Changers

Performance/Feature	Comments
Number of discs	Choose 6 or 10 discs.
Stand-alone mode	Can be controlled using its own remote. Allows the changer to be used with any head unit.
CD-R, CD-RW compatibility	Can play CD-Rs and/or CD-RWs as well as prerecorded CDs.
MP3/WMA playback	Allows you to listen to CDs with MP3 or WMA compressed music files.
Video CD compatibility	Able to play Video CDs (VCDs).
DVD-R, DVD-RW, DVD+R, DVD+RW compatibility	Look for a changer that's compatible with any recordable and rewriteable DVD formats you use.
Selectable aspect ratio	Allows you to set the video output for 16:9 or 4:3 modes.
Two sets of video outputs	For driving front and rear monitors.
Digital optical output	For connection to a Dolby Digital/DTS surround-sound processor.
FM modulator	Important for providing audio from the changer to a head unit without aux inputs.
Mounting angle	Defines the range of mounting angles for proper operation.

changer to be used with any head unit, or even without a head unit. Most DVD changers have this feature.

CD-R, CD-RW Compatibility. DVD changers with this capability can play CD-Rs and/or CD-RWs as well as prerecorded CDs. This is an important feature if you record your own CDs. Most DVD changers are CD-R and CD-RW compatible.

MP3/WMA Decoding. Allows you to listen to CDs with MP3 or WMA compressed music files. Some changers support MP3 only, others support MP3 and WMA. For more information about MP3 and WMA, see the chapter on head unit projects.

Video CD Compatibility. Able to play video CDs (VCDs). Most DVD changers have this feature.

DVD-R, DVD-RW, DVD+R, DVD+RW Compatibility. These are some of the different standards for recordable and rewriteable DVDs. If you record your own DVDs, look for a changer that's compatible with the formats you use.

Selectable Aspect Ratio. Allows you to set the video output for 16:9 Wide (when connected to a wide-screen monitor), 4:3 Pan & Scan, or 4:3 Letterbox.

Two Sets of Video Outputs. Provides two composite video outputs for driving front and rear monitors.

Digital Optical Output. For connection to a Dolby Digital/DTS surround-sound processor for 5.1 channel audio. Some changers allow this output to be configured for linear PCM for connecting to an amp or decoder that's not Dolby Digital/DTS compatible.

FM Modulator. Important for providing audio from the DVD changer to a head unit without aux inputs. The modulator converts the audio signal to FM, then sends it through your head unit's antenna input. You can choose the frequency of the modulator to avoid a conflict with a commercial station.

Mounting Angle. Defines the range of mounting angles for proper operation. Almost all models allow 0 degrees, 45 degrees, and 90 degrees (90 degrees means "face up"). Some allow mounting over the entire 0 to 90 degree range or more, important for glove compartment installations.

Adding a Digital Music Player to Your System

Digital music players give you easy access to your entire music collection without the hassle of discs in the car. They connect to your system like a CD changer, but store MP3, WMA, or WAV files of your music rather than discs. Files are transferred to the digital music player using your home computer.

Digital music players are generally hard-drive-based MP3/WMA players. The hard drive provides tremendous amounts of music storage, especially for compressed music files. A 20 GB hard drive can hold about 5,000 MP3 or WMA files. Some digital music players have 80 GB of storage space, enough for 20,000 music files!

Using software (included with the player) with your home computer, you convert your CDs to MP3, WMA, or WAV files. You can also download music from the Internet. The software lets you convert from one format to another and organize your music into playlists. Music files are then transferred from your computer to your digital music player through the USB port.

Some digital music players use *cartridge docking*, others use *player docking*. Cartridge docking systems use a relatively small cartridge (containing the hard drive) to transfer music files from your computer to the music player in your car. The advantage of this approach is the compact size of the cartridge. The Kenwood Music Keg (Fig. 10-8) is an example of this kind of system.

With player docking systems, the player itself docks with your computer. After transferring music files, the player then docks in your car. The advantage of player docking is that you can have a docking station for your home stereo as well as your car stereo, and have access to your entire music library in both places. You could even share the same digital music player between multiple vehicles.

Digital music players connect to your car stereo just like a CD changer. Some are controlled by a dash-mounted controller, others use the CD changer controls of compatible head units. The Alpine HDA-5460 (Fig. 10-9) is an in-dash player, so all the controls and display are on the face of the unit itself. It fits in a single DIN slot, has a removable 16 GB hard drive

FIGURE 10-8

Kenwood KHD-C710 Music Keg digital music player. (*Courtesy of Kenwood.*)

FIGURE 10-9

Alpine HDA-5460 in-
dash digital music
player. (*Courtesy of
Alpine Electronics, Inc.*)

with a USB port for connection to your home computer, and will work
with any brand of head unit.

The audio outputs of music players are generally connected to the aux
inputs of the head unit. If the head unit lacks aux inputs, an FM modulator or aux input converter may be used. With compatible head units, the
audio is connected through the changer cable.

Digital Music Player Performance and Features

Table 10-4 shows important performance characteristics and features to
consider in a digital music player.

For most people, choosing the right model comes down to your docking system preference and whether a player can use the CD changer controls of your head unit. Other factors may also be important to you. If
you've got a huge music library, more memory is a plus. If you own a Mac,
the operating system requirement is critical. And features like WAV compatibility, WiFi file transfer, and voice index may strongly appeal to you.

Memory. The standard is 20 GB, which will store about 5,000 MP3 or
WMA files. The exact number of files depends on the length of songs and
the amount of compression used (higher compression produces smaller
files but lower sound quality). Some players support 80 GB or more.

MP3/WMA/WAV Compatibility. Most players support MP3 and WMA
files with compression bit-rates up to 320 kbps, as well as variable bit-rates.

TABLE 10-4

Performance and
Features of Digital
Music Players

Performance/Feature	Comments
Memory	20 GB is standard and will store about 5,000 songs.
MP3/WMA/WAV compatibility	Most players support MP3 and WMA, some also support WAV.
ID3 tag display	Standard feature. Displays the song title, album, artist, year, genre, and comments for MP3 files.
Docking system	Choose cartridge docking or player docking.
Computer OS requirement	Most are compatible with newer versions of Windows.
Controller	Some units use a dash-mounted controller, others use the CD changer controls of compatible head units.
Audio connection to head unit	Can be through aux inputs, FM modulator, or aux input converter. With compatible head units, connection is through the changer cable.
WiFi file transfer	Allows wireless transfer of music files from your computer to the digital music player in your car.
Voice index	Lets you browse your music library using speech technology, so you can keep your eyes on the road.
Mounting angle	Defines the range of mounting angles for proper operation.

Some players also support WAV files. WAV files are uncompressed music files that are truly CD quality and require no encoding, but are about 10 times larger than high-quality (128 kbps) MP3 files.

ID3 Tag Display. Standard feature. Displays the song title, album, artist, year, genre, and comments for MP3 files having ID3 tags and for WMA files having WMA tags. Later versions of ID3 (ID3v1.1, ID3v2) add even more information capabilities.

Docking System. Choose cartridge docking or player docking. (See explanation above.)

Computer OS Requirement. Most are compatible with newer versions of Windows, including Windows XP, Win2000, WinME, and Win98. Some are also compatible with Mac OS 9 and OS 8.

Controller. Some units use a dash-mounted controller; others use the CD changer controls of compatible head units. Dash-mounted controllers can be surface mounted or mounted in a DIN chassis adjacent to your head unit.

Audio Connection to Head Unit. The audio outputs of the player are generally connected to the aux inputs of the head unit. If the head unit lacks aux inputs, an FM modulator or aux input converter may be used. With compatible head units, the audio is connected through the changer cable.

WiFi File Transfer. Optional accessory with some players. Allows wireless transfer of music files from your computer to the digital music player in your car, up to 150 feet away. This method is slower than USB transfer, so it's most useful for updates rather than initial transfer of files. Requires that your computer has a WiFi wireless router.

Voice Index. Lets you browse your music library using speech technology, so you can keep your eyes on the road.

Mounting Angle. Defines the range of mounting angles for proper operation. Some specify mounting horizontally or vertically; others allow mounting at any angle.

Installation

Installing a CD changer, DVD changer, or digital music player is a matter of choosing a mounting location, mounting it and connecting it up. It's a good idea to understand the basics of installation beforehand, to help you choose the right changer or player, and so you know what to expect.

Choosing a Mounting Location

No single mounting location is best for every vehicle, changer, or person (Table 10-5). Think about where you might want to put your changer/player before shopping for one—it can determine the size and mounting angle range you'll need. Grab a tape measure and scope out your vehicle,

TABLE 10-5

Changer and Player
Mounting Locations

Mounting Location	Comments
Trunk	May be least vulnerable to theft.
	For changers, you need to change disc magazines from outside the vehicle. If your trunk is packed with luggage, changing disc magazines is a chore.
Under seat	Takes advantage of otherwise unused space.
	Susceptible to dirt, spills, and getting kicked from behind.
Console	For changers, lets you comfortably change discs from the driver's seat.
Glove compartment	Most glove compartments are too small to hold even a six-disc changer or compact digital music player.
	Usually requires an odd mounting angle, so choose a model that allows mounting over the entire 0- to 90° range.

then look at sizes of changers or players. The Crutchfield catalog has dimensions for every model that Crutchfield carries, so you can easily get an idea of what is possible.

Trunk. In the trunk, finding space for a changer or player is rarely a problem. In vehicles without a trunk release lever, the trunk provides the mounting location least vulnerable to theft. A disadvantage of trunk mounting changers is accessibility—you need to change disc magazines from outside the vehicle. If your trunk is packed with luggage, changing disc magazines is a chore. You also need to be careful about the changer or player getting wet if you open the trunk when it's raining.

If you want to mount your changer/player at an angle (against the sloping front of the trunk, for example), make sure you choose a model that allows mounting over the entire 0- to 90° range.

Under Seat. The beauty of mounting a changer/player under a front seat is that it takes advantage of otherwise unused space. The amount of space under a seat varies quite a bit from vehicle to vehicle. When measuring for space, you need to check all the possible positions of the seat for interference, including front-to-back position, tilt, and height settings. A disadvantage of mounting under the seat is its susceptibility to dirt, spills, and getting kicked from behind.

> **Tip:** When choosing a spot to mount a changer or player, be sure you can easily remove the disc magazine/hard-drive cartridge. This is a common oversight for under-seat mounting.

Console.   For changers, console mounting lets you comfortably change discs from the driver's seat. Space is tight, so you may need to choose a six-disc changer. The obvious disadvantage of this location is the loss of most of the useable console space.

Glove Compartment.   Most glove compartments are too small to hold even a six-disc changer or compact digital music player. If your vehicle is one of the select few, glove compartment installation provides convenient access to the changer or player. Glove compartment installation usually requires an odd mounting angle, so choose a changer that allows mounting over the entire 0- to 90° range.

Mounting

Almost all changers and players can be mounted at 0 and 90° (90° means "face up"). Many allow mounting over the entire 0- to 90° range. You'll need to adjust a changer's suspension to match the mounting angle. Check the owner's manual for instructions.

Make sure the mounting surface you've chosen is strong enough to support the changer/player firmly, so it can't rip loose during a sudden stop. If you are mounting under the rear deck, make sure it won't interfere with the torsion spring of the trunk lid. Before you choose an exact mounting spot, observe how the spring moves as you close the lid. Don't mount your changer anywhere it would be subjected to direct sunlight or rain.

When drilling holes for mounting brackets, be careful not to drill into the gas tank or a brake line.

Connecting

If you're using the changer controls of a compatible head unit, you'll need to run the changer cable to the head unit and plug it in the back. You'll have to pull the head unit out to do this. If you are using the CD changer controls of a factory head unit to control a changer, you'll need to insert an OEM interface CD changer converter between the aftermarket CD changer and the factory head unit.

If you're mounting your changer/player in the trunk, run the changer cable down one side of your car, along the door sill. Look for a hole to pass the cable from the trunk into the passenger compartment. You may have to remove the back seat to find it. To conceal the cable under the carpeting, you'll have to take off the door sill plate (or plates).

If you're mounting the changer under a front seat, do not run the cable too close to a seat rail where it could be cut or pinched when the seat is moved.

If you have an amp in the trunk, run the CD changer cable on the side opposite the amp's 12-volt power cable. You'll be less likely to introduce engine noise into your system. Secure any excess cable with wire ties so it doesn't end up in the way of the pedals or hood latch.

After you plug the changer cable into the head unit, test the changer thoroughly before you fully reinstall your head unit.

Changers/Players with FM Modulators. Changers or players with FM modulators require a few additional connections. These can include battery +12 volts and ignition/accessory +12 volts. The best place to find these power sources is at your fuse panel. Use fuse taps at appropriate locations in the panel. You'll also need to connect the black ground wire to the metal chassis of the vehicle with a screw.

Your factory antenna cable will need to plug into the FM modulator (usually integrated into the changer, or a separate module in some units).

A cable from the FM modulator also needs to plug into the head unit's antenna jack. When deciding where to mount a separate FM modulator module, be sure its antenna cable will reach your head unit's antenna input. Use cable ties to secure any slack in the antenna lead, so it can't fall down and interfere with your pedals.

Try to make the selector switch for the FM modulator frequency as accessible as possible. (Some models allow the frequency to be changed from the dash-mounted control panel.) If the selector switch will be difficult to access, set it before you mount the unit. Determine which of the available FM frequencies is least likely to be used by a strong local radio signal, and choose that one.

Video and Surround Hookup for DVD Changers. In addition to the controller and stereo audio connections required for all changers and players, DVD changers require a video connection as well. Depending on your system, you'll need to connect the video output of the changer to the video input of your head unit or the video input of your monitor.

If your system is equipped for 5.1 channel sound, you'll also need to connect the optical output of the changer to your surround-sound processor.

Controlling Multiple Changers Using a Multi-Changer Adapter.
By using a multi-changer adapter to share the changer port on your head
unit, you can connect multiple changers and players to your system and
control and listen to them all through a single head unit. For example,
you could connect a CD changer and digital music player to your head
unit or multiple CD changers.

You must use a multi-changer adapter that's compatible with your
head unit, and all the changers and players must be individually compatible with the head unit as well. Some multi-changer adapters allow two
changer/players to be connected, others allow as many as seven
changer/players by daisy-chaining adapters. MCAs are available for Kenwood, Sony, Alpine, and other head units.

CHAPTER 11

Accessories

The level of hype for accessories is even higher than that for car stereo as a whole. This section will help you separate science from snake oil when it comes to items such as power line caps, premium speaker wire, and sound deadeners.

Power Line Capacitors

The term *power line capacitors* refers to one or more large capacitors (0.5 farads or greater) connected to an amplifier's power wire (Fig. 11-1). The purpose of using these is to provide a reserve power source from which the amplifier can rapidly draw power when it needs it (such as during a deep bass note). The electrical theory is that when the amplifier attempts to draw a large amount of current, not only will the battery be relatively slow to respond, but the voltage at the amplifier will be a little lower than the voltage at the battery itself (this is called *line drop*). A capacitor at the amplifier will try to stabilize the voltage level at the amplifier, dumping current into the amplifier as needed.

Should You Install a Power Line Cap?

Considering the relatively high cost of power line caps, you should first make sure that you have done everything possible to reduce the voltage

FIGURE 11-1

Power line caps.
(*Courtesy of Parts Express.*)

drop between the battery and the amplifier. This means keeping power and ground cables as short as possible, using the proper wire gauge, and soldering crimped connectors to reduce their resistance.

If you've done what you can to reduce line drops, and your dash lights still dim every time your subwoofer hits a strong bass note with the music turned up and your engine running, a power line cap could help you out.

Choosing the Right Cap

The commonly accepted rule of thumb for determining proper capacitor size is 1 farad per kilowatt of amplifier power. For example, a system running at 500 watts would need a 0.5-farad (or 500,000-μF) capacitor. Choose a cap with a working voltage (WVDC) rating of 20 volts. Anything less than this is risky, and anything more is a waste of money.

You should consider the Equivalent Series Resistance (ESR) of the capacitor. Capacitors should have an ESR less than that shown in Table 11-1 for maximum effectiveness of the cap.

Equivalent Series Inductance (ESL) is also important, because it dominates the impedance of the capacitor at the high frequencies used by switching power supplies in high-power amps. For a capacitor to provide a benefit at high frequencies, it should have an ESL lower than that of the power cables to the amp. A reasonable value is 1 microhenry. Unfortunately, ESL is not normally advertised.

Another factor to consider is temperature rating. Power line caps have a temperature rating anywhere from 85 to 105°C. No one expects to operate a power line capacitor at temperatures near the boiling point of water, but temperature rating is actually an accurate indicator of the useful lifespan of your power line cap. This is because high temperatures accelerate the process of the electrolyte inside drying out, reducing the capacitance and dramatically increasing the ESR. A cap with a high temperature rat-

TABLE 11-1

Maximum Recommended ESR for Power Line Caps

Capacitance	Maximum ESR
0.5 farad	4 mΩ
1 farad	2 mΩ
2 farads	1 mΩ

ing is less susceptible to this process and has a longer lifespan. Opt for a cap with a temperature rating of 95°C or higher.

If cost is no object, you can buy electronically monitored power line caps. These provide an indication of the state of charge on an LED bar graph display. Some electronically monitored models also provide reverse polarity protection in case you connect the cap backwards.

Installation

If you connect a power line cap backwards you will destroy it (the electrolyte will ooze out), so double-check your polarities before making any connections. To install a capacitor, you should not simply attach it to the power and ground wires near your amplifier, as it will draw a very large amount of current from the battery and blow the fuse. Instead, precharge the cap using this procedure:

1. Connect the negative lead to the negative terminal of the cap, but do not connect the positive lead to the positive terminal yet.

2. Insert an automotive lightbulb between the positive lead and the positive terminal of the capacitor to pre-charge the cap. When the lightbulb goes out, the capacitor is done charging.

3. Now connect the positive lead to the positive terminal of the cap.

Battery Savers and Monitors

If you like to crank your stereo for extended periods with the engine off, then you need to be concerned about draining the battery past the point where you can start the car. One deep discharge also sacrifices from one-fourth to one-third the life of your battery.

Some newer cars may keep the battery's voltage from dipping too low, but if your car just sits there as the battery drains, you might consider a battery saver. A battery saver is a computerized switch that automatically disconnects the battery before it's drained to its no-go threshold. Open a door or press a reset button (depending on brand) to reconnect the battery after the battery saver disconnects it. Battery savers are mounted on the side of the battery, and require only a wrench for installation.

A leading consumer test magazine compared the PriorityStart! battery saver (about $80; Fig. 11-2) to another brand. Testers simulated a situation in which the driver had left the lights on, then tried to start the car at 0°F. PriorityStart! left the battery with plenty of power to start the engine, but the battery capacity left by the other brand was sometimes inadequate to start a car.

Another factor important to owners of high-powered car stereos is the contact resistance of a battery saver. This directly translates to voltage drop that can rob your stereo of headroom. The contact resistance of Priority-Start! is less than 1 milliohm, which would cause less than a 25-mV line drop when using a 100-watt per channel amp. The contact resistance of some battery savers may be as high as 50 milliohms, which could cause a line drop of over 1 volt when using a 100-watt per channel amp.

Another option is the "Battery Guard" (about $40; Fig. 11-3) from PAC (Pacific Accessory Corporation). It's a battery saver specifically designed for car audio. It uses a microprocessor to precisely monitor the battery voltage. When the voltage drops below 11.6 volts, it turns the sound system off. When the battery is recharged to 12.4 volts, it turns the head unit back on. An advantage of this approach is that power to the rest of the car is never disrupted, so you won't need to reset your clock or lose information stored by your car's computer. A disadvantage is that you aren't protected against other sources of battery drainage, like accidentally leaving the dome light on overnight.

A cheaper alternative is the "Bat Alert" battery monitor (about $15) from PAC. (See Fig. 11-4.) This device is mounted under the dash and connected to the ignition/accessory 12-volt supply. Its LED is green for bat-

FIGURE 11-2
PriorityStart!
mounted on battery.
(*Courtesy of BLI International.*)

tery voltages above 12 volts, yellow between 11.9 and 11.5 volts, and red
below that. A red LED tells you it's time to start your engine or hook up
a charger. The disadvantage of this approach is that you need to keep your
eye on the LED.

Premium Speaker Wire

If you believe the advertising hype, premium speaker wire offers you greater
overall depth and clarity, more dynamic range, and tighter, deeper bass.

What the advertising doesn't tell you is that these benefits come from
using the proper wire gauge rather than from time-correct windings,
magnetic flux tube construction, linear polyethylene dielectric, and so
on. If you use the proper wire gauge, then the benefits of premium
speaker wire are purely cosmetic.

For speaker wiring, the dominating factor for selecting wire gauge is resistance. For 4-ohm speakers, the speaker wires should have a resistance of less than 0.1 ohms for best performance. Values higher than this can start to affect bass response by allowing the impedance characteristic of the speaker to come into play. A 4-ohm speaker can easily have a 20-ohm impedance peak at its resonant frequency.

Resistance is strictly a matter of wire gauge and length. Table 11-2 provides minimum recommended wire gauges, depending on wire length, for all power amps. The wire lengths shown in Table 11-2 guarantee a resistance of less than 0.1 ohms. Using thicker wire (smaller gauge) and shorter lengths will give you lower resistance.

If you are running 2-ohm loads, subtract 2 from the recommended wire gauge in the chart. For example, use #10-2 up to 30 feet.

Premium Patch Cables (Interconnects)

Interconnects is just a fancy name for patch cables, to make you feel better for paying a premium price. What you get for the extra money is largely cosmetic.

Factors such as characteristic impedance and low-capacitance dielectric just don't make any difference in audio patch cables. These factors become important at higher frequencies, in applications involving extremely long cables, or where impedance matching is used. None of these apply here. There is no scientific evidence that oxygen-free copper conductors provide any audible benefit whatsoever.

Gold-plated connectors do provide an additional degree of corrosion resistance, but you can buy patch cables with gold-plated ends without spending a fortune.

TABLE 11-2

Minimum Recommended Gauge for Speaker Wire

Amplifier	Speaker Wire	
All wattages	up to 12′	#16-2
	up to 20′	#14-2
	up to 30′	#12-2

One area where there can be an important difference between cables is noise immunity, especially in the noisy automotive environment (Fig. 11-5). This is of most concern where:

- Long cables are used (such as between the head unit and the trunk)

- A low (less than 2-volt) preamp-level signal source is involved

- High-power (greater than 100W × 2) amplifiers are used

Unfortunately, cable manufacturers don't directly specify noise immunity. The best you can do is guess, based on terms like *double-shielded* or *100% foil shield*. Experiments by the Autosound 2000 test lab provide evidence that unshielded twisted-pair cables may furnish the best noise immunity in the automotive environment. Note: System noise performance is often determined by factors other than the type of cable used. See Chap. 12 for more details.

A useful feature of some premium cables is an extra embedded wire for remote amp turn-on. This saves you from having to run a separate wire from the head unit to the power amp.

Portable Music Player Head Unit Adapters

A head unit adapter lets you listen to your portable MP3 player through your car stereo. This is a good solution if you want to keep your head unit but it lacks aux inputs. If your head unit doesn't play CDs (or it doesn't play MP3 files recorded on CD-Rs), a head unit adapter can be

FIGURE 11-5
Premium patch cables. (*Courtesy of Parts Express.*)

TABLE 11-3

Portable Music
Player Head Unit
Adapters

Adapter	Comments
Cassette adapter	Requires cassette head unit—wired solution.
	Tape deck transport is active during use and subject to normal wear.
FM transmitter	Uses FM radio—wireless solution.
	Very limited transmission range.
Auxiliary input converter	Requires head unit with CD changer controls—wired solution.
	Requires installation.

Tip: If you plan to use a portable music player in your car on a regular basis, you will want to use a power converter to save on batteries. These plug into the lighter jack and convert 12 volts to the voltage needed by your player.

Important: Power converters not designed to go with your music player may not be compatible, even if the connectors are the same. Always check for the correct voltage AND correct polarity before plugging a power adapter into your player. Failure to do this can result in a destroyed music player.

used with a portable CD player. Head unit adapters are often a great solution for leased or rental cars.

There are three types of adapters available: cassette adapters, FM transmitters, and auxiliary input converters.

Cassette Adapters

A cassette adapter looks like a cassette tape that it has a cable coming out with a plug on the end (Fig. 11-6). These adapters are inserted into your tape deck like a normal tape and the plug is inserted into the headphone jack of your portable CD player. Cassette adapters are available for less than $20.

A disadvantage of using cassette adapters is that the tape deck transport mechanism is active and subject to normal wear during use with the adapter. (The tape head may or may not be subject to wear, depending on the design of the adapter.)

Some inexpensive cassette adapters may not work with all tape decks. For example, Delco tape decks will shut down if they sense that there is

FIGURE 11-6

RCA cassette adapter. (*Courtesy of MCM Electronics.*)

abnormal tape motion—not all adapters have what it takes to fool the deck. Choose a reputable brand of adapter to be safe.

FM Transmitters

This adapter is basically a miniature radio station (Fig. 11-7). It converts the audio from your music player's headphone jack to an FM stereo signal picked up by your head unit. These are available for about $30 from Radio Shack and other sources.

Because of the heavy compression used by commercial broadcasters to reach the maximum audience, the audio quality using an adapter can be much better than a normal FM broadcast.

The biggest problem with FM transmitters is their very limited transmission distance. Because of strict FCC limits on maximum transmitted signal strength, their effective range is quite limited. For some vehicles, this doesn't present a problem. For others, it's virtually impossible to achieve good reception.

In addition to portable FM transmitters, there are hard-wired FM modulators that mount behind the dash. These connect through your car's antenna cable for more reliable FM transmission, and use 12-volt power from the car so you don't need to worry about batteries.

Auxiliary Input Converters

If your head unit has CD changer controls, an auxiliary input converter can often be used to provide one or more sets of aux inputs. Aux input converters are available for most aftermarket and many factory head units. The Aux2Car (Fig. 11-8) by Peripheral Electronics is a universal aux input converter, programmable for most vehicle applications using internal dip switches. Low-cost vehicle-specific harnesses are available separately.

FIGURE 11-7
irock! Beamit 450FM FM stereo transmitter. (*Courtesy of FID.*)

FIGURE 11-8

Aux2Car universal auxiliary input converter. (*Courtesy of Peripheral Electronics.*)

Some aux input converters require that a CD changer be connected, some require that no CD changer be connected, and some can be used either way, so be sure to read the fine print before buying.

Installing an aux input converter may require pulling the head unit out to connect to the CD changer port. (In some cars you can reach behind the head unit from the passenger side to plug the converter in.) Power and ground connections may also be required.

If you have an iPod, Peripheral Electronics' iPOD2CAR is specifically made to connect it to most factory and aftermarket head units. What's unique about the iPOD2CAR is that it lets you use the CD changer controls of your head unit (and steering wheel controls, if you have them) to control your iPod. It will even charge your iPod's battery.

Antennas and Antenna Boosters

If your car already has a working antenna, then there's probably no reason to replace it. The two exceptions to this are if you have an embedded windshield antenna or if you want to convert to a motorized antenna.

FIGURE 11-9

iPOD2CAR auxiliary input converter for iPod. (*Courtesy of Peripheral Electronics.*)

Embedded Windshield Antennas

Embedded windshield antennas keep your car's body lines clean and they can't get broken off by vandals or at car washes, but they are very directional. This means their performance is good in some directions and poor in others. If you want to pull in weaker stations from all directions, a mast-type antenna is a must.

Another factor with embedded antennas is window tinting. Metallic window-tint films can degrade the performance of embedded windshield antennas. Not all window-tint films are metallic, and there are several degrees of metallic film. The more metal in the film, the greater the degradation in reception. If you have a tinted windshield and your FM reception seems poor, consider switching to a mast antenna. And if you're planning to have your windshield tinted and have an embedded antenna, specify a high-quality non-metallic film.

Motorized Antennas

Motorized antennas (Fig. 11-10) are automatically raised when the radio is on and lowered when it's off. They keep your car's body lines clean, provide good reception in all directions, and only get broken off if you forget to turn off your radio at the car wash. The performance of motorized antennas is comparable to that of fixed mast antennas.

Because of the additional bulk of the motor assembly, it may be difficult or impossible to install a motorized antenna in the front fender of every vehicle. If you mount it in the rear fender, you'll need to use an antenna extension cable and run it under the carpet to the receiver. Some other disadvantages are cost and reliability. The expected life of a motorized antenna is only five to ten years.

FIGURE 11-10

Motorized antenna.
(*Courtesy of MCM Electronics.*)

Antenna Installation

If you are replacing an existing antenna, attach a length of thin wire to the end of the old antenna cable before you pull it out. As you pull the cable through the car, the wire will snake through the cable's mounting path. Once you've pulled the cable all the way out, attach the wire to the end of the new antenna's cable, then have someone feed the new cable as you pull the wire back into the car.

If you're installing an antenna in a vehicle that didn't have one before, scout out the antenna location and cable path the car's designers intended. Look for a rubber or plastic plug on the front fender. Another likely location on Japanese cars is the front pillar between the windshield and front door. Do not run the antenna cable through a hole with other wiring or you will risk picking up interference from those wires.

In the unlikely event that you don't find an existing mounting hole, you'll need to drill one. Check where other cars of the same make have theirs. Once you've chosen a location, protect the area with a piece of duct tape. Use a center punch to mark it and drill a ⅛-inch pilot hole. Gradu-

Antenna Adapters

If you are adding or changing an antenna or replacing a factory head unit, you'll quickly discover that every antenna doesn't directly connect to every head unit. That's where antenna adapters come in. Aftermarket head units and antennas all use the standard Motorola connector, but many factory systems do not (Table 11-4). Adapters are available to adapt aftermarket head units to factory antennas and also to adapt aftermarket antennas to factory head units.

TABLE 11-4

Types of Antenna Connectors

Type	Comments
Standard (Motorola)	Used on all aftermarket equipment.
GM mini	Used on 1988 and up GM.
Ford	Used on some 1995 and up, usually for radios with DSP controls.
Chrysler	Used on 2002 and up Chrysler/Jeep.
Nissan	Diversity (two-antenna) system.
Volkswagen/Euro	Factory antenna needs 12 volts to turn on impedance-matching circuit.

ally enlarge the hole with successively larger bits to reduce the chance of the bit slipping. Check the hole as you approach the correct size to avoid drilling too large a hole.

Antenna Boosters

Antenna boosters are low-noise amplifiers designed to improve weak signal reception. They are inserted between the antenna and the head unit by plugging the antenna into the booster and the booster output into the head unit.

Antenna boosters can improve *sensitivity,* but not *selectivity.* What this means is that if you are trying to pick up a weak signal in the city (where there are many nearby strong signals), a booster won't help a bit. On the other hand, if you are out in the country trying to pick up a weak signal among other weak signals, a booster might help. How much it might help depends on how good the booster is and how bad your head unit front end is. A cheap booster can actually degrade the weak signal performance of a top-notch receiver.

Sound-Deadening Materials

Sound-deadening materials are used by all automobile manufacturers to reduce the ambient noise level in the passenger compartment. Effective sound deadening means you don't need to turn up the volume control as much to overcome road noise. It also means you'll be able to experience more of the dynamic range available with CDs and even cassettes—you'll be able to hear more of the subtle details in the music. Unlike other accessories, sound deadening provides a benefit even when the stereo is off, by reducing driver fatigue due to noise.

Whether or not a particular vehicle would benefit from additional sound deadening depends on how much soundproofing was done by the vehicle manufacturer. Luxury cars tend to have lots of soundproofing, and are not normally good candidates for improvement. Less expensive cars, older cars, and sports cars are better candidates.

In addition to reducing road noise, sound-deadening materials can provide other sonic benefits. They can improve the sound of your system by reducing unwanted panel vibrations caused by your speakers. By apply-

ing sound-deadening material to door panels, the audible vibrations
caused by door speakers are greatly reduced. And if you have a subwoofer
in your trunk, you can reduce the sound loss through the trunk walls
and actually increase the amount of bass you hear by lining the trunk
lid and walls with sound-deadening material.

Materials generally run $1 to $5 per square foot. Dynamat™, Stinger
Roadkill™, and Accumat™ (Fig. 11-11) are some of the popular product
lines. Each line contains a number of materials targeted for specific applications such as on doors, floor panels, trunks, or under the hood. Most
materials take the form of adhesive-backed sheets, but spray-on products
are also available for hard-to-reach areas.

When trying to reduce road noise, it's important to focus your efforts
on the weak links. Otherwise you'll be spending your time plugging pin-
holes when there's a hole the size of a grapefruit nearby. Determining the
weak link can be difficult, but try to identify the source and location of
noise as you drive on the highway. Try to judge whether engine noise,
noise from the tires on the pavement, or wind noise is dominating. Is
most of the noise coming through the floor, through the doors, or elsewhere? In many ways this is a job for an acoustic engineer with sophisticated measuring equipment and lots of time. In addition, many noise
problems, such as wind noise due to the aerodynamics of the car, are difficult or impossible to correct yourself.

The advertising for noise-deadening products generally claims that
improvements of 3 dB are possible. This is a noticeable improvement for
most people. You need to judge whether the cost of material and your
time are worth it.

CHAPTER 12

Battling Noise

Most people don't think about noise until after they've installed their system and experience a problem. For basic low-power systems, noise is less likely to be a problem, and this is a reasonable approach. But if you're installing a high-power multiamp system, the best time to think about avoiding noise is when you're planning your system.

This chapter explains the common causes of automotive noise problems, how to avoid them, and how to fix them. Fixing noise problems can be frustrating, time-consuming work. Following the techniques explained in this chapter can help you systematically solve problems and eliminate much of the frustration.

NOTE   *Turn-on and turn-off pops associated with added amplifiers are covered in Chap. 7, "Amplifiers and Amplifier Projects."*

Noise Basics

This section explains some basic principles of noise and the important noise mechanisms in car audio. Reducing noise is a complex subject and many highly technical books have been devoted to it. Understanding the basics will go a long way toward helping you reduce noise when you design, install, and adjust your system or have to troubleshoot it.

What Is Noise?

Noise is the undesired sound you hear during (what should be) silent passages in music or other programming.

Thermal noise sounds like the hiss you hear between stations on your radio. It occurs due to random electron motion in electronic components. It's called thermal noise because the amount of electron motion (and therefore noise) depends on the temperature.

Induced noise can sound like clicking, popping, whirring, buzzing, whistling, or whining. What it sounds like is often a good clue as to its source. Induced noise always has a *source* (such as the alternator), a *channel* (such as a power wire), and a *receiver* (such as an amp). This is important to remember because induced noise problems can be tackled at the source, channel, receiver, or some combination of the three.

Signal-to-Noise Ratio

When dealing with noise, it usually makes sense to think in terms of the signal-to-noise ratio (SNR) rather than the absolute noise level. The signal-to-noise ratio is a measure of the degree of contamination of a signal by noise.

The signal-to-noise ratio is the signal voltage level divided by the noise voltage level. This number is usually expressed in decibels. For example, a 1-volt signal contaminated by 1 millivolt (0.001 volt) of noise would have a signal-to-noise ratio of 1000:1 or 60 dB. To put this in perspective, the signal-to-noise ratio of a Dolby B cassette recording is usually between 60 and 65 dB. Every 10-dB improvement in signal-to-noise ratio (higher is better) sounds like cutting the noise volume in half.

An important property of the signal-to-noise ratio is that it is not changed by amplification or attenuation. For example, suppose a 1-volt signal contaminated by 1 millivolt of noise is fed into an amplifier with a voltage gain of 10. The amplifier output would have 10 volts of signal contaminated by 10 millivolts of noise. The SNR is 1000:1 (or 60 dB) at the input as well as the output of the amp.

Signal Level and Signal-to-Noise Ratio

Even though the signal-to-noise ratio is not directly changed by amplification or attenuation, amplification and attenuation play crucial roles in determining the overall system signal-to-noise ratio. That's because the signal level at each point in a system determines the noise immunity at that point. The higher the signal level, the higher the noise immunity at that point.

When it comes to adjusting your system or choosing equipment, higher signal levels are always better for noise. But you need to make sure that levels aren't set too high, or you'll end up with distortion. The proper procedures are explained later on, in the section on installation and adjustment.

Figure 12-1 shows how high preamp levels improve noise immunity.

Systems (a) and (b) are identical, except that (a) uses a head unit with a 1-volt preamp output level and (b) uses a head unit with a 4-volt level. In both cases, we'll assume that 1 millivolt of noise is induced into the cable

FIGURE 12-1

How high preamp levels improve noise immunity.

(a) head unit with 1V preamp level:

(b) head unit with 4V preamp level:

between the head unit and amp. We'll also assume that in both cases the amp level controls were properly set to provide full output power with full input voltage from the head unit.

The signal level coming out of each head unit determines the noise immunity at the cables. Even though the induced noise into each cable is the same for both systems, the signal-to-noise ratio of system (*b*) is 4 times better at the amp input, due to the higher signal level. Since the signal-to-noise ratios are unchanged by the amplifiers, system (*b*) provides a 4 times (12 dB) better signal-to-noise ratio at the speaker.

Why High-Power Systems Are More Noise Prone

Figure 12-2 shows why high-power systems are more prone to noise. This explains why it's important to think about avoiding noise beforehand when you're planning a high-power multiamp system.

Diagram (*a*) shows a 50-watt system with a head unit having a 1-volt preamp level. Diagram (*b*) shows a 200-watt system with the identical head unit, but a more powerful amp. In both cases, we'll assume that 1 millivolt of noise is induced into the cable between the head unit and amp. We'll also assume that in both cases the amp level controls were properly set to provide full output power with full input voltage from the head unit.

FIGURE 12-2

Why high-power
systems are more
prone to noise.

(a) 50 watt amp operating at full volume:

(b) 200 watt amp operating at full volume:

(c) 200 watt amp operating at 50 watt volume level:

Since the signal level coming out of each head unit is 1 volt and the noise induced into each cable is 1 millivolt, both systems have a signal-to-noise ratio of 1000:1 (or 60 dB). The difference between the two systems is strictly output power. With a 1-volt input, the 50-watt system provides 50 watts to the speaker and the 200-watt system provides 200 watts to the speaker. This makes perfect sense, because we expect to be able to achieve full amplifier power with full input voltage from the head unit.

Now let's see what happens when we adjust the volume control of the 200-watt system to match the output power of the 50-watt system. This is shown in diagram (c). (To produce a 50-watt output, a fourfold reduction in power is needed. Because power is proportional to voltage squared, a twofold reduction in voltage at the head unit is required.) Since the signal coming out of the head unit is now 500 mV, and the noise induced in the cable remains at 1 mV, the signal-to-noise ratio drops to 500:1 or 54 dB. Thus, the signal-to-noise ratio of the high-power system is inferior *when comparing at the same output power.*

Of course, the higher-power system is capable of 4 times more output power, but for normal listening levels you pay a price in noise immunity.

Differential Versus Single-Ended Signals

Using differential (or balanced) signals provides a huge improvement in noise immunity. It's no wonder that all Bose and Ford Premium sound systems rely on differential signaling to provide clean signal transfer.

Unfortunately, most aftermarket equipment is single-ended. It is possible to buy a differential head unit and amp. You can also buy a differential line driver/receiver for use with single-ended equipment. Another often overlooked possibility: The speaker-level outputs of high-power head units are differential. Using the speaker-level inputs of an amp or crossover with true differential inputs gives you a big noise advantage.

Here's how differential signaling works (Fig. 12-3): The differential outputs of a head unit (or differential line driver) provide two equal but opposite versions of the music signal—an inverted version and a noninverted version. At the differential inputs of the amplifier (or differential receiver), the two versions of the signal are subtracted. Since any noise presumably affects both versions of the signal the same, subtraction causes cancellation of the noise. Because one of the music signals was inverted, subtraction also results in a music signal that is twice the original signal.

Theoretically, differential signaling can result in complete cancellation of induced noise. In practice, nonidentical noise into both wires and imbalances in the subtracter limit the effectiveness of the cancellation process. It's very important in differential applications to make sure both wires are receiving identical noise—twisted-pair cabling is often used for this purpose.

FIGURE 12-3

How differential signaling works.

Ground Loops

Ground loops are one of the major causes of system noise problems in vehicles. It's important to understand the structure of ground loops and why they are an invitation to noise.

Basically, a ground loop is a loop formed by redundant ground wiring. For example, ground loops are formed by the chassis ground and signal ground wiring between a head unit and amp as shown in Fig. 12-4.

Why is a ground loop a problem? One of the fundamental laws of electromagnetics (Faraday's law) states that when a changing magnetic field passes through a loop of wire, a voltage is induced in the wire. The automotive environment is *loaded* with changing magnetic fields (and they're all potential noise sources). When a changing magnetic field passes through a ground loop, a noise voltage is induced across the ground conductor.

How do you fight against ground loops? For one thing, avoid them as much as possible. Amps, equalizers, and crossovers with true differential inputs (either preamp level or speaker level) break ground loops because they do not create an input connection to ground. IMPORTANT: This strategy applies to single-ended source applications too—not just differential. You don't need a differential output to take advantage of the ground loop breaking ability of a differential input.

You can also buy true differential line output converters and preamp-level ground loop isolators for installation at the input of an amp having ground-referenced inputs.

For short runs between two pieces of equipment, it usually suffices to make the loop area of ground loops as small as possible. This is because the amount of noise voltage induced in the loop depends on the size of the loop. Make the loop small by minimizing both the length and width

FIGURE 12-4

Anatomy of a ground loop.

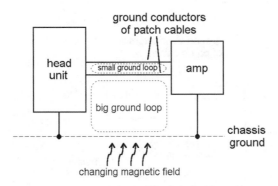

of the loop. (Minimizing the width of the loop implies running your cables close to the chassis ground.) The amount of noise voltage induced in the loop also depends on the strength of the changing magnetic field through the loop. This means keeping the loop away from noise sources such as motors and other wiring.

Common Ground Impedance

In the preceding discussion, you may have wondered about simply cutting redundant ground conductors as a cure for ground loops. In the previous example, you could have cut the ground conductors of the patch cables and used chassis ground for signal ground as well. This would have eliminated the ground loop problem, but it would have introduced another noise problem—one due to common ground impedance (Fig. 12-5).

The chassis ground is shared by virtually every accessory and electrical device in the vehicle. This means that return currents from all these potential noise sources flow through the chassis. Even though the chassis resistance is quite low, it's not zero. Return currents from potential noise sources flow through the resistance between two points on the chassis and produce a noise voltage between them. In this example, the noise voltage would directly couple to the inputs of the amplifier.

As Richard Chinn of AudioControl likes to say, "Ground isn't ground!"

Power Supply Noise

Another way that noise can find its way into your stereo system is through the 12-volt power supply.

FIGURE 12-5

Common ground impedance.

ground conductors of patch cables cut

head unit

amp

resistance between two distant points on chassis

chassis ground

return currents from potential noise sources

The alternator is a primary source of noise on the 12-volt line. It supplies raw electrical power for the vehicle and is used to charge the battery. It produces alternating current pulses that are rectified and coarsely regulated. The battery provides strong filtering action for alternator-based noise, but there is still plenty to go around.

Electrical accessories can also introduce large amounts of noise onto the 12-volt line. Accessories actually create noise on the 12-volt line by *using* power. This is analogous to the water system in your home, where flushing a toilet causes a pressure drop in the shower. Devices that switch large amounts of supply current off and on are prime offenders. Good examples are motors, horns, turn signals, and brake lights.

Car stereo equipment is designed to be somewhat immune to noise on the power line, but high levels of power line noise can cause objectionable noise at equipment outputs. All equipment is not created equal with respect to power line noise immunity, but manufacturers generally don't give you any specs to compare in this area.

Power supply noise problems are usually dealt with by adding an appropriate power line filter at either the source of the noise problem or the equipment that is affected by it.

Buying Equipment

When it comes to buying equipment with an eye toward good noise immunity, the most important factors are high preamp levels and ground loop prevention. Choose amps, crossovers, and equalizers with differential inputs (speaker level or preamp level) for ground loop isolation. For competition-caliber systems, there are a number of specialty products to keep even the most complex and powerful systems quiet.

Head Units

If you plan to use the preamp-level outputs of your head unit, the most important thing you can do to improve noise immunity is to choose a model with high preamp output levels. (Alternately, you can use the speaker-level outputs of the head unit for driving an amp, crossover, or equalizer. The high voltage levels and differential drive provided by high-power speaker-level outputs is actually superior to 5-volt preamp outputs for noise immunity.)

FIGURE 12-6

Eclipse CD8053 balanced output head unit. (*Courtesy of Eclipse.*)

Unfortunately, most aftermarket head units have single-ended preamp-level outputs. An exception is the Eclipse CD8053 (Fig. 12-6). You can select unbalanced (8 volts) or balanced (16 volts) preamp output signals for a better signal-to-noise ratio. (Using the balanced signal requires an amp that accepts balanced inputs.)

Amplifiers

When it comes to buying an amp, there are two factors to consider from the standpoint of system noise. The first is whether the amp has differential inputs and the second is the amp's signal-to-noise ratio.

Differential inputs are the key to avoiding ground loops with both differential and single-ended sources. Both preamp-level and speaker-level inputs can be single-ended or differential, so make sure the inputs you plan to use are differential. Differential inputs should be considered a must for high-power amps located more than a foot or two from a preamp-level component feeding them. More and more amplifiers now feature differential inputs to reduce noise—there's no good reason not to choose a model with this feature.

An amp's signal-to-noise ratio spec is of lesser importance. Almost all decent amplifiers have about 100 dB signal-to-noise ratio, which is more than enough for most applications. In most systems, the signal-to-noise ratio is dominated by induced noise prior to the amp or the SNR of the source itself.

Crossovers and Equalizers

As with amps, the two factors to consider from the standpoint of system noise are differential inputs and signal-to-noise ratio.

Differential inputs are the key to avoiding ground loops with both differential and single-ended sources. Both preamp-level and speaker-level inputs can be single-ended or differential, so make sure the inputs you plan to use are differential. If the crossover or equalizer you like doesn't have differential inputs, you may need to resort to a ground loop isolator later on.

The signal-to-noise ratio spec is of lesser importance. Almost all decent crossovers and equalizers have signal-to-noise ratios of about 100 dB, which is more than enough for most applications. In most systems, the signal-to-noise ratio is dominated by induced noise prior to the crossover or the SNR of the source itself.

Cables

The type of cable you use can affect the level of induced noise. Cable noise immunity is most important where:

▪ Long cables are used (such as between the head unit and the trunk).

▪ A low (less than 2 volts) preamp-level signal source is involved.

▪ High-power (greater than 100W × 2) amplifiers are used.

Unfortunately, cable manufacturers don't directly specify noise immunity. The best you can do is guess, based on terms like *double-shielded* or *100% foil shield*. Experiments by the Autosound 2000 test lab provide evidence that unshielded twisted-pair cables may furnish the best noise immunity in the automotive environment.

Line Drivers

A line driver boosts the signal level and often provides a balanced output, both of which greatly improve noise immunity of a preamp-level signal over a long cable. AudioControl's Overdrive™ line driver (Fig. 12-7) does both of these and more.

FIGURE 12-7
AudioControl
Overdrive line driver.
(*Courtesy of*
AudioControl.)

The Overdrive provides differential inputs for ground loop isolation, adjustable gain up to 24 dB, and a peak signal voltage of 13.5 volts. It is capable of driving the high capacitive loads presented by some cables.

Installation and Level Adjustment

Proper installation and level adjustment are just as important as choosing the right equipment in achieving good noise immunity. Proper installation minimizes the induction of noise into your system and proper level adjustment minimizes its audibility.

Equipment Placement

When deciding where to put each of the components in your system, noise immunity considerations aren't likely to be near the top of your list. But try to keep noise pickup in mind, especially where you have flexibility in mounting locations.

From the standpoint of noise pickup, cable length and cable routing are prime factors. *Equipment placement is important because it dictates cable length and routing.* Choose equipment locations that:

- Allow you to route cables away from noise sources (such as motors and wiring)
- Let you use short cables for highly noise-sensitive signal paths

An example of a highly noise-sensitive signal path would be the low-voltage (500 mV) preamp-level outputs of a head unit. Suppose you want to use these outputs for driving a crossover and amps. Putting the crossover under the dash, close to the head unit, lets you use a short cable for the highly noise-sensitive path. The voltage gain of the crossover provides enhanced noise immunity for the cables to the amps, so cable length and routing is less important for them.

Another example would be a trunk-mounted subwoofer system with separate crossover and amp. Using speaker-level signals to the crossover provides good noise immunity for the long run to the trunk. The preamp-level output of the crossover to the amp is a comparatively highly noise-sensitive path, and should be a short cable.

Cable Routing

Avoid running preamp-level signal cables side by side with high-current power wiring. If you plan to install amps in the trunk, run the signal cables down one side of the car and the power wires down the other.

Try to route signal cables away from electromagnetic noise sources such as motors and other wiring. Where possible, run your cables close to the chassis.

Experiment with different cable routing paths to minimize noise pickup. Start the engine and turn on the head lights and stereo. To make it easier to hear noise, set the sensitivity controls of the amps and processors to max, but turn the volume control of the head unit to minimum. Sometimes moving a cable just a few inches can make a big difference. The best time to experiment with cable routing is during the installation, not after it.

Grounding

The chassis is the generally preferred grounding point for amps and other components because of its low resistance. But it's important to use the proper grounding techniques (Fig. 12-8) to reduce noise pickup due to common ground impedance with potential noise sources.

Figure 12-8(a) shows two components sharing a ground wire to the chassis. This allows the ground currents of one component to affect the ground reference voltage of the other component. This is mainly a concern where an amp is affecting the ground reference of a component such as a crossover. At a minimum, each amplifier should have its own connection to the chassis.

Figure 12-8(b) shows two components using individual but widely separated chassis grounding points. This allows return currents that flow through the chassis to produce a noise voltage between the two points.

Figure 12-8(c) shows the proper grounding technique—each component has its own connection to the chassis, and all connections are closely located. It's okay for low-current components to share a common ground point.

Not all metal in a car is electrically connected to the chassis, so use a multimeter to confirm a low-resistance connection to a known good ground. Look for values less than 0.3 ohms. Note: When making ultra-low resistance measurements, first short the two test probes together and observe the reading. If it's an analog meter, zero the meter at this point. For a digital meter, you will need to mentally subtract this reading from your measurement readings.

FIGURE 12-8

Improper and proper grounding techniques.

wrong

(a) two components sharing a ground wire to the chassis:

resistance of shared ground wire

chassis ground

wrong

(b) ground impedance between two distant points on chassis:

chassis ground

resistance between two distant points on chassis

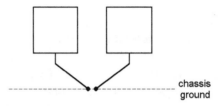

right

(c) proper grounding technique:

chassis ground

Step-by-Step Level Adjustment

Important: Some cars (Audi, Porsche) have galvanized bodies. In these cars, you must find one of the manufacturers' grounding points or else some noise can result.

When it comes to adjusting your system, higher signal levels are always better for reducing noise. But you need to make sure that levels aren't set too high, or you'll end up with distortion. The goal is to find the level that maximizes the signal-to-noise ratio while keeping you out of distortion.

The procedure given next covers the general case of the cascade of many components, each with a level control at its input (Fig. 12-9). For simplicity, this procedure is written assuming two processors between the head unit and amp. For example, processor 1 might be an equalizer and

FIGURE 12-9

The cascade of many components.

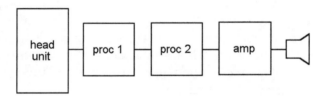

head unit | proc 1 | proc 2 | amp

Important: When mounting a power amp (or any car stereo component), secure it in such a way that the metal case does not make electrical contact with the car chassis. This guarantees that the amplifier's ground wire is the exclusive connection between the amp's internal ground and the system ground. Electrical isolation is important to prevent ground loops.

> **NOTE**   A few components have electrically isolated cases—these should be electrically connected to the car chassis to provide shielding to the internal circuitry. When in doubt, use an ohmmeter to measure the resistance between the case and ground wire of the component.

Use rubber grommets inside metal mounting bracket holes to prevent screws from making an electrical connection with the chassis. Alternately, you can mount your components on a board, then mount the board to the car chassis.

processor 2 might be a crossover. Your system may have more or fewer components cascaded together, but the process remains the same. Note: Some systems require a deviation from this procedure to satisfy other constraints (such as proper level matching between channels in an amplifier-saving configuration). See the appropriate project chapter when in doubt.

1. Set the amp level control and all processor level controls to minimum.

2. With music, turn up the head unit volume control. When you reach the point where you start to hear distortion, turn the volume control down slightly until the distortion disappears. Leave the volume control at this setting.

> **NOTE**   If the sound from the speaker is so low that you cannot clearly hear the onset of distortion, turn up the amp's level control as needed. If turning up the amp's level control to max still isn't loud enough, then start to turn up processor 2's level control as well. Return level control settings on the amp and processor 2 to minimum when you finish this step.

3. Now, turn up the processor 1 level control. When you reach the point where you start to hear distortion, turn the processor 1 level control down slightly until the distortion disappears. Leave the processor 1 level control at this setting.

NOTE   *If the sound from the speaker is so low that you cannot clearly hear the onset of distortion, turn up the amp's level control as needed. Return the amp's level control setting to minimum when you finish this step.*

4. Now, turn up the processor 2 level control. When you reach the point where you start to hear distortion, turn the processor 2 level control down slightly until the distortion disappears. Leave the processor 2 level control at this setting.

NOTE   *If the sound from the speaker is so low that you cannot clearly hear the onset of distortion, turn up the amp's level control as needed.*

5. Turn up the amp level control until the system is as loud as you'll ever play it or you begin to hear distortion. If you hear distortion, slightly decrease the amp level control.

Troubleshooting Noise Problems

If you've followed the advice in the previous sections on buying, installing, and setting equipment, then chances are good you won't need this section. But sometimes even well-designed systems have noise problems. The vehicle itself may aggravating the problem—deteriorated ignition or charging system components, a loose battery cable clamp, or missing or defective factory noise suppressors can increase the conducted and radiated noise levels.

This section introduces the most important supplies, tools, and techniques for troubleshooting and repairing noise problems. It concludes with a step-by-step troubleshooting procedure. Fixing noise problems can be frustrating, time-consuming work. Following the techniques explained in this section can help you systematically solve problems and eliminate much of the frustration.

> **Important:** Troubleshooting techniques should be used only *after* you're satisfied that the system level adjustments are right.

Identifying Noise Sources

Knowing what each of the common noise sources sounds like can make the job of troubleshooting easier. This is especially true for AM/FM noise entering the head unit through the antenna or power line. Table 12-1 lists the most common noise sources, what they normally sound like, and what to try to fix them.

Shorting Plugs

Shorting plugs (or muting plugs; Fig. 12-10) are probably the cheapest and most useful troubleshooting aid for system noise problems. Shorting plugs are used for muting the inputs of an amplifier or other component to determine if the noise is entering after that point.

TABLE 12-1

Common Noise Sources

Noise Source	What It Sounds Like	What to Try
Alternator	A whine whose pitch changes with engine speed	Capacitor to ground at the alternator output
Ignition	Ticking that changes with engine speed	Using a sniffer to further localize the source of the problem
Turn signals	Popping synchronized with the turn signals	Capacitor across the turn signal flasher
Brake lights	Popping synchronized with the brake lights	Capacitor across the brake light switch contacts
Blower motor	Ticking synchronized with the blower motor	Capacitor to ground at the motor hot lead
Dash lamp dimmer	A buzzy whine whose pitch changes with the dimmer setting	Capacitor to ground at the dimmer hot lead
Horn switch	Popping synchronized with horn	Capacitor between the hot lead and horn lead at the horn relay
Horn	Buzzing synchronized with the horn	Capacitor to ground at each horn hot lead
Amplifier power supply	A nasty buzz, not affected by engine speed	Grounding the amp chassis

FIGURE 12-10

Shorting plugs.

You'll want at least a pair of them and can make them yourself. Make each one by soldering a short piece of wire between the center and outer conductors in a standard RCA plug.

See the step-by-step troubleshooting procedure at the end of this section for full details on using shorting plugs.

Ground Loop Isolators

Ground loop isolators (Fig. 12-11) are as much a diagnostic tool as they are a repair means. By inserting one in the signal path of a known or suspected ground loop, you can quickly determine if a ground loop involving that path is degrading system noise immunity.

For diagnostic purposes, any ground loop isolator will do. If you decide you need to install one permanently to solve a system noise problem, then it pays to buy a high-quality model. Low-quality units usually have premature bass response roll-off. Passive ground loop isolators use transformers, and are susceptible to magnetic fields, so you need to keep them away from motors and other wiring. Both of these problems can be avoided by using an active ground loop isolator.

A good way to do an A/B test for the level of noise improvement provided by a ground loop isolator is to use a ground bypass wire (Fig. 12-12).

FIGURE 12-11

Ground loop isolator. (*Courtesy of Parts Express.*)

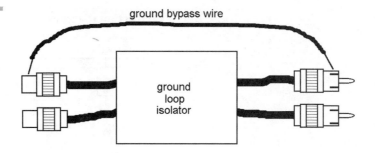

FIGURE 12-12

Ground bypass wire for ground loop isolator.

After you've installed the ground loop isolator, start the engine and turn on the headlights and the stereo. Turn the head unit volume control to minimum. Now use the ground bypass wire to momentarily short the ground connection across the ground loop isolator. You only need to short one channel, not both. If you hear a noise difference, then a ground loop was degrading system noise immunity.

Power Line Filters

Power line filters are used to reduce the amount of noise present on the 12-volt power line. Filters may be used at the source of the noise problem, at the equipment that is most affected by it, or on the power line between the two.

There are four common types of power line filters (Table 12-2): capacitors, chokes (inductors), three-terminal passive filters, and electronic noise suppressors.

Capacitors. Capacitors are easily connected from any 12-volt point to chassis ground. The idea behind them is to provide a low-impedance path to ground for the noise. Capacitors used for noise suppression are generally 0.5 µF in value. For good high-frequency performance, electrolytics are not used here.

Capacitors specifically designed for automotive noise suppression often have only a single wire coming from them—the ground connection is made via the mounting tab of the cap. Feed-through designs are also common. These also make the ground connection via the mounting tab, but an in wire and out wire (connected internally) are provided for wiring convenience.

Unlike the other filter types, capacitors can be added anywhere on the

TABLE 12-2

Types of Power Line
Filters

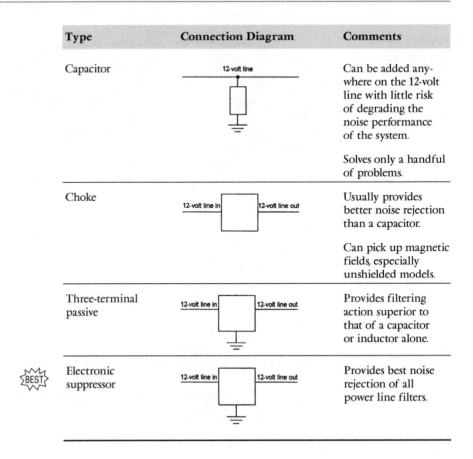

Type	Connection Diagram	Comments
Capacitor	12-volt line	Can be added anywhere on the 12-volt line with little risk of degrading the noise performance of the system. Solves only a handful of problems.
Choke	12-volt line in / 12-volt line out	Usually provides better noise rejection than a capacitor. Can pick up magnetic fields, especially unshielded models.
Three-terminal passive	12-volt line in / 12-volt line out	Provides filtering action superior to that of a capacitor or inductor alone.
Electronic suppressor (BEST)	12-volt line in / 12-volt line out	Provides best noise rejection of all power line filters.

12-volt line with no risk of exceeding the current rating of the filter and little risk of degrading the noise performance of the system. Unfortunately, only a handful of problems are solvable with capacitors—these tend to be noises affecting radio reception.

Chokes. Chokes (inductors; Fig. 12-13) are installed in series with the 12-volt line, normally right at the power lead of the stereo component sensitive to noise. The idea behind them is to provide a high-impedance path for the noise getting to the component. Chokes usually provide better noise rejection than capacitors.

Because all the current used by the stereo component flows through the choke, you need to buy a choke that has a current rating suitable for your application. Current rating is a good indicator of the DC resistance of a particular choke—it's not an indicator of its noise filtering ability. Don't buy a choke with a significantly higher current rating than you need—it can have lower inductance and provide inferior filtering. Since manufacturers don't normally provide inductance specifications for their chokes, beware of unusually small models.

Mount chokes away from motors and other wiring. The unshielded models especially can easily pick up magnetic fields.

Three-Terminal Passive Filters. Three-terminal passive filters (Fig. 12-14) are installed in series with the 12-volt line, normally right at the power lead of the stereo component sensitive to noise. They require a ground connection as well. Three-terminal passive filters contain both capacitors and inductors. This can provide filtering action superior to that of capacitors or inductors alone. As with chokes, you need to buy a model that has a current rating suitable for your application.

Electronic Noise Suppressors. Electronic noise suppressors (Fig. 12-15) are three-terminal devices installed the same way as three-terminal passive filters. Electronic noise suppressors can provide better performance than even three-terminal passive filters. As with chokes and three-terminal passive filters, you need to buy a model that has a current rating suitable for your application.

FIGURE 12-15
Electronic suppressor. (*Courtesy of Navone Engineering.*)

Noise Sniffers

Noise sniffers are hand-held electronic devices used to track down sources of radiated noise. These are frequently used by professionals to solve difficult cases.

Electromagnetic Radiation (EMR) sniffers are used to find sources of audio frequency magnetic fields. PAC's NA-1 Noise Analyzer (Fig. 12-16) performs this job and more. The NA-1 comes with inductive and conductive probes. It has a built-in speaker or can be used with headphones. (For sensitive measurements, headphones are preferred because they block some of the mechanical sounds of the engine.)

FIGURE 12-16
PAC NA-1. (*Courtesy of Pacific Accessory Corporation.*)

Use the inductive probe for EMR sniffing. Start the vehicle's engine. Start probing near the cable or stereo component that is picking up the noise. Move the probe to find the loudest source of the noise. The orientation of the probe can make a big difference, so try various orientations. You can use the probe to find the exact wire bundle and often the specific wire causing the problem. Once found, you can shield it with copper tape (be sure to ground the tape), or as a last resort, reroute the offending wire by splicing in an extension.

The conductive probes can be used for listening to power wires, signal wires, or multiple ground points for any noise that is present.

Copper Shielding Tape

Copper shielding tape (Fig. 12-17) is useful for wrapping around wires and cables to provide shielding. It can be wrapped around patch cables you want to shield from noise, or around power and accessory wiring to reduce radiated emissions. Shielding power and accessory wiring to reduce radiated noise is the generally preferred strategy because there is little risk of making things worse. Shielding patch cables can actually make things worse by coupling chassis noise into them.

Copper shielding tape uses an electrically conductive adhesive to provide a low-resistance path between the backing and substrate. Tinned copper shielding tape is also available to make the job of soldering to it easier.

FIGURE 12-17
Copper shielding
tape. (*Courtesy of 3M.*)

Any bundles of wire nearby and parallel to patch cabling are good candidates for wrapping with copper tape. When wrapping a bundle of wires with tape, there should be a minimum $\frac{1}{4}$-inch overlap between layers. To maximize the shielding effectiveness, the shield wrap should be electrically grounded to the chassis. Solder short wires to the wrap every few feet and electrically connect them to the chassis via ring crimp connectors and self-tapping screws.

Step-by-Step Troubleshooting Procedure

The key to effective troubleshooting for noise problems is to use a methodical approach to identify the problem. This saves time, frustration, and money.

To troubleshoot a noisy system, follow these steps:

1. Start at an amp where you hear noise. Replace each of the signal cables feeding into the amp with a shorting plug. Start the car's engine, turn on the headlights, and turn on the stereo. Is the result clean? If you hear noise at this point (which is rare), noise is either getting in on the amp's power supply wire, there is something abnormal about the speaker load (e.g., a speaker wire is shorting to the chassis), or the amp is defective.

2. If the result is clean, then it's time to move the shorting plugs upstream (toward the head unit). Turn off the stereo first. For this example, let's assume a crossover is located between the head unit and amp. Plug the cables from the crossover back into the amp. Unplug the cables from other outputs of the crossover for the moment. Now replace each of the signal cables feeding into the crossover with a shorting plug. Start the car's engine, turn on the headlights, and turn on the stereo. Is the result clean? If you hear noise at this point, and your amp lacks differential inputs, the noise is probably due to a ground loop involving the cables between the crossover and amp. (This theory can be tested by temporarily inserting a ground loop isolator at the amp's inputs.) It could also be due to a high level of induced noise on the cable or noise getting in on the crossover's power supply wire.

3. If the result is clean, replace the cables you just unplugged from the other outputs of the crossover. If noise returns, you've got a ground loop involving the cables you just plugged in. If it's still clean, then

the problem has to involve the head unit connection to the crossover. If your crossover lacks differential inputs, the noise is probably due to a ground loop involving the cables between the head unit and crossover. (This theory can be tested by temporarily inserting a ground loop isolator at the crossover's inputs.) It could also be due to a high level of induced noise on the cable or noise getting in on the head unit's power supply wire.

Once you've located the component or cable most affected by the noise and made a preliminary diagnosis of the problem as ground loop related or not, you'll need to follow up each of your leads. If you discovered a ground loop problem, you'll need to break the loop with a ground loop isolator or equipment having differential inputs. If you don't have a ground loop but are experiencing high induced noise in a cable, you'll need to experiment with cable routing and shielding nearby wiring with copper tape. If this fails to fix the problem, the next step is to track down the source of the noise itself. You may have deteriorated electrical system components or inadequate factory noise suppressors. This level of troubleshooting usually requires professional help. Finally, if you suspect your problems are power line related, try an appropriate filter.

RECOMMENDED MAIL-ORDER SUPPLIERS

Crutchfield
1 Crutchfield Park
Charlottesville, VA 22911-9097
(888) 955-6000
www.crutchfield.com

Great selection of quality car stereo equipment combined with unequaled service. Well-trained staff and Master-Sheet instructions provide all the guidance you'll need.

Parts Express
725 Pleasant Valley Drive
Springboro, OH 45066-1158
(800) 338-0531
www.parts-express.com

Car stereo supplies and tools, component speakers, boxes, and electronic components.

MCM Electronics
650 Congress Park Drive
Centerville, OH 45459
(800) 543-4330
www.mcmelectronics.com

Car stereo supplies and tools, component speakers, boxes, and electronic components. Their huge catalog contains lots of hard-to-find items.

David Levy Company
12753 Moore Street
Cerritos, CA 90703
(800) 421-3533
www.dlcparts.com

Car stereo supplies and tools, component speakers, vehicle security, and restyling.

Madisound Speaker Components
8608 University Green
P.O. Box 44283
Madison, WI 53744-4283
(608) 831-3433
www.madisound.com

Component speakers and speaker building supplies. A favorite of home speaker building enthusiasts. Top-notch products at wholesale prices.

MFR Engineering
10308 Indian Lake Blvd. South
Indianapolis, IN 46236-8329
www.mfr-eng.com

Subwoofer Design Toolbox™ direct sales.

RECOMMENDED READING

Books and Technical Papers

The Loudspeaker Design Cookbook
Vance Dickason
Published by Audio Amateur
Press
$39.95

If you're serious about designing and building your own subwoofers, this book is unsurpassed. Now in its sixth edition, this book is an industry standard. Includes a chapter on auto sound.

Designing, Building and Testing Your Own Speaker System
David Weems
Published by McGraw-Hill
$19.95

Another excellent book for subwoofer builders. Now in its fourth edition, this is a completely revised version of Weems's best seller. A hands-on approach to design and construction of speaker systems.

AudioControl Technical Papers
AudioControl

Cover a range of topics from car acoustics to crossovers. Visit their website at www.audiocontrol.com for a list of papers or to download PDF versions of many of them.

JL Audio Tutorials
JL Audio

Cover a range of topics from setting amplifier gains to subwoofer box design and construction. Visit their website at www.jlaudio.com.

Magazines

Car Sound & Performance
460 Park Avenue South
9th Floor
New York, NY 10016
(212) 378-0400
www.carsound.com
$15.00/year (6 issues)

Covers car stereo, plus security, navigation, and performance. Includes product reviews, buying tips, installation techniques, and new product guides.

Car Audio and Electronics
P.O. Box 420235
Palm Coast, FL 32142-0235
(800) 243-6400
www.caraudiomag.com
$15.95/year (12 issues)

Published for the car audio and mobile electronics enthusiast. Includes test reports and custom installations. Annual product directory issue each April.

Mobile Entertainment
1633 Broadway, 40th Floor
New York, NY 10019
(212) 767-6000
www.m-emag.com
$12.00/year (6 issues)

audioXpress
P.O. Box 876
Peterborough, NH 03458-0876
(888) 924-9465
www.audioxpress.com
$34.95/year (12 issues)

Somewhere between a magazine and a technical journal. For those interested in building loudspeakers as well as those who want to understand the technology behind them.

BIBLIOGRAPHY

Chapter 1: Before You Begin

Higgins, Michelle. "Custom Auto Add-Ons Get Tricky." *Wall Street Journal,* October 14, 2004, p. D3, cols. 1–3.

Chapter 3: Speakers and Speaker Projects

Crutchfield. *Car Stereo Installation Made Easy.* 1995.

Crutchfield. *Car Stereo and Home Audio/Video Catalog & Buyer's Guide.* Fall 2004/Winter 2005.

Kinsler, Lawrence E., et al. *Fundamentals of Acoustics.* 3rd ed. New York: John Wiley & Sons, 1982.

Klasco, Mike and Rob Baum. "What's New With Speaker Cones?" *Voice Coil,* April 1999, pp. 29–34.

Navone, David and Richard Clark. "Updating Your Image." *AutoMedia,* August 1998, pp. 34, 36, 64.

Chapter 4: Subwoofers and Subwoofer Projects

Clark, Richard. "Blocking That Bass." *CarSound,* December 1997, 10–12.

Clark, Richard. "Speaking Out On Speakers." *Car Sound & Performance,* October 2000, pp. 22, 76.

Dickason, Vance. *The Loudspeaker Design Cookbook.* 5th ed. Peterborough, NH: Old Colony Sound, 1995.

Kinsler, Lawrence E., et al. *Fundamentals of Acoustics.* 3rd ed. New York: John Wiley & Sons, 1982.

Klasco, Mike and Rob Baum. "What's New With Speaker Cones?" *Voice Coil,* April 1999, pp. 29–34.

Putman, Rob. "Beating Bose." *AUTOMEDIA,* September 1997, 36–43.

Rumreich, Mark. "Box Design and Woofer Selection: A New Approach." *Speaker Builder,* Issue 1, 1992.

Chapter 5: Head Unit Projects

Crutchfield. *Car Stereo Installation Made Easy.* 1995.

Crutchfield. *Car Stereo and Home Audio/Video Catalog & Buyer's Guide.* Fall 2004/Winter 2005.

Crutchfield. *How to Upgrade Your Factory Stereo: OEM Integration Made Easy.*

Higgins, Michelle. "Custom Auto Add-Ons Get Tricky." *Wall Street Journal,* October 14, 2004, p. D3, cols. 1–3.

Klasco, Mike. "Tripath Profile: Class T." *Multi Media Manufacturer,* September/October 2004, pp. 1, 4, 6, 7.

Putman, Rob. "Aftermarket Ambush." *AutoMedia,* January 2000, pp. 34–46.

Putman, Rob. "Beating Bose." *AUTOMEDIA,* September 1997, 36–43.

Putman, Rob. "Update on GM's Class 2 Serial Data Bus." *AutoMedia,* July 2000, pp. 44–49.

Sonada, Paul. "Satellite Radio Round-Up." *Car Sound & Performance,* July 2004, pp. 66–68.

Strassberg, Dan. "RECEIVERS' FUTURE LOOKS DIGITAL." *EDN,* December 26, 2002, pp. 44–48.

Chapter 6: Mobile Video and 5.1 Channel Audio

Aruti, Scott. "Feds Concerned About Driving Distractions." *AutoMedia,* July 2000, p. 22.

"CAR VIDEO Watch your movie!" *Consumer Reports*, July 2003, pp. 54–55.

Crutchfield. *Car Stereo and Home Audio/Video Catalog & Buyer's Guide*. Fall 2004/Winter 2005.

Sonada, Paul. "VIDEO: WHAT YOU GET PAID FOR." *AutoMedia*, October 2004, pp. 64–65.

Sonada, Paul. "YOU'RE SURROUNDED Four things you need to know about 5.1 to make a sale." *AutoMedia*, April 2004, pp. 66–67.

"What's New with Displays." *PC Magazine*, May 4, 2004, pp. 115–120.

Chapter 7: Amplifiers and Amplifier Projects

Crutchfield. *Car Stereo Installation Made Easy.* 1995.

Crutchfield. *Car Stereo and Home Audio/Video Catalog & Buyer's Guide*. Fall 2004/Winter 2005.

Kinsler, Lawrence E., et al. *Fundamentals of Acoustics*. 3rd ed. New York: John Wiley & Sons, 1982.

Noguez, Rob "O". "Upping the Amps." *AutoMedia*, September 2003, pp. 64–66.

Putman, Rob. "Beating Bose." *AUTOMEDIA*, September 1997, 36–43.

Putman, Rob. "Finger On The Trigger." *AutoMedia*, January 1999, pp. 54–56, 62.

Wehmeyer, Andy. "CEA 2006." *AutoMedia*, January 2004, pp. 63–68, 76.

Chapter 8: Equalizers and Equalizer Projects

Geddes, Earl and Henry Blind. "The Localized Sound Power Method." *J. Audio Eng. Soc.* 34, no. 3, 1986.

Janis, Robert. "Signal Processors: Trends and Merchandising." *Mobile Electronics Specialist*, June 1996, 10–15.

Kinsler, Lawrence E., et al. *Fundamentals of Acoustics*. 3rd ed. New York: John Wiley & Sons, 1982.

Chapter 9: Biamping and Crossovers

Chinn, Richard. *Crossovers and Biamplification,* AudioControl technical paper number 104, 1987.

Chapter 10: Changer and Player Projects

Crutchfield. *Car Stereo Installation Made Easy.* 1995.

Crutchfield. *Car Stereo and Home Audio/Video Catalog & Buyer's Guide.* Fall 2004/Winter 2005.

Chapter 11: Accessories

"Time for a Battery Check?" *Consumer Reports,* October 1997, 23–27.

Crutchfield. *Car Stereo Installation Made Easy.* 1995.

Navone, David and Richard Clark. "Misconceptions in Cabling." *AUTOMEDIA* 2, no. 6, 1997, 29–42.

Navone, David. "The Tint Dilemma." *AutoMedia,* May 2001, pp. 52–53.

Chapter 12: Battling Noise

Chinn, Richard. *Level Matching for Autosound...Or Why Is My System So Noisy?* AudioControl technical paper number 103, 1986.

Navone, David. "A Nose for Noise: How to Use Car Audio Sniffers to Detect System Noise." *AUTOMEDIA,* September 1997, 60.

Navone, David. "Troubleshooting: Sound Advice." *CarSound,* December 1997, 86–88.

Navone, David and Richard Clark. "Misconceptions in Cabling." *AUTOMEDIA* 2, no. 6, 1997, 29–42.

INDEX

About the Author

Mark Rumreich is a senior design engineer for TCL-Thomson Electronics who specializes in analog and digital audio and video systems and circuits. He has written numerous articles for *Electronics Now, Speaker Builder, Radio-Electronics,* and *Audio Amateur* magazines and taught seminars in loudspeaker design and automotive acoustics. Mr. Rumreich holds more than 40 U.S. patents and received his master's degree in electrical engineering from Purdue University.